What people are

The Riddle of

Walking in the footsteps of Carl Gustav Jung, Kiritsis ranges effortlessly in his essays from an analysis of enigmatic alchemical motifs to contemporary issues in physics, evolutionary biology, and neuroscience, all the while drawing on a profound knowledge of Greek mythology and philosophy. A thought-provoking and beautifully written work.

Hereward Tilton, PhD, author of *The Path of the Serpent, Vol. 1: Psychedelics and the Neuropsychology of Gnosis,* and *The Quest for the Phoenix: Spiritual Alchemy and Rosicrucianism in the Work of Count Michael Maier* (1569–1622)

The Riddle of Alchemy is a dense and lavish text that elucidates a storied natural philosophy and protoscience, showing its creative influence on modern psychology.

Foreword Clarion Reviews

Alchemy, the alleged transmutation of base metals into precious ones, has long captured the human imagination, sometimes serving as a metaphor for other types of change. In this provocative book, Paul Kiritsis discusses the topic from several different perspectives, spanning various eras and cultures. From the chemical laboratories of ancient Greece, to the "internal alchemy" of Eastern sages, to the psychological insights of Carl Gustav Jung, alchemy is a topic that never fails to delight and intrigue, as Dr Kiritsis points out in this reader-friendly book, each chapter of which is an eloquently stated discussion of the topic.

Stanley Krippner, PhD, co-author of *Personal Mythology: Using Ritual, Dream, and Imagination to Discover Your Inner Story,* 3rd ed. (with David Feinstein)

A licensed medical psychologist with graduate degrees in clinical psychology, history, and English, Kiritsis expertly leads an interdisciplinary exploration of alchemy supported by a solid understanding of history, literature, and modern psychology. This analysis is backed by more than 150 scholarly footnotes that carefully balance astute commentary with an engaging writing style. The book does not overwhelm readers with academic jargon, and the text is accompanied by a wealth of visual aids, from historical drawings to full-color reproductions of art found in illustrated manuscripts. Even skeptics will find much to appreciate in this beautifully crafted work. A well-written, expertly researched analysis of the history and legacy of alchemy.

Kirkus Reviews

The Riddle of Alchemy

Also by Paul Kiritsis

Confessions of a Split Mind
ISBN-13: 978-1546205531

A Critical Investigation into Precognitive Dreams:
Dreamscaping without My Timekeeper
ISBN-13: 978-1527564923

Tales of a Spiritual Sun
ISBN-13: 978-1804390054

The Creative Advantages of Schizophrenia:
The Muse and the Mad Hatter
ISBN-13: 978-1527543447

The Riddle of
Alchemy

Paul Kiritsis

MANTRA
BOOKS

London, UK
Washington, DC, USA

CollectiveInk

First published by Mantra Books, 2024
Mantra Books is an imprint of Collective Ink Ltd.,
Unit 11, Shepperton House, 89 Shepperton Road, London, N1 3DF
office@collectiveinkbooks.com
www.collectiveinkbooks.com
www.mantra-books.net

For distributor details and how to order please visit the 'Ordering' section on our website.

Text copyright: Paul Kiritsis 2023

ISBN: 978 1 80341 637 3
978 1 80341 688 5 (ebook)
Library of Congress Control Number: 2023946964

A CIP catalogue record for this book is available from the British Library.

Design: Lapiz Digital Services

UK: Printed and bound by CPI Group (UK) Ltd, Croydon, CR0 4YY
Printed in North America by CPI GPS partners

We operate a distinctive and ethical publishing philosophy in all areas of our business, from our global network of authors to production and worldwide distribution.

For Harry Toulacis and Jessica Jacobson

One becomes Two, Two becomes Three, and out of the Third comes the One as the Fourth.

— Axiom of Maria Prophetissa

Contents

Figures

Acknowledgements

Figure A-1. Photo of Paul Kiritsis.

I am most indebted to my editor, the conscientious James Baron, for his laborious and meticulous work. None of this would have been possible without his eagle eye for constructive criticism and knack for conveying it in a sensitive manner. He has been a phenomenal asset in this subsequent instalment of my development as a writer and researcher.

Profound gratitude must also be given to my ever-faithful friends, confidantes, and colleagues: the congenial Adam Arzadon, Ashleigh Kramer-Walthall, Francesca Lalli, Jessica Johnson, and Jessica Jacobson — I laud them for their candidness and camaraderie, receptivity to my requests, nonjudgmental attitude, and embodying unconditional positive regard and love. They are truly exceptional individuals, pearls of pulchritude in the deep cobalt-blue ocean.

393ds4ds55

ss ds ssssਤ

Without hesitation, I also offer heartfelt thanks to Sean Lynn and Charity Anne Ross, who offered countenance during the years (2011–14) I was writing the papers and articles that appear in this treatise. I have not forgotten the innumerable and very stimulating nocturnal discussions we had on esotericism, especially theosophy, astrology, alchemy, and magic. The experience of revisiting a second time places and spaces that are pregnant with multiple meanings and anointed with personal significance was especially poignant for me. It was also punctuated by bouts of wistful longing—a yearning to return and complete an ancient Odyssey that was prematurely aborted after being beguiled by the deafening Sirens of clinical psychology. My quest for arcane knowledge began many, many years before I serendipitously stumbled upon the modern quantitative tools of empiricism, and I return to it now with the same fervent zest I felt when I first glanced at the celebrated death mask of the boy-king Tutankhamun.

Finally, I salute my beloved family—father, mother, and brother—who are omnipresent in my life and immensely supportive from both an emotional and financial standpoint. Their solicitude knows no bounds.

Preface

Figure A-2. Separation and synthesis as a central theme in alchemy.

The word "alchemy" has very powerful connotations for individuals who are familiar with the craft through personal study or popular media—the concoction of potent fizzling panaceas able to cure all ailments, medieval maverick men at work in their subterranean laboratories trying to create a scintillating saffron powder able to transmute base metals into gold, and cleverly concealed chemical formulas in convoluted allegorical narratives are just some of the themes the word itself might evoke. I became deeply fascinated with the esoteric discipline in my mid-twenties, after having read some of Carl Jung's rather abstruse monographs on psychological alchemy. I knew that Jung, save for being the father of analytical psychology, was one of the great interpreters of the Western esoteric traditions (i.e., alchemy, astrology, theurgy). In the 1920s, Jung's intellectual curiosity was piqued by a Chinese mystical treatise titled *The Secret of the Golden Flower*, which he stumbled upon quite serendipitously. The discovery culminated in a full-blooded cross-cultural investigation into alchemical symbolism. Chief among the golden fruits of this foray was a translation of some pretty arcane medieval treatises rife with alchemical symbols and tropes (i.e., Michael Maier's *Atalanta Fugiens* and Salomon Trismosin's *Splendor Solis*) into coherent psychological terms. Specifically, Jung sought consilience with the idiosyncratic processes afforded by analytical psychology, a sociohistorical bridge that in hindsight had to be made to preserve the theoretical legitimacy and feasibility of a shared mind or collective unconscious.

There's probably no need to make punitive judgments on Jung's conceptual jerrymandering or to invoke Occam's razor here because my intention is not to discredit him as any dogmatic, black-and-white-thinking scientist might do. Alchemists— whether ancient, medieval, Renaissance, or contemporaneous— readily subscribed to animistic worldviews, and their quests may have been very multifaceted in nature, at once inner and outer, and physical but also psychospiritual. Perhaps some alchemical treatises were solely by-products of psychological projection, a proto-scientific form of Rorschach inkblot tests where the true meaning and significance of the creative product wasn't available to conscious awareness. One can definitely make a compelling case for it. In truth, we'll probably never know whether the treatises themselves alluded to psychological processes and other cosmic truths ineffable to our limited human intellect. However, what we can conclude with some degree of conviction is that some were chemical cookbooks for tinctures, colloids, elixirs, aphrodisiacs, paints, and natural medicines. Just like modern-day cooks who transcribe their delicious recipes into notebooks for precise replication, posterity, and potential publication, so too did alchemists keep detailed written records of all their radical concoctions in leather-bound and personally inscribed portfolios to bequeath to a worthy colleague or protégé at some auspicious time. Some prescriptions were simply just that: chemical formulae with heterogeneous applications— nothing more, nothing less. No psychical embellishments are necessary or mandatory to explain their existence.

The obscure intentions of the alchemists are echoed in the etymology of the word "alchemy" itself. There is some consensus regarding its origins—the Old French word *alchimie*, the medieval Latin word *alkimia*, the Arabic word *al-kimiya*, and the Greek word *khemeioa* have all been acknowledged as semantic precursors of the English equivalent and literally mean "alchemy." *Khemia* ["land of black earth" in Greek] was also mentioned by Plutarch and implicates Egypt as the originator of the dual philosophical-technical craft. Moreover, the Greek term *khymatos* means "that which is poured out," which is perhaps an allusion to its operative and practical concerns. If we can trust etymological clues in offering historical guidance, then all endeavors desiring to pinpoint Western alchemy's exact origins and subsequently trace its cross-cultural dissemination should begin in Egypt proper. Yes?

The single most important figure in Western alchemy is probably Bolus of Mendes, or Pseudo-Democritus as he was sometimes called. Bolus was born during the first half of the second century BCE in the eastern Deltaic city of Mendes, in Egypt, and lived at a time when the first two Ptolemaic rulers, Ptolemy Soter and Ptolemy Philadelphus, were establishing the city of Alexandria as the intellectual center and envy of the world. Bolus's contribution to the growing field of knowledge was a treatise called *Physika kai Mystika* [Physical and Mystical Matters], which became so popular that it rivaled more orthodox works on natural history such as Aristotle's *Meteorologica*. The few remaining fragments of Bolus's text that have come down to us reveal a deep concern not only for the magical and supernatural, but also for the physical. There is a section on spagyrics, which describes the therapeutic and magical properties of various herbs. He also singles out a select few known to cause psychedelic visions upon ingestion. His material is also littered with spells that demand the correct intonation of words and specific breathing techniques so as to incite quasi-material change and command Nature herself. Most interesting of all is the formulae he provides for the creation of gold, silver, gemstones, and purple dyes—a section which brings to mind the metallurgical and chemical practices of the ancient Egyptian priestcraft that occurred deep in the temple crypts and sanctuaries, well hidden from the eyes of the profane.

As an alchemical text, *Physika kai Mystika* delineates a process whereby a base substance or the *prima materia*, usually lead, is used in the preparation of gold—the Great Work or Philosopher's Stone. In this, the earliest known model of alchemical transmutation, transformation, and exaltation of the "stone" is marked by four distinct phases of coloration that serve as exoteric markers of a reduction process instigated by the laws of cosmic sympathy and antipathy. Thus, the "stone" or noble metal is conferred form only after having undergone putrefaction through *melanosis* (nigredo), bleaching through *leucosis* (albedo), yellowing through *xanthosis*, and finally, reddening through *iosis* (rubedo). Purple sometimes takes the place of red in the last of these stages, hinting at the royal and spiritual scheme bubbling directly beneath a process that at first appears to be nothing more than a descriptive transcription of the coloration and purification of metals.

What separated Bolus from other artisans who busied themselves with metallurgy, glassmaking, and chemistry is that he married these techniques with Pythagorean mysticism, thus couching the indigenous practical arts in a holistic framework of the cosmos as a system of interrelated wholes. Bolus believed in the underlying unity of all things. The created world was composed of the four Aristotelian elements—fire, water, air, and earth—which combined to form a compound of matter, and matter's ability to manifest in different ways was the direct result of variances in the compound's elemental mixture. By manipulating the dominant element in the mixture, it was possible to convert one form or substance into another. If conversion was possible, so too was multiplication, and before long alchemy was the science of multiplication. This Aristotelian nature philosophy underpinned the alchemists' worldview and informed their versatile practices.

Bolus's treatise is also the first known instance in which the material process of metal transmutation, or the Great Work, is understood to be under the direct astrological influence of the seven *aetheric* "planets," or powers of the celestial realm, implying that the time of year at which the process was initiated also determined success. His amalgamation of the physical and the metaphysical recalls the conception of reality proposed by the Pythagorean mystics. There can be no doubt that Bolus was an active member of this movement for he hints, time and time again, of his allegiance to an esoteric school of wisdom that preserved the greatest of cosmic secrets. We can be certain that the movement to which he alludes is none other than the Pythagorean school of metaphysics, for Pythagoras was the first known person in history to impose obligatory oaths of silence to all who came to him for instruction.

The first alchemical treatises were written in and promulgated from Egypt during the Hellenistic period, though it wasn't until the times of medieval Europe that manuscripts began to appear in profusion. All of them make a good job of being cryptic, codified, and vague. Contrary to the philosophical understanding so popularized by Greco-Egyptian philosophers of late antiquity such as Zosimos of Panopolis (c. CE 300), some European alchemists often interpreted the central premise of the art as no more than a quest for material gold. Their written works were so heavily riddled with symbols, images, and allegories that one could easily lose one's bearings amid the narrative density and verbosity. For those with little or no interest in Hermetic principles, the treatises may seem like claptrap, yet the occult-minded and spiritually inclined would beg to differ. In fact, it challenges logic that so many practitioners of the art would go to great lengths in writing about formulae that unlock great secrets and keep alluding to them unless something of importance were being conveyed. But what exactly? A vital clue appears to come from the nature of the images themselves and particularly the quintessential principles that underpin them.

Two of these principles that appear repeatedly are *Sol* and *Luna*. *Sol* can be understood as an active, masculine principle that seeks expression in the universe and desires to make itself known. It is the "I" of the personal ego that manifests human personality. It can also be light, consciousness, fire, gold, day, the sun, the soul, intelligence, the triangle, and time. *Luna* stands as its polar opposite; it is a passive, feminine principle that morphs to reflect the inverted form of that which is impressed upon it. The concept brings to mind water deities like the nymph Thetis and the sea god Proteus, both of whom encompassed the ability to change shape at will. *Luna* can be darkness, unconsciousness, water, the night, the moon, matter, mercury, the ocean, the circle, eternity, silver, and astral light. Alchemy is a language whereby images of the two polar principles are connected to one another by way of analogy and will often represent differing aspects of the same object.

Hence, what we have is a process whereby *Sol*, the personal ego that grows conscious of its own existence and can experience its surroundings, conjuncts *Luna*, the matter that exists in various states and can be experienced. Just as the mercury in a thermometer measures the temperature gradient by rising and falling, so too are *Luna's* transitory shapes an accurate marker

Figure A-3. The sixth meditative emblem from German alchemist Basil Valentine's book *Azoth of the Philosophers*, allegorically revealing the potentiality of spirit rising from the primordial egg through *Sol* and *Luna's* repeated conjunctions as the hermetic androgyne, the seven *aetheric* powers that grant individual soul-sparks their personalities, the dragon of Nature as personification of the hermetic fires through which the Great Work comes to fruition, and the four elements (represented by the square and number four) uniting to form the alchemical trinity of fixed salt, active sulphur, and passive mercury (signified by the triangle and number three) from the winged sphere of the *prima materia*, c. CE 1659.

of the manner in which *Sol* experiences his or her being. By removing the alchemical jargon, one also sees the framework for Jung's concept of *individuation*. The "I" of the personal ego is subjected to continuous, prolonged interactions with base matter, which leads to evolution or involution of its own consciousness. There is often an internal struggle of some sort between various self-states in which the experience itself incites a fundamental change at the core, ensuing in the generation of greater self-awareness. It recalls the hero myth of all cultures in which a superhuman benefactor travels far and wide, enduring death-defying and inexorable ordeals before returning to his/her hometown wholly transformed, transposed, renewed, and more often than not exalted.

In hindsight, the alchemical manuscripts may have desired to draw attention to a different sort of relationship between spirit and matter. Outwardly, the two may appear to be polar opposites, yet a much more rigorous investigation of the two principles reveals something startlingly different. The "lead" and other base materials in the universe—which formed a benchmark against which the soul-spark measured its conscious awakening—weren't really dead and inert at all; they were merely in a state of suspended animation and would spark to life the moment a newly integrated perception of the self had to be accommodated, thus recreating and reforming the seemingly inanimate world in ways that were truly magical.

Just like Carl Jung before me, I, too, may be committing intellectual suicide and endorsing the fallacy of conceptual anachronism by ascribing psychological interpretations to alchemical manuscripts that were inspired, written, and compiled centuries before an idiosyncratic and culturally bound system of knowledge called "psychology" ever reared its head. Yes, using the interconnected and mutually dependent paradigms of mind, behavior, and social relationships to understand what alchemists may or may not have been thinking is, strictly speaking, a historical inaccuracy, but it doesn't necessarily invalidate the psychological view. The mental landscapes of the authors inspired to create such awe-inspiring manuscripts may have been facilitated and catalyzed by the same internal processes parading under our more mundane, disenchanted psychological labels today. Inner mental processes may, in fact, be stable across time — we understand and make sense out of them using a mutual language of scientific orthodoxy imposed upon us by our pedagogical institutions. Your cultural blueprints enable one kaleidoscope rendition of the rugged terrain and mine another. Each is one inimitable way of perceiving, but not the only way. We cling desperately to our own cultural conditioning in an attempt to tolerate ambiguity, preserve the private and essential illusion of personal control, and negate the existential dread of annihilation, chaos, and social pandemonium. Paradigms confined to disparate epochs might not necessarily be incommensurate; perhaps peoples existing across the full spectrum of sociohistorical milieus are simply using different labels and jargon to describe the same universal truths.

Under these circumstances, what reasonable conclusion can be drawn? First, we don't have to become the blind victims of modern Cartesian-Kantian philosophy, or dogmatic proponents of an either/or agenda intent on drawing premature judgments and conclusions. Second, and more importantly, we should examine the entire scope of kaleidoscopic lenses we have at our discretion and leave no stone, however small and misshapen, unturned.

This monograph encompasses a collection of essays on this fascinating subject. The core philosophical principles that inform the mystical and operative ambitions of alchemy are all described in explicit detail in the appendices. Appendix A delineates the four Aristotelian elements — water, fire, earth, and air — while Appendix B contains the seven planet–metal relationships — the sun or gold, the moon or silver, Venus or copper, Mercury or quicksilver, Mars or iron, Jupiter or tin, and Saturn or lead. Appendix C, on the other hand, contains the triune aspect of sulphur of the *Tria Prima*, mercury of the *Tria Prima*, and salt of the *Tria Prima*.

Part One, *Alchemy: Histories*, is concerned with the interdisciplinary and cross-cultural intercourse that occasioned the rich tapestry of alchemical tropes, themes, narratives, and pursuits. Chapters in this section address: the harmonious fusion of Hellenistic nature philosophy, Gnostic mythology, and Egyptian crafts and metallurgical practices in late antiquity; the role of alchemy during the Renaissance; the influence of alchemy on Jacob Boehme's theosophy; and the integral role medieval alchemical imagery played in the theoretical legitimacy of Jung's collective unconscious.

Part Two, *Alchemy: Processes of the Mind*, looks at the alchemical opus and its individual stages in the context of analytical, developmental, and clinical psychology. Chapters in this section offer psychological interpretations of the *Splendor Solis* plates, as well as integrated alchemical interpretations of personality, personal growth, and the human condition.

Part Three, *Alchemy: The Noetic Science*, examines the empirical validity of alchemical theory and pursuits. Chapters in this section critically address: the viability of metallic transmutation; whether esoteric correspondences (i.e., the planet–metal connections) might exist in any objective sense and whether they hold up when subjected to empirical scrutiny; and how its animistic paradigm and principles of transformation might be connected to more innovative and radical ideas that are now emerging within the nomothetic disciplines. This section also contains a comprehensive chapter on the mechanical narratives of orthodox science, their incompatibility with the known facts, and the link with alchemy.

Part I: Histories

Chapter 1

The Influence of Hellenistic Philosophy on Alchemy

Save for being a product of the marriage of the technical crafts with Greek philosophy in an Alexandrine milieu that was as deep and complex as it was variegated and broad, Western alchemy was the discipline that best captured the Hellenistic plight to perfect and compete with Nature herself. It appropriated many of the ideas that were around at the time—speculative nature science, Stoic philosophy, Gnostic soteriological notions of purification and illumination via contemplation, Egyptian symbolism of the Osirian rebirth cycle[1]—and in doing so offered a new point of reference pertaining to perspectives on the nature of matter through which the relationship between the ethereal and material, the divine and corporeal, and the natural and artificial could be scrutinized. Alchemy was different from the Hellenistic and Egyptian *technai* of metallurgy, glassmaking, pottery, chemistry, dyeing, jewelry-making, and generating lifelike automata because it went beyond the cosmogony of superficial imitation to a perfective one in which a different atomic structure could be imposed onto the existing blueprint of a created object or substance, thus altering its inherent "form." Adopting the role of a secondary or inferior deity, the alchemist could fashion gemstones, metals, elixirs, and other products by first reducing them to primal chaos or *prima materia*[2] in a manner reminiscent of God's creation *ex nihilo*, an act of creating something out of nothing. This fanciful list of natural replications would later evolve to encompass artificial procreation in the homunculus,[3] a rudimentary proto-cloning of human beings with biotechnological consequences and moral-ethical concerns much more relevant now than they probably were back then.

Even though the origins of Western alchemy are ambiguous, ill-defined, and shrouded in mystery, we must attempt at least a cursory demarcation of its development in Hellenistic Egypt for the sake of pinpointing which Hellenistic ideas it entered into dialogue with and when this might have transpired. What seems clear beyond reasonable doubt is that prior to its confluence with Hellenistic philosophy, the proto-alchemy of the Egyptian Late Period was closely related to the chemical arts and the metallurgical crafts that sought to counterfeit precious stones and dyes.[4] During its formative stages of evolution, it was purely a mimetic endeavor. According to Andre-Jean Festugiere (1898–1982), the French philosopher who critically examined the historiography of alchemical documents, this inaugural period lasted until about 200 BCE, and produced prescriptions described in a purely technical, mechanical, and quantitative manner. Such appears to be the case with the Leyden X and Stockholm papyri. Both offer a plethora of instructions for the counterfeiting of gold and the synthetic replication of silver, pearls, and textile dyes.[5] The discipline's trajectory changed direction sometime between 200 BCE and CE 100, when substances, metals, and natural processes were anthropomorphized and appreciated for their qualitative markers; everything that came-to-be, was coming-to-be, and had been in the cosmos subscribed to universal laws of love and conflict. Individual members of the three kingdoms—plant, animal, and mineral—rigidly obeyed these laws, forming "sympathies" and "antipathies" with individuals who belonged to the same kingdom or were from disparate ones, respectively.

Festugiere argued that this phase was embodied par excellence by Bolus the Democritean's (c. 200 BCE) alchemo-mystical treatise *Physika kai Mystika*, though it is now contested that the text in question dates to the first centuries CE and was probably reworked a number of times.[6] Finally, the fragmentary works of Zosimos of Panopolis (c. CE 300), a Gnostic alchemist, complete the cross-cultural pollination of the chemical technologies of ancient Egypt by Hellenistic philosophy.[7] Zosimos's dream-like *Visions* transcribe at length purifications of the human soul and Nature in Gnostic and Stoic terms,[8] alluding to the notion that alchemy was a viable and respectable route through which both Nature and her most celebrated creature, the human being, could emerge transposed and transfigured from what might be described as an accursed, abased, fallen, and disenchanted state.

Today, many scholars of Western esotericism are convinced that the transmutational plights described by alchemists are fictional and only make sense in the context of an Aristotelian nature philosophy, which later lapsed into disrepute. While this may be true, the concepts that crop up, again and again, in discourses of Aristotelian teleology and explicate the relationship between "matter" (*hyle*) and "form" (*eidos*) are surely permutations of earlier Greek thought. By far the most imperative of these is the ubiquitous *prima materia*, a synonym for what the ancients understood as the undifferentiated first matter from which everything in the corporeal world was made and to which it would eventually return. The alchemists themselves were convinced that the phenomenon and experience of transmutation as a world-creating and self-actualizing process was impossible without a transient return to the primordial state of Oneness. Further, they also believed that the essences of the soul and base matter were both projections of the *prima materia*, and *prima materia* was often equated with the culmination of the opus, the *ultima materia* or Philosopher's Stone.[9] Thus, for a base substance or "soul" to be transmuted into silver and gold, it had to be reduced to its primal state first.

This marked a seminal stage in the alchemical opus known as *necrosis* or *nigredo* in which the old form or matter dies and putrefies, and is superseded by an unadulterated one that ignites from its ashes. As both the matrix and fruition of the Stone, it seems entirely natural that the *prima materia* would be imbued with epithets that are conceptually heterogenous yet qualitatively linked: moon, sea, mother, mercury, water, earth, virgin, menstrue, poison, chaos, dew, and *hyle*[10] are just some of these.

So where might the idea of mutual interconnectedness and interdependence of all created matter and life, the intimation that all is One, have actually come from? The Greeks have always been inquisitive seafarers, and there is ample evidence to suggest they were traveling to Egypt as early as the eighteenth and seventeenth centuries BCE.[11] Their adventures in the land of the Nile would have brought them face to face with the Egyptian priesthood, and a great many Greek travelers would have been entrusted with intimate details of the Heliopolitan creation myth. This state myth, sacrosanct in the mind of any ancient Egyptian, makes use of a dramatic metaphor to explain how the universe came into being. It speaks of a primeval ocean of undifferentiated mass called Nun, which existed since time immemorial before its self-generated vortices pushed up a mound of fertile silt. In turn, the silt segregated into a conscious and self-engendered creator god. The god proceeded to masturbate and ejaculate a pair of substances, air and moisture, from whence all created matter emerged.[12] Vivacious in spirit and philosophical by nature, the early Greeks would have brooded upon the homogenous first substance of creation, which the Egyptians defined as primeval chaos (χάος). The early Greeks would have wanted to tear aside the metaphoric veil and know its true nature. It was an obsession that befuddled the Ionian pre-Socratics for centuries on end.

Smyrna-born poet Homer (c. 850 BCE) stayed faithful to the Egyptian conception, describing the primordial substance as "River Ocean, a deep and mighty flood, encircling land and sea like a Serpent with its tail in its mouth."[13] An evocative illustration of this concept appeared later in an eleventh-century Hellenistic manuscript together with the slogan *hen to pan*, the notion that everything is one.[14] Thales (c. 630–546 BCE), on the other hand, visualized a flat earth floating atop a base substance that resembled a vast and desolate ocean. He, too, aligned himself with the view put forth by the Egyptian creation myths and Homer. A pupil of his, Anaximander of Miletus (c. 610–546 BCE), called it the *apeiron*, a term connoting "boundless" and recalling the mutability of water. Anaximenes (584–28 BCE), also of Miletus, was the first philosopher to initiate a radical departure from the established convention, visualizing the base substance of the cosmos as a kind of vapor or air but not of the physical type. Meditating on the problem at hand, Anaximenes reasoned that condensation of the primal substance produced physical air, water, and earth, while its rarefaction formed fire. His emphasis on transformation of one substance into another formed the foundation of Empedocles of Acragas's (c. 490–430 BCE) doctrine of the elements. These elements were eventually absorbed into Aristotle's nature philosophy. Of all the pre-Socratic philosophers it was a contemporary of Anaximenes in Heraclitus of Ephesus (535–475 BCE) who came closest to what many contemporaneous esotericists believe to be true. Seeing that the active mover behind the rotation of the elements is fire, he deduced that the underlying cause of all phenomena must be an ethereal fire of sorts.[15]

Empedocles's instructional poem *On Nature*, a philosophical work written in hexameter, made a very important contribution to Aristotelian nature science. Unlike the pre-Socratics who believed each element to be a primary substance in its own

Figure 1-1. An engraving of an ouroboros, a snake biting its own tail, by Lucas Jennis in the 1625 alchemical tract *De Lapide Philosophico.*

right, Empedocles posited that it was the *prima materia* that differentiated into the four elements under the influence of four auxiliary qualities. It should be made patently clear that the four elements in question are not to be confused with the four corporeal manifestations of the same name; they are merely philosophical principles founded upon an ancient but now antiquated theory of corpuscles that enable the *prima materia* to take on innumerable guises while remaining fundamentally unchanged. Under this paradigm, an esoteric practitioner could invoke undisputed authority and empirical legitimacy in declaring inanimate or organic forms in Nature to come from the One. The conviction in Empedoclean principles persisted, like the tides and seasons, for many centuries after the condensed summa of alchemical knowledge presented in the enigmatic *Tabula Smaragdina* [Emerald Tablet] under the aegis of the legendary Hermes Trismegistus staunchly claimed that the Stone's father was the solar orb (also fire or Philosophical Sulphur) and its mother was the lunar orb (also water or Philosophical Mercury). Conversely, the wind or air would be implicated as the womb that carried it, and the earth, the volatile and moist humus, would be cast in the presiding role of wet nurse.[16]

The Empedoclean world was clearly all about diametrically opposed forces: fire—an active, masculine principle with a propensity to rise—is dry and hot. Air—also an active, masculine principle but with a tendency to expand—is hot and wet. In sharp contradistinction to this, the feminine, passive principle of water is wet and cold because of its inherent nature to expand and drop, while earth—also of the same essence as water but characterized by a condition of solidity that causes it to drop toward the navel of the earth—is cold and dry.[17] Each element shares a secondary quality with two others. This permits integration into an eternal cycle known as elemental rotation, where a succeeding condition is potentially latent in an existing one. As had been posited by Heraclitus, the only active mover in this assembly is fire, an element whose physical counterpart spurs the transformation of water from a liquid form to a gas, and whose absence enables its transition back into a liquid and a solid. In observing the subtle intricacies of these processes, it would have seemed like an anathema, if not an outright heresy, not to ascribe the manifestations of the noumenal world or natural transmutations occurring through chemical processes, like calcination, coagulation, distillation, sublimation, and dissolution, to the modus operandi of fire.

This brings us to the genius of Plato, who followed century-old premises pioneered by Ionic pre-Socratics. He borrowed the pre-Socratic vision of the universe as a living being, as well as Anaximenes's vision of the First Cause as an ethereal fire, and married them with Pythagorean mystical insights that defined the First Cause in strictly quantitative and geometric terms. Plato's deductions and inferences were unprecedented; if, on one hand, the uncreated potential was a spherical speck of fire that mysteriously took on a plethora of forms when it differentiated into other substances and qualities, and if, on the other hand, everything coming-to-be was infused with the same vital life force emanating from the primeval origin, then the universal nature must be a binary system; somewhere "out there" and concealed from the human mind with its fallible sensory organs existed a world of Eternal Ideas, Forms, and Archetypes that stood apart from Nature herself but also played a fundamental role in determining physical laws, as well as the nature and dynamic of the relationships therein. Time and space separated the two dimensions.

Further speculations were then made from within this ontological framework, placing the earth under the mediation of a Universal Soul (*psyche*) which united the human soul in its virginal state with the web of the cosmic animal that was Nature. The Universal Soul and the human psyche were superior and inferior reflections of a Universal Spirit (*nous*) that stood above them on the cosmological totem pole and espied the first cogitation, a primeval and benevolent act of self-love that was God. Directly beneath the Universal Soul was the earth and below that the formless *hyle*, the *prima materia*.[18] Western alchemy would use logic proceeding from the threefold hypostasis of the Platonic cosmos to forge connections between the sickly metals of the mineral realms and the untethered human soul seeking *unio mystica* with the Godhead, both having to be purged of their "sickness" and restored to an original state of perfection if the true essence of Spirit in all its glory (i.e., gold) was going to shine through. In hindsight, it appears alchemy's conviction in a Godhead and in supernatural agencies, the idea of a transcendental realm, the relationship between macrocosm and microcosm, and much of its terminology derive explicitly from Platonic metaphysics.[19]

Neo-Platonic philosophy, in particular, exerted a profound influence on practical aspects of the alchemical process, though it wasn't until the sixteenth century that manuscripts supporting this contention came to light. Strictly speaking, the Neo-Platonic cosmos was merely a system of orthodox Platonism that congealed under Plotinus (CE 205–70), a Greek-Egyptian philosopher from the Deltaic city of Lycopolis in Lower Egypt. His closest disciple and biographer, the Lycian-born Porphyry (CE 232–305), established and elaborated a cosmological system whereby the aether-filled spheres of the seven planets and the four Empedoclean elements of the earth separated Man from the Empyrean of God and the *primum mobile*, an etheric substance that permeated space and facilitated the heavenly rotation.[20] It's likely that the sevenfold astrological schema through which incarnating souls descended and picked up their distinct personality traits was extended to the corresponding metals.

Hence, when alchemists relayed details of their practical work, they described an abstruse process characterized by distinct phases based on coloration and mediated by seven planetary powers. The Saturnine, Jovial, and Lunar forces "lunarized" the base matter by galvanizing chemical processes such as calcination, solution, and putrefaction, which brought about the *nigredo* (putrefaction) and the *albedo* (whitening) in the sealed vessel.[21] Successful completion of the whitening phase bestowed upon the alchemist the gift of the "white stone," the power of healing ailments and of transmuting base matter like lead or mercury into silver. Further operations were then carried out under the auspices of the Venusian, Martian, and Solar forces, which "solarized" the just formed "white stone" through chemical reduction, sublimation, coagulation, and fermentation.[22] The subsequent reactions brought about distinctive colorations known as the *citrinitas* (yellowing) and *rubedo* (reddening), and culminated in the synthesis of a scintillating red powder of significant weight known as the "red stone." Known by other cryptic terms like *ultima materia* or Philosopher's Stone, the "red stone" was the alchemists' coveted and zealously guarded secret—with it, a practitioner could wield extraordinary esemplastic powers and either transmute base metals to gold or prolong human life indefinitely. Orchestrated under the patronage of Saturn, Jupiter, and the moon, the creation of the "white stone" comprised what alchemists typically alluded to as the Lesser Work; on the other hand, the preparation of the "red stone" under the patronage of Venus, Mars, and the sun was referred to as the Greater Work. The protean Mercury, a planet-metal comprising the preliminary stage, was never ascribed with rulership over a specific phase in its own right because it was deemed vital to the alchemical process as a whole.

Plato's student Aristotle (384–322 BCE) played an integral role in the transmission of Hellenic philosophy to alchemical theory. His teleological schema explicated all created matter (substances, objects, beings) in terms of four primary quotients, including the material, the formal, the efficient, and the final.[23] The material and formal relayed its material composition and unique anatomical configuration, the efficient attempted to delineate the moving force behind it, and the final had to make do with the ultimate purpose for its existence. The last of these principles had been embedded in the created matter by the prototype existing in the Platonic universe of Forms and was itself a thought of God.

According to Aristotle, everything Nature could engender contained a *nisus*—in other words, an intrinsic yearning to become the Platonic Form in the Empyrean upon which it had been modeled. Under this esoteric paradigm, transformation was possible through the interaction effects of fiery activity or "form" and passive potentiality or "hyle." In such a dynamic, ever-fluctuating world, the neonate strived to become a full-grown human, the egg a chicken, the seed a tree, the caterpillar a butterfly, and the element of carbon a diamond. There were far-reaching implications for the mineral kingdom, too; base metals weren't inert or dead reagents as they appeared to the naked human eye, but inspirited embryos in variant stages of maturation deep in the subterranean womb of the Great Mother Goddess.[24] Measured against gold, a metal perceived by the most eminent contemporary philosophers to be the material reflection of the immaterial, spiritual prototype of God, the other six known metals were essentially inchoate versions of gold that had yet to ripen. This was the natural process that the ancient alchemist sought to accelerate under artificially simulated conditions.

We see a confluence of many pre-Socratic, Platonic, and animistic ideas surrounding minerals and metals in Aristotle's *Meteorologica*. In this particular treatise, the Stagirite argues that the material occupying the space occupied by the *primum mobile* and the planetary spheres wasn't the four earthly elements but an indivisible, incorrupt, and previously unidentified fifth substrate known as "aether" or the "quintessence."[25] This concept is commensurate with the Greek *pneuma* or transcendental Spirit. He also lays bare the proposition that rocks, minerals, and metals all originated from exhalations of moist "watery vapor" and dry "earthy smoke" in the subterranean. Those that could be dissolved, a category encompassing gold and the imperfect metals, were composed of the wet substrate, while those impermeable to change, like fossils and rocks, were creations of the dry one. When the Arab polymath Jabir ibn Hayyan (c. 721–815) described the growth of metals in the *Liber misericordiae* of the *Corpus Jabirianum* (c. eighth–tenth centuries) some 11 centuries afterward, he connected the first of Aristotle's exhalations to sulphur, the active principle of flammability and combustibility, and the second to mercury, the principle of fusibility and volatility.

Jabir believed that the nature of the metals themselves corresponded to two distinct and intrinsic qualities. Each metal congealed under the influence of a particular planetary power, which was itself acting upon a dynamic aggregation of mercury, consisting of the passive elements of water and earth, and sulphur, consisting of the active elements of fire and air. This was known as the Sulphur-Mercury theory, a model that would go on to dominate Western alchemy until the development of phlogiston theory in the latter stages of the seventeenth century.[26] Alternatively, in his renowned medieval alchemical treatise *Summa perfectionis*, the Latin Geber (c. 1200) claims that exaltation of the Philosopher's Stone was feasible because mercury was composed of minute corpuscles that would induce transmutation by diffusing through the perforated exterior of a base metal. Geber's idea was informed by the Aristotelian idea of "least parts" as described in *Physics* and *Meteorologica*.[27]

Aristotle's speculations procured some far-reaching consequences for the aurific art by strategically positioning it on a pedestal of eternal feasibilities that would precariously balance between poles demarcating the good and the evil, the genuine and the fraudulent, and the natural and the artificial for centuries to come. In *Physics*, Aristotle differentiates between the artificial and the natural by illuminating the former's condition of inertness and the latter's proclivity toward motion and change. He then explicates (at *Physics* II 8 199a15–17) the nature of mimesis by positing that purposive intervention on the part of an artist can either duplicate the prototype without changing its inner structure (*mimetai*), or more importantly, catalyze the transformation of objects and substances in ways that violate the teleological cycle (*epitelei*). Moreover, in his celebrated treatise *Meteorologica*, Aristotle uses verbs associated with the artificial activity of cooking like "roasting" and "boiling" to intimate that both the technical operations seeking to mimic natural processes and the natural processes themselves are reflections of one another, fundamentally one and the same.[28] By rendering and describing a natural process in the context of operant human behavior, Aristotle makes known his unconscious philosophical conviction that artificial methods could still generate a natural product.

The marriage between Aristotelian nature philosophy and the technical recipes probably occurred during the life and times of Bolus the Democritean, an active Pythagorean who lived in the Deltaic Egyptian city of Mendes during the second century BCE.[29] Known for his mystical approach to the artisanal crafts, Bolus wrote a rather lengthy alchemical treatise titled *Physika kai Mystika* [Physical and Mystical Matters] of which only segments have survived. While revealing a deep preoccupation with both the physical and paraphysical, Bolus's work delineates a process whereby a base substance or the *prima materia*, usually metallic lead or mercury, is used to prepare gold, otherwise known as the Great Work or Philosopher's Stone. In this, the earliest known permutation of metallic transmutation, exaltation of the "stone" is marked by four distinct phases of coloration that serve as ostensible markers of inner transformation. Thus the "stone" or noble metal is conferred form only after undergoing putrefaction through *melanosis* (nigredo), bleaching through *leucosis* (albedo), yellowing through *xanthosis* (citrinitas), and lastly reddening through *iosis* (rubedo). Purple sometimes takes the place of red in the last of these stages, hinting at the dual purpose of alchemy as both an applied craft zealously striving to perfect gross matter and an esoteric discipline for psychospiritual development.

The full grafting of Hellenistic philosophy onto the technical and chemico-operative prescriptions of the proto-alchemical period in Egypt is clearly discernible in the work of Zosimos, a Gnostic alchemist who viewed alchemy as an artificial operation able to transform inspirited Nature as a whole. In his fragmentary commentary titled *On Virtue*, Zosimos describes a series of dream-like visions and interpretations, and renders salient his philosophy that the intangible principle of zestfulness, color, character, distinctiveness, and ensoulment—in other words, the *pneuma* (Spirit)—can be separated from its corporeal shackles through ordinary evaporation processes like sublimation and distillation.[30] His clever use of metaphor to draw parallels between base metals and the human condition, between the distillation apparatus and temples and altars, and between the liberation of the spirit-soul from the human body, and the transformation of the volatile substance comprising base metals is intentional, shrewdly drawing attention to corresponding processes of creation reflected in the Divine Intellect or the One.

Yet another dream transcribed in Zosimos's *Visions* involves the ritual torture, punishment (*kolasis*), and death of a horde of men inside an alchemical flask. If the dream is, in fact, an allegory, then the men suffering trials and tribulations can be equated with the liberation of *pneumata* from their restrictive matrix through heat and the application of corrosives, their purification with rudimentary transformation into a nobler form, and the resurrection or reanimation of their mutilated bodies into the coagulation of a new form. Zosimos first discusses this parable in the context of individual reagents before augmenting his parameters to include created Nature as a whole. He postulates that success in transmutation is entirely contingent on the individual alchemist, who, in seeking success, must permit for Nature (*physis*) to be "forced to the investigation" (*ekthlibomene pros ten zetesin*) by regressing to a primordial state of confusion and suffering (*talaina*) where her instinctual reaction will be to assume transitional states of being until she drifts closer and closer to death.[31] Only through this torturous suffering can she become more pneumatic and endure. Genuine transmutation, according to Zosimos, entailed manipulating the invigorating life principle, or *pneuma*, and resynthesizing it with the physical base through a sequence of controlled chemico-operative techniques.

Several sections in the 13 opuscules of Zosimos's *Authentic Memoirs* deal with distillation equipment in a pneumatic capacity.[32] He describes several apparatuses intended for sublimation; numerous multi-piped alembics fashioned from glass and fitted with clay or terracotta stems that were used for either distillation or the fixation of mercury; and a sophisticated, cylinder-like vessel called a *kerotakis*. The last of these was a sublimation apparatus, especially significant because it was known to facilitate changes to the color and properties of the substance within that were undoubtedly construed by the overseeing alchemist as a genuine recombination of *pneuma* and body. The *kerotakis* tower was a closed vessel comprising three cubicles: a lower compartment in which the material to be sublimed was placed, a perforated plate near the top of the vessel on which a piece of metal or ore was placed, and a hemispheric cap to collect the vapors. Sublimation was performed by fixing a substance, usually arsenic sulphide, mercury, or sulphur, on the lowermost compartment directly above a burning furnace and letting the vaporous fumes react with the metal or ore resting on the middle of the plate. Once the fumes reached the hemispherical lid on the top, they would condense into liquid and sluice their way back into the compartment containing the liquefied substance. Eventually, the sublimate would infuse itself into the metallic base, precipitating alterations to color that were probably perceived by Zosimos as fundamental changes in the structure of matter.

In retrospect, the imitative arts have a long and illustrious history in Western civilization. In late antiquity, those who identified as artists were primarily interested in creating products that amalgamated synthetic features and either mimicked those of their natural prototypes or attempted to supplant them. Often, the products themselves were aesthetically pleasing but lacked the intrinsic principle of movement and the inner qualities that characterized their prototypes. Examples par excellence of the counterfeiting of natural products like gold and silver, as well as natural dyes and precious stones, predominate within the technical prescriptions of the Leyden X and Stockholm papyri, both of which represent a mechanistic or "exoteric" proto-alchemy. Later, when alchemical writings fused with the philosophical musings of the Greeks and the nature philosophy of Aristotle, the Hermetic Art reorientated itself in the Alexandrine world as a *techne*, a self-appointed authority propagating absolute claims about the mutable nature of atomic structure. When Zosimos started writing his 28-volume corpus, a tome encompassing his personal insights and earlier musings, alchemy was no longer just a perfective endeavor seeking to generate the *ultima materia*—the medicinal panacea or the coveted alchemical gold. Alongside medicine, alchemy sought to artificially recapitulate the processes of creation in whole and down to the last explicit detail. In doing so, the art claimed an exalted place in the hierarchy of ancient *technai*. But none of it would have been possible had alchemy not borrowed its authoritative looking glass from Greek philosophy.

Endnotes

1   Bernard D. Haage, 'Alchemy II: Antiquity-12th Century', in *Dictionary of Gnosis and Western Esotericism*, ed. by Wouter J. Hanegraaff et al., 2 vols (Leiden: Brill, 2005), I, p. 22.

2   The passive, receptive, unformed basis known as the *hyle* from which all matter, be it immaterial and of the soul or material and of the world, is formed.

3   Haage, p. 28.

4   Stanton J. Linden, *The Alchemy Reader: From Hermes Trismegistus to Isaac Newton* (Cambridge, UK: Cambridge University Press, 2003), pp. 46–49.

5   Ibid, pp. 46–49.

6   Ibid, p. 38.

7   Joseph L. Henderson and Dyane N. Sherwood, *Transformation of the Psyche: The Symbolic Alchemy of the Splendor Solis* (East Sussex, UK: Routledge, 2003), p. 9.

8   Albert de Jong, 'Zosimus of Panopolis', in *Dictionary of Gnosis and Western Esotericism*, ed. by Wouter J. Hanegraaff et al. 2 vols (Leiden: Brill, 2005), I, p. 1185.

9   Titus Burckhardt, *Alchemy: Science of the Cosmos, Science of the Soul* (Shaftesbury, UK: Element Books, 1986), p. 97.

10   Lindy Abraham, *A Dictionary of Alchemical Imagery* (Cambridge, UK: Cambridge University Press, 1998), p. 156.

11   Michael Rice, *Egypt's Legacy: The Archetypes of Western Civilization* 3000–30 BC (London, UK: Routledge, 1997), pp. 178–179.

12   Lorna Oakes and Lucia Gahlin, *Ancient Egypt* (New York City, NY: Hermes House, 2002), p. 301.

13   Charles Mills Gayley, *The Classic Myths in English Literature and Art* (Boston, USA: Adamant Media Corporation, 2005), p. 3.

14   Haage, p. 18.

15   Emile Brehier, *The History of Philosophy: The Hellenic Age* (Chicago, USA: University of Chicago Press, 1965), p. 208.
16   Linden, p. 28.
17   Burckhardt, pp. 94–95.
18   Ibid, p. 116.
19   Ibid, pp. 115.
20   Aldis Uzdavinys (ed.), *The Heart of Plotinus: The Essential Enneads (Perennial Philosophy)* (Bloomington, IN: World Wisdom, 2009), p. 248.
21   Burckhardt, pp. 185–189.
22   Ibid, pp. 189–191.
23   Andrea Falcon, 'Aristotle on Causality', in *The Stanford Encyclopedia of Philosophy (Fall 2011 Edition)*, ed. by Edward N. Zalta, http://plato.stanford.edu/archives/fall2011/entries/aristotle-causality/ [Accessed May 24, 2021].
24   Henderson and Sherwood, p. 5.
25   Haage, p. 19.
26   Allison P. Coodert, 'Alchemy IV: 16th–18th Century', in *Dictionary of Gnosis and Western Esotericism*, ed. by Wouter J. Hanegraaff et al., 2 vols (Leiden: Brill, 2005), I, p. 42.
27   Ibid, p. 42.
28   Aristotle, *Meteorologica*, ed. and trans. by H. D. P. Lee (Cambridge, MA: Harvard University Press, 1952), IV 381B3-9.
29   Linden, p. 38.
30   Noretta Koertge (ed.), *A House Built on Sand: Exposing Postmodernist Myths about Science* (New York City, NY: Oxford University Press, 2000), p. 221.
31   Ibid, p. 221.
32   Michele Mertens (ed.), *Les Alchimistes Grecs: Zosime de Panopolis*, trans. by Michele Mertens (Paris, FR: Les Belles Letres, 1995), pp. 4:130–152.

Chapter 2

The Dignity of Alchemy During the Renaissance

Contrary to what an occult dilettante may think, the esoteric undercurrent known as Hermeticism has never been a distinctive philosophical discipline in its own right, nor has it competed for cultural prominence against the major monotheistic religions: Judaism, Islam, and Christianity. For a more comprehensive grasp of the topic, one must return to the milieu in which it originated—the world of Graeco-Roman Egypt. If Hermeticism was represented by an equilateral triangle, each of its three sides would represent the concepts of revelation, secrecy, and initiation. Alternatively, one can think of the discipline as a worldview that acknowledges God's absolute transcendence: *gnosis*, an intellectually guided and intuitively felt participation, is what made this reality coherent in the eyes of the human being.[33] There were also obligatory oaths of silence and initiatory rites accompanying and governing the whole endeavor, and these were undoubtedly inherited from the mystical Pythagorean tradition during the cross-cultural pollination of ideas in fertile Alexandria sometime between c. 300 BCE and CE 300.

Just like the wisdom literature of the autochthonous Egyptian culture, Hermetic discourse was usually didactic and instructional in scope and yoked by ethical and moral undertones; the teachings were imparted by a pseudepigraphical persona, usually a semidivine father or teacher to his pupil or son, for the sole purpose of realigning the latter with a salvific quest that sought to reconcile the soul with its divine source, the Sphere of the Fixed Stars, and the Empyrean of God. The philosophical and theological writings brewing in Alexandria after the third century BCE also precipitated a fusion between the ibis-headed moon god Thoth and the Greek messenger god Hermes. Traits belonging to either of the two—the invention of writing, mercurial thought, the enforcement of divine and corporeal law, the authorship of knowledge, and intercession between worlds—were inevitably recast under the aegis of the composite Hermes-Thoth. Sometime during the second century onward, this composite deity also acquired the epithet "thrice-greatest" and became known as Hermes Trismegistus.[34] Trismegistus was the venerated champion of Hermeticism, or at least the *egregore* to which its adherents paid homage. Just as the moon reflects supernal light from the sun during the nocturnal hours, so too did Hermes Trismegistus possess the minds of the literati so that the genealogy of primordial knowledge would be transcribed onto parchments of papyrus from the Nile, or so they thought.

What made a text Hermetic wasn't the philosophical or religious undercurrent from whence it had sprung, but rather an absolute appeal to the Egyptian sage himself and a conviction that primeval knowledge, which by some lamentable lapse had been lost some time ago, had existed since time immemorial. It appears the legitimacy of the Hermetic institution was precariously hinged on emphatic claims that were fabricated, bundled into legends, and then inserted into treatises for the sole purpose of perpetuating that conviction. Moreover, they all advocated for a cosmos with a quintessentially animistic bent; the divine, which contains within both physical and paraphysical constituents, permeates all levels of creation. Within this idiosyncratic system, Nature herself is a living entity, and further still, all things created are qualitatively and quantitatively interdependent and interconnected in an intricate web through the law of cosmic sympathies and antipathies. At the pinnacle or highest echelon is the transcendental and benevolent God, the ineffable One, who ruminates in fundamental harmony. Emanating from the One is a hierarchical order of dimensions encompassing the planetary deities and lesser supernatural intelligences. It was believed a human soul wishing to incarnate would acquire specific traits or qualities as it passed through each of these dimensional rungs of the cosmic ladder until it reached Earth (i.e., the Mercurial sphere would grant cunning, the Venusian sphere would bequeath desire, the Jovian sphere would gift ambition, and so forth).

Figure 2-1. A 1617ce drawing of Hermes Trismegistus from Michael Maier's alchemical treatise *Symbola Aurea Mensae Duodecim Nationum*.

For Alexandrine Hermeticists, the universe (the macrocosm) and the corporeal protohuman (the microcosm) were inextricably linked through a system of correspondences that both reflected and coherently expressed the Divine Intellect, the Empyrean of God. Further still, their texts implicate a practical approach to the primeval knowledge that enabled practitioners to either bend Nature to their will—for instance, by accelerating its perfection through *chrysopoeia* (gold-making) or discerning time frames decreed by the heavenly arrangement to be auspicious for certain activities like divination. Hermeticism, then, was akin to the Egyptian sacred science from its humble beginnings, a *philosophia pia* that syncretized theology, philosophy, mysticism, natural science, and medicine with the dignified disciplines of alchemy, astrology, and theurgy. The French philosopher Andre-Jean Festugiere (CE 1898–1982) classified the heterogeneous texts according to their content, a division that remains effective to this day.[35] On one hand, there were the "philosophical Hermetica," texts concerned with philosophical speculation, and on the other hand, there were the "technical Hermetica," texts reinforcing philosophical knowledge of God through real-world application of principles and practice. Both subdisciplines actively sought *regressus ad uterum* for their postulants, with curricula tailored toward transcendental reaccession through the seven celestial spheres and a mystical union with the Godhead in the eighth.

Alchemy, though a distinct practice in its own right, was the embodiment of operative Hermeticism. Although discussed at length in the previous chapter, it's probably useful to summarize some of its core philosophical assumptions again. First and foremost, it emerged from the Alexandrine marriage of Aristotelian natural science to Gnostic and Egyptian mythology, as well as Neo-Platonism.[36] From the primordial slime, the *prima materia*, or the One, we have a fourfold differentiation into the

Aristotelian elements of fire, air, water, and earth, all of which comprise two auxiliary qualities: fire is dry and hot, air is hot and wet, water is wet and cold, and earth is cold and dry. Each Aristotelian element shares a secondary quality with two others, placing them into a linear cycle known as elemental rotation, where an ensuing state is latent in the existing one. The square born from the circle, or the number four which segregates from the One, is a geometric expression and equivalent of the conferral of form from the amorphous base substance. This makes possible a realm of endless feasibilities: the transmutation of base metals, the creation of precious stones, the purification of all substances, and, dare I say it, the "raising of vibrations" or consciousness (this and analogous statements are now thrown around liberally by members of the contemporaneous neopagan communities). The alchemist's universe comprised four elements and seasons (Nature, the inferior plane) emerging from a fourfold celestial arrangement (Empyrean, the superior plane) to generate a unique equilibrium of four cardinal humors in the human being (Man, both inferior and superior planes): phlegm (phlegma), black gall (melancholia), yellow gall (cholera), and blood (sanguis). Undisputed in their idiosyncratic worldview was that the correct admixture of corpuscles equated to a salubrious body or the restoration of health. There was even an apocryphal chemico-medical formula for life eternal.

By the second century CE, alchemy was already a syncretized mystical and chemico-operative art. The surviving written testament of an active Pythagorean named Pseudo-Democritus, or Bolus of Mendes, who lived in the Deltaic Egyptian city of Mendes during the second century BCE certainly attests to such.[37] Known for his mystical approach to the artisanal crafts, Bolus wrote a rather lengthy alchemical treatise titled *Physika kai Mystika* [Physical and Mystical Matters] of which only segments have survived. What remains of this text reveals a profound preoccupation with both the physical and paraphysical; *spagyreia*, a principal concern of the Chinese and later of the Arabian alchemists, is given special prominence here. He educates his audience about the therapeutic efficacy of many herbs along with the propensity of some to evoke the voice of the gods and cause psychedelic visions. His knowledge of theurgy was also commendable for he transparently discusses word intonation and breathing techniques in the casting of magical spells. The focal point of the treatise is the description of a process whereby a base substance or the *prima materia*, usually lead or mercury, is used to prepare gold, otherwise known as the Great Work or Philosopher's Stone. In this, the earliest known prototype of metallic transmutation, transformation, and exaltation of the "stone" is marked by four distinct phases of coloration that serve as external cues of inner transformation. The "stone," Bolus tells us, is conferred form only after undergoing putrefaction through *melanosis* (nigredo), bleaching through *leucosis* (albedo), yellowing through *xanthosis* (citrinitas), and finally reddening through *iosis* (rubedo). Purple sometimes takes the place of red in the last of these stages.

Hermeticism espouses a fairly undogmatic approach to monotheistic notions of the divine and served as a propaedeutic to the first truths revealed in the New Testament.[38] Under these circumstances, one should not be blamed for presuming that its assimilation into the incumbent Christian tradition was a straightforward and harmonious affair. Indeed, it's logical to assume Hermeticism and alchemy eschewed the vehement polemics of the early theologians, but they didn't! The opposite actually holds true. Writing at the end of the fourth and beginning of the fifth centuries, the Christian philosopher Augustine of Hippo (354–430) decried the Hermetic *Asclepius* for its reinforcement of Platonic daemonology and theurgic conjuration, which sought to ensorcel spirits into statues.

Spirits could listen to prayers and grant wishes by possessing statues. For Augustine, Hermes was a pagan sorcerer whose idolatrous ways could not be reconciled with an alternate image of him as the harbinger the Son of God in Jesus Christ. Paramount for the early Christian apologetics, these sentiments naturally extended to *chema*, the operative art. Tertullian (160–220), Clement of Alexandria (150–215), and a coterie of other apologetical narrators were convinced that knowledge of the chemical arts was compiled into books by fallen angels who'd embarked on indecent liaisons with corrupted mortals.[39] Secondly, they believed alchemy's lofty ambition to recapitulate the wonder of the cosmos before the Fall flirted too openly with heretical revelations made by certain Gnostic sects, namely that the original *gnosis* was lost when the androgynous protohuman ruptured into its male and female constituents, Adam and Eve. The Gnostic affiliation was the proverbial straw that broke the camel's back. When Constantine inducted Christianity into the Roman Empire as the only official and legitimate state religion, he outlawed *chema* and consigned all its textual references to the fate of a giant conflagration. Albeit demonized, the art was not extinguished; it subsisted and was even exalted in the progressive Arab world, and returned to the West through Latin translations of texts made during the late twelfth and early thirteenth centuries in Toledo in Spain.

The Arabian polymaths uniformly ascribed alchemical knowledge to the tutelage of Hermes Trismegistus. A lost ninth-century frame narrative called *Kitab al-Uluf* reveals that there were in fact three sages called Hermes.[40] The first, an antediluvian ancestor, transcribed the primeval Adamic knowledge onto stelae inside the Upper Egyptian temple of Akhmim (Panopolis); the second rediscovered the knowledge for the betterment of humanity; and the third authored a plethora of alchemical treatises. A supernal legitimation legend from the

Arabic frame narrative *Treasure of Alexander the Great* tells of a golden book that had been locked into a chest and subsequently smuggled into the walls of a monastery by Antiochus I. Inside this book is a passage intimating that the King of Macedon had been initiated into mysteries of Adamic knowledge by the third of these figures, King Hermes the Alchemist. At the prompting of his tutor Aristotle, Alexander had meticulously studied the primeval wisdom through 10 Hermetic volumes composed chiefly of chemico-operative and medical content. The aforementioned treatise was in widespread circulation during the early modern period under the title of *Liber de Compositione Alchemiae* [Book on the System of Alchemy], having been translated into Latin by Morienus the Greek. We can be certain of this because the Hermetic legitimation legends based on Alexander the Great were emphatically retold in *Praefatio Castrensis*, a prefatory note to Morienus's work written by Robert of Chester; in the translator's preface accompanying the *Septem Tractatus Hermetis* [Seven Tractates of Hermes]; and in the preface to the *Liber Hermetis Mercurii Triplicis de VI rerum principiis* [Book of the Triple Hermes-Mercury on the six principles of things].

Another ninth-century legend, this one from Greece proper, relays how Alexander once had a beautiful sister called Gorgona.[41] At one point, the beloved siblings conspired to steal the Elixir of Life from a grotesque dragon that lived in the subterranean. They succeeded but their exuberance was short lived; as they fled from the field, Gorgona dropped the flask, splattering its contents on the ground. Alexander's cussing left an indelible mark by turning her into a gargantuan mermaid. The character of Alexander the Great as an archetypal world hero held widespread appeal in the Middle Ages, just as Prince Khaemuas, the fourth son of Ramses the Great, gained a dignified place as the protagonist of many fables belonging to the magical demotic literature of Egypt's Late Period. Alexander's beloved tutor, Aristotle, was also a very popular subject in the Arabic world, so popular as to be hailed as the author of treatises with underlying philosophies that were incompatible with his own. The most prominent were *The Theology of Aristotle* and *Liber de causis*; these texts saw the universe as an interacting realm of physical and paraphysical forces, which could be accessed in part through personal revelation. The Muslim philosophers Al-Kindi (c. 801–873), Al-Farabi (c. 872–950/1), Avicenna (c. 980–1037), and Averroes (c. 1126–1198) were direct inheritors of this intellectual dowry. In the Arabic world, the Hermetic philosophy was elaborated under the confluence of alchemical doctrine and Platonic metaphysics, and had a far-reaching effect on the discipline of alchemy, which returned after a marked absence to the Latin West couched in Neo-Platonic jargon.

By far the most important text pertaining to transmission of Arabic alchemy was the *Tabula Smaragdina* or Emerald Tablet, an apocryphal summa of alchemical knowledge couched within a philosophical treatise titled *Book of the Secrets of Creation*. Attributed to Balinas, the Pseudo-Apollonius of Tyana, and translated from Arabic into Latin by Hugo von Santalla in the late twelfth century,[42] this text gave an elucidation of the formative principles that underpin the universe. It explores, among other things, the many epithets of the ineffable One, God, and recounts the celebrated birth of the cosmos through Aristotle's theories of matter. Concluding Balinas's *Book of the Secrets of Creation* is the enigmatic prose of the *Tabula Smaragdina*, which offers an abridged summa describing natural processes within a teleological framework. Emphasis is placed on the dependence of all life on the two celestial luminaries, and fire or heat is implicated as the primal mover and root power of chemical processes like sublimation, dissolution, and calcination. A great many philosophers, like Albertus Magnus

(c. 1193/1206–1280) and Roger Bacon (c. 1214–1294), attempted to decode this cryptic text in the thirteenth century with little to no success. A noteworthy interpretation, at least one with far-reaching consequences for Renaissance alchemy, was given by Hortulanus in the fourteenth century. He postulated that the equivocal doctrine alluded to the creation of the Philosopher's Stone. Hortulanus's shrewd understanding has accompanied nearly all early modern publications of the text.[43]

I would be remiss not to mention two other Arabic texts that played a crucial role in the alchemy inherited by the Renaissance period. These were the *Secreta Secretorum*, a tenth-century Arabic treatise that was translated into Latin in c. 1120 by John of Seville and then again in c. 1232 by Phillipus Tripolitanus, and the *Turba Philosophorum* or *Assembly of Philosophers*, a late-thirteenth-century Latin translation of a tenth-century Arabic text tentatively ascribed to Uthman ibn Suwaid of Akhmim (c. 900). The first of these, a monograph on a syncretic occultism combining alchemical, astrological, and theurgical concepts, is presented from within the literary device of a pseudepigraphical letter from Aristotle to his pupil Alexander the Great. Unique aspects of this text are an early translation of and select commentaries on the *Tabula Smaragdina*, along with a meticulous transcription outlining the process whereby the "red stone" is brought into existence. The second, the *Turba Philosophorum*, attempts to fabricate posterity for the Hermetic craft by arguing that pre-Socratic and classical philosophers of the caliber of Pythagoras, Socrates, Anaxagoras, Democritus, and Parmenides were all ardent disciples of an ancient doctrine called the *prisca theologia*. Stretching across the sands of time, the *prisca theologia* was a doctrine endeavoring to yoke institutionalized religions together under the pseudohistorical umbrella of common origins. In a nutshell, its core assumption was that religions all conveyed the same fundamental truth about the cosmos and the nature of reality, despite the disparate sociopolitical narratives and literary devices they used to propagate ideas. The mythographers who invented the narratives distorted, deconstructed, transposed, encoded, and anthropomorphized the laws and principles pertaining to this truth, a truth that had been directly transmitted from God to humankind during the prehistoric epoch.

This concept first flowered and gained widespread acceptance during the early Renaissance under the auspices of the humanist Marsilio Ficino (1433–1499).[44] More importantly, the text preserved kernels of the Hellenistic alchemical tradition in fragments of Pseudo-Democritus's *Physika kai Mystika* as it was before coming to the attention of the Arabian polymaths. In the *Turba*, for instance, synthesis of the universal elixir or panacea does not reference acts of copulation whereby the sulphurous male and the mercurial female—stand-ins for Philosophical Sulphur and Philosophical Mercury—are subjected to a sequence of *solve et coagula*, or dissolutions and coagulations, until the matter in the alembic can be jettisoned of its impurity. The florid language, evocative imagery, and allegorical motifs that crop up in the *Turba* were markedly absent from the Hellenistic manuscripts and make their inaugural appearance in the *Corpus Jabirianum*, a cache of over 500 alchemical texts attributed to the Arab Geber, or Jabir ibn Hayyan (c. 721–815).[45] These narrative gildings were Arabic innovations.

There was a major shift in philosophical perspectives under the Arab thinkers. Elaborating upon Aristotelian nature philosophy, the Arab Geber postulated that the four Aristotelian elements further differentiated into Philosophical Sulphur and Philosophical Mercury or *argent vive*. Balance created by the sulphur-mercury dyad allowed the metals to coagulate under the aegis of the seven planetary powers. The theoretical refurbishing brought with it a noticeable shift of orientation away from the creation of metallic gold to a far more ambitious endeavor: the preservation of human life. Many Arabian polymaths sought to apply their knowledge of chemical processes to manufacture alchemical tinctures for the treatment of ailments and injuries, inadvertently paving the way for the practice of iatrochemistry. According to Jabir, potent medicines could be prepared using base matter from any of the three great kingdoms.[46] He also elaborated Aristotle's teleology and put his vivid imagination to prolific use, arguing that if man were indeed a microcosm, his esemplastic powers should allow for the replication of cosmic processes on a smaller scale. Perhaps, he thought, an alchemist could artificially manipulate elemental corpuscles in his hermetically sealed flask under auspicious stellar arrangements and in so doing birth artificial creatures called *homunculi*. The seeds for creating life artificially, prolonging life, curing ailments, and palingenesis were first planted by the Arabic alchemists many centuries ago. These avant-garde alchemical pursuits entered conventional scientific thought and have in our time taken on a voluminous life of their own in the guise of sophisticated enterprises like in-vitro fertilization, a surgical procedure which allows for conception outside the human uterus, and recombinant DNA technology, which may, against all odds, permit the resurrection of recently extinct species.

From about the twelfth century until the dawn of the early Renaissance in the fourteenth century, theologians and philosophers seemed deeply preoccupied with the writings of their Hellenistic and Islamic forebears. Albertus Magnus and Roger Bacon both conducted extensive research into chemical processes and searched diligently for the universal panacea, publishing their findings in the treatises *Libellus di Alchemia* and *Compendium Philosophiae*, respectively. During this period, Thomas Aquinas (1225–1274) made feasible attempts to marry practical approaches to the acquisition of divine knowledge with Christian dogma. Noteworthy inroads were made by the Iberian physician and alchemist Arnold of Villanova (1235–1312) who juxtaposed *necrosis* (nigredo), a stage in which matter in the alembic blackens and putrefies, with the crucifixion of Jesus Christ. In Arnold's eyes, the passion of Christ was an exemplar par excellence of *solve et coagula*, or the disintegration and (re)creation of a new form among the Aristotelian elements. The idea of a coveted vital life principle[47] (also known as an essence or a quintessence) that can allegedly be isolated through chemical processes like infusion, distillation, and maceration was also a psychological novelty of Arnold's mind. This was a compelling notion for an inquisitive Renaissance philosopher yearning for something novel and receptive to the radical. The fourteenth-century Franciscan monk Johannes de Rupescissa was so inspired by Arnold that he embarked upon a lifelong quest to isolate the quintessence, describing his adventures in a treatise titled *De consideration quintae.*

Three main cultural developments in the fourteenth century heralded the passage from the Late Middle Ages to the Renaissance and early modern Europe. The first, Johannes Gutenberg's invention of the printing press, enabled translations of Hellenistic, Arabic, and Latin texts from all disciplines to emerge from their niche monastic circles and achieve much wider distribution and influence. The second is inextricably linked with the fall of Constantinople in 1453, a lamentable collapse that saw many Byzantine scholars desert their posts and move to Western Europe, particularly Florence. The seed of transformation was swept there in the guise of a Greek manuscript titled *Corpus Hermeticum* by a monk named Leonardo de Pistoia. Translated into Tuscan Italian by the scholar Marsilio Ficino (1433–1499), the philosophical-theological worldview underpinned by its first 14 texts argued fervidly in support of an animistic universe. As a source of authority in its own right, the book served as ammunition for philosophers who espoused systems of thought that were vehemently opposed to Aristotelian Scholasticism.[48] It also served as an auspicious conduit for esotericism to mix with more orthodox ideas during the sixteenth-century reformation and aid in the birth of Newtonian-Cartesian epistemology. The third and final development was an epiphenomenon inextricably linked with the re-emergence of classical sources; Ficino's translations of the *Corpus Hermeticum*, the Platonic dialogues, the Orphic Hymns, and other important Neo-Platonic texts brought Renaissance humanism into the spotlight—the *philosophia perennis* or *prisca theologia*, which treated Hermes Trismegistus as one of its sages and the Christian revelation as its final cause and culmination.

The imported idea of Man or microcosm in the role of the hermetic Archmagus would have appealed to and seduced many Renaissance humanists. This promotion can be traced to a Neo-Platonic ontology standing firm in its conviction that realms above the sublunary and below the Empyrean—the Sphere of the Fixed Stars, the *primum mobile,* and the seven planets—were subject to transitory states and the condition of becoming. In themselves, plants, trees, minerals, stones, and animals were little more than elemental corpuscles of detritus and dust, unique configurations of the four elements revealed through the key qualities of hot, cold, dry, and moist, in addition to secondary ones like soft, hard, sweet, and sour. What inspirited them was a vital life force emanating from the stars. Known as the *anima mundi* or World Soul, this intangible essence infused matter and dynamically manipulated its features. Additionally, it yoked the *spiritus mundi* or World Spirit, and the material realm, the *corpus mundi* or World Body, into an indissoluble triangle. The human condition was equipped with a mind able to both access the dimensions presiding over the corporeal world and manipulate natural processes therein through a system of esoteric correspondences. In short, the Neo-Platonic vision restored to the milieu the primordial but suppressed idea that human beings were gods in their own right.

Conciliatory steps were made to bridge Aristotle's theory of matter with Platonic metaphysics by Ficino in the treatise *De vita coelitus comparanda*. He decreed the *spiritus mundi* and the quintessence described by both Arnold of Villanova and Johannes de Rupescissa to be one and the same entity.[49] Agrippa of Nettesheim (1486–1535) later elaborated upon Ficino's innovation, imbuing the elements with an alchemical flavor and claiming that success in natural magic was contingent on understanding the structure of the elements. In his *De occulta philosophia*, Agrippa declared the ubiquitous essence of the *anima mundi* to manifest in five different hypostases—in the four Aristotelian elements as well as the fifth, the quintessence. In the mineral realm it manifested through the element of earth, while in the plant realm it manifested under the aegis of water. On the other hand, the primitive urges and drives familiar to animals were a by-product of the action of air, and the human reason was a powerful projection through the element of fire. In the first four hypostases, the *anima mundi* acted as a universal curative or panacea, but in its fifth and purest incarnation, otherwise known as aether or spirit, it attained unbridled expression as a formative force to be reckoned with. Here, it became *spiritus mundi* or the Philosopher's Stone, a power able to attract and influence the planetary intelligences, transmute metals, and offer convalescence to those with languishing health. The sixteenth- and seventeenth-century interpretations of the *Tabula Smaragdina* as a cryptic and hallowed ode to the World Soul all attest the popularity of this view.

The abovementioned premises would go on to dominate the sixteenth- and seventeenth-century outlook of Hermetic philosophy.[50] In my eyes, the *apotheosis* of this syncretic alchemy came with Paracelsus of Hohenheim (1493–1541), an individualist who respected the contributions of predecessors like Marsilio Ficino and Agrippa but hoped to leave his own unique mark on the craft. Paracelsus believed in the first differentiation of the *prima materia* into the elements of Spirit, Soul, and Body, and the quintessence or panacea, which interpenetrated Nature's threefold kingdom but manifested differently within each one. For the Swiss alchemist and physician, the triad of Spirit, Soul, and Body were more aptly described as mercury, sulphur, and salt, as well as *archeus* for the latter.[51] Like many before him, Paracelsus was inclined to view the cosmos as an epiphenomenon of voluminous operations carried out by God. But God wasn't just any alchemist, he was "the Alchemist" who galvanized *creation ex deo* by distilling the *prima materia* in his alembic, over and over, until splendid nuggets of consciousness had been set free. Every substance, every particle of matter that existed represented a particular stage in Paracelsus's cycle of distillations.

Paracelsus possessed a keen eye for observation and emphasized practice over dependence on conventional wisdom. He concurred with Agrippa on the topic of healing — understanding nature on a microscopic or atomic level, and correctly interpreting correspondences was a necessary prerequisite to any therapeutic intervention (a belief that still holds true today!). The key to unlocking Nature's cryptic language, Paracelsus argued, lay in correctly interpreting the "occult signature" of the object or substance in question. Knowing the occult property of something in the natural world enabled the Hermetic practitioner to directly affect a complement in a different kingdom, if sympathetic correspondences permitted. Let's proceed with an example. If Paracelsus was alive today, he'd interpret the kava kava root's ability to induce euphoria

Figure 2-2. The Louvre copy of the lost portrait of
Paracelsus by Quentin Matsys.

and psychedelic visions in people as evidence of subordination
to the lunar force. Rendered into a tincture it might make a
potent remedy for an ailing organ ruled by that planetary
power, in this case the brain. Paracelsus pioneered a spagyrical-
based method of fabricating metal-based detoxifying drugs and
homeopathic tonics to correct chemical imbalances caused by
celestially derived parasites and poisons, a true testament of his
ingenuity and sagacity. His applications derive from theoretical
deductions linking anatomical features of the human body
and its overall vitality to the waxing and waning energies of

planetary intelligences, deductions that rejected wholesale the highly resistant Middle Age strain of Hippocratic and Galenic medicine based on a quaternary model of disproportionate humors and temperaments.

Paracelsus was definitely a man with one leg planted in an inchoate paradigm of proto-scientific method with objective measures and the other firmly entrenched in a psychospiritual realm pervaded by hidden intelligences. The latter, soon to be confined to a dustbin of occult tradition attractive only to an eccentric iconoclast, dictated Paracelsian reasoning to a substantial degree. With respect to the synthesis and administration of homeopathic dilutions, for instance, Paracelsus monitored the astrological movement. Planetary conjunctions, oppositions, or eclipses involving celestial bodies ascribed rulership over plants or metals intended for therapeutic use had to be carefully monitored, for certain times were more likely to render a herbal elixir potent (or impotent) than others. Therefore, timing, a qualitative factor swept under the rug and ignored by orthodox biological science today, was imperative to efficacy and hence the outcome. Paracelsus's panentheistic world was based on dynamic interactions between the planetary powers, the human body, and the three kingdoms of Nature herself. By manipulating the subtle energies with minute doses of a substance, perhaps at levels where body and mind interact, he could spur a spritely return to homeostatic balance for those suffering from serious and perplexing illnesses, or so he believed. One may be selectively critical of Paracelsus for his volatility, social recalcitrance, and acts committed with a degree of impunity; however, even his most vehement detractors cannot ignore his efficacy in ameliorating leprosy, gout, and epilepsy in many of his patients, conditions that his contemporaries were unable to cure. Love him or hate him, whatever he did worked.

Paracelsus of Hohenheim is generally acknowledged as the founding father of iatrochemistry and the principles he remained faithful to accord closely with the homeopathic approach to medicine today. He outright rejected the conventional Galenic medicine of curing through opposites on the premise that a substance that elicited a specific condition could itself serve as an antidote or a poison for that same condition. It was nuances in quantity that determined whether the effects would be noxious and lethal, or therapeutic. The development of vaccines, a biological preparation that allows for the acquisition of immunity to particular infectious diseases by injecting the patient with a very minute dose of the pathogen to stimulate an immune response, is a contemporary and bona fide echo of Paracelsian homeopathy. During Paracelsus's lifetime, alchemical doctrine was successfully integrated into the sacred science of Renaissance man, the new Adam. This multi-eyed microcosm, with each lens tuned to a different vocation— hermetic Archmagus, physician, mystic, philosopher, alchemist, and astrologer—enabled practitioners to bend nature, to coerce and correct it, to align it with the *heimarmene* or even pervert it. Nonetheless, the jack-of-all-trades approach gave human beings the Midas touch—officially divine, at last.

Endnotes

33 Roelof van den Broek, 'Gnosticism I: Gnostic Religion', in *Dictionary of Gnosis and Western Esotericism*, ed. by Wouter J. Hanegraaff et al., 2 vols (Leiden: Brill, 2005), I, p. 402.

34 Florian Ebeling, *The Secret History of Hermes Trismegistus: Hermeticism from Ancient to Modern Times*, trans. by David Lorton (London, UK: Cornell University Press, 2007), p. 6.

35 Roelof van den Broek, 'Hermetic Literature I: Antiquity', in *Dictionary of Gnosis and Western Esotericism* (see Broek, above), pp. 487–488.

36   Bernard D. Haage, 'Alchemy II: Antiquity-12th Century', in *Dictionary of Gnosis and Western Esotericism* (see Broek, above), p. 22.

37   Stanton J. Linden, *The Alchemy Reader: From Hermes Trismegistus to Isaac Newton* (Cambridge, UK: Cambridge University Press, 2003), p. 38.

38   Antoine Faivre, 'Hermetic Literature IV: Renaissance–Present', in *Dictionary of Gnosis and Western Esotericism* (see Broek, above), p. 534.

39   C. J. S. Thompson, *The Lure and Romance of Alchemy* (London, UK: Random House, 1990), p. 11.

40   Ebeling, p. 45.

41   John L. Tomkinson, *Haunted Greece: Nymphs, Vampires and Other Exotica* (Athens, GR: Anagnosis Books, 2004), p. 68.

42   Ebeling, p. 49.

43   Ibid, p. 51.

44   Antoine Faivre, 'Ancient and Medieval Sources of Modern Esoteric Movements', in *Modern Esoteric Spirituality*, ed. by Antoine Faivre and Jacob Needleman (Chestnut Ridge, NY: Crossroad Publishing, 1992), pp. 47–48.

45   Thompson, pp. 60–61.

46   Haage, p. 27.

47   Thompson, p. 83.

48   Kocku von Stuckrad, *Western Esotericism: A Brief History of Secret Knowledge*, trans. by Nicholas Goodrick-Clarke (London, UK: Equinox Publishing, 2005), pp. 49–50.

49   William R. Newman and Anthony Grafton (eds.), 'Introduction: The Problematic Status of Astrology and Alchemy in Premodern Europe', in *Secrets of Nature: Astrology and Alchemy in Early Modern Europe* (London, UK: MIT Press, 2006), p. 24.

50   Ebeling, p. 80.

51   von Stuckrad, pp. 68–69.

Chapter 3

Alchemy in Christian Theosophy

Before attempting to explain how alchemy facilitated the emergence of Christian theosophy, it would be wise to define what is meant by the term "theosophy." As an esoteric *gnosis* within Christianity, theosophy is a speculative philosophical system closely allied to Hermeticism and Platonism. It perceives God's creation in the context of an emanationist cosmology.[52] Under this system, the transcendental One stands at the very top of the cosmos and emanates through rungs of celestial hierarchies usually guarded by planetary daemons. The lowest rung is the earthbound plane of matter, an inspirited tapestry divided into three kingdoms that can be controlled by a mystic who has acquired requisite knowledge of the divine through applied psychospiritual awakening and also intellectual effort.

Coursing along the same roads paved by the Gnostic religions, theosophical doctrine proposes that the chief purpose of physical incarnation is to reawaken the divine spark within. This is first and foremost a salvific quest and secondly, a pilgrimage of spiritual ascent along a ladder of celestial hierarchies, which culminates in *unio mystica* with the Godhead.[53] Theosophy is also separated from more conservative and exoteric forms of Christianity by rendering an intermediary realm of disembodied entities available for exploration through practical techniques, like active imagination. This is something more inquisitive seekers and proselytes have found meaningful. Moreover, it recognizes that divine revelation isn't just some abstruse historical event experienced by the apostolic elite but a state of mind ready to manifest within each individual during latter stages of their diligent quest. Essential to an individual's success, traversing the royal road that leads to communion with the Holy Spirit, is the omnipresence of Sophia or Divine Wisdom.

As a product of seventeenth-century enterprises, theosophy ran antithetical to the Lutheran Reformation—it was a countercultural reaction to a guise of Christianity that had become too dogmatic, ascetic, and idealistic in its view and approach toward the divine.[54] This topic was first broached for discussion by a humble German cobbler named Jacob Boehme (1575–1624). Typically, what most people would like to know about Boehme is how a man with limited means, a man born in a sociocultural milieu tactfully described as rustic, ended up inspired to the extent that he eloquently transcribed and later propounded intellectual musings about Nature and God. Of course, the answer to this question lies in the cultural milieu of the time and in fields of inquiry that comprised his formative influences.

Jacob Boehme was born in 1575 in Germany's Görlitz, a town of about 10,000 inhabitants in the geopolitical region of Upper Lusatia. The religious climate in areas north of the Alps during the alpenglow of the Renaissance and the Reformation was one that considered Paracelsian pansophy to be an important keystone in successfully unlocking the secrets of God's creation.[55] Having distanced themselves from Renaissance Neo-Platonism and the Hermetic suppositions of Italian humanist philosophers like Marsilio Ficino (1433–1499) and Cornelius Agrippa (1486–1535), thinkers of this proto-theosophical school—i.e., Valentin Weigel (1533–1588), Heinrich Khunrath (1560–1605), and Johann Arndt (1555–1621)—perceived Latin and vernacular translations of authentic Hermetic and alchemical treatises as remnants of genuine primeval knowledge that had passed into the torch-bearing hands of both Hermes Trismegistus and Paracelsus (1493–1541). In their minds, a physico-theology that did not differentiate between the natural and the divine was the only dignified path for Christian tradition and piety. It had to emerge from obscurity and become the orthodox method.

In Boehme's day, the town's cognoscenti were devoted to the theory and practice of this more mystical approach toward accessing objective truth and divine knowledge. Of paramount significance here is that Bartolomaus Scultetus (1540–1614), the mayor of Görlitz, was a Paracelsian aficionado.[56] Two of Boehme's closest allies, the orientalist Balthasar Walther and the physician Tobias Kober, were active members of the *secta Paracelsi*.[57] Walther's own mentor, a physician named Abraham Behem, was also an adherent of the German mystical tradition and had once been decried by the townsfolk for being part of a Paracelsian cult. There's another fact worth mentioning: Boehme's Görlitz could be found on a commercial route in close proximity to Prague, a city which transformed into an intellectual hub for the dissemination of astrological and astronomical knowledge during the reign of Rudolf II (1552–1612). This would have made Görlitz something of a layover for traveling theorists wishing to spread the word about the latest developments in natural science and philosophy. The Scottish alchemist Alexander Seton (1566–1636), for instance, meandered about Central Europe for some time promoting a "hidden food of life" in the element of air that could also be found in a more stable form within physical saltpetre.[58] The striking similarity between this concept and Boehme's own idea of a divine *Salitter* definitely gives credence to the notion that Seton sojourned in Görlitz and wooed the mayor and the literati with evidence in support of his nitre theory before finally settling into the court of Rudolf II in Prague. These formative influences emerged in the vernacular dialect and go far in elucidating why the seventeenth-century breed of Christian theosophy promulgated by Boehme is saturated with alchemical leitmotifs.

During the early modern period, there was a major nomothetic transition from a geocentric to a heliocentric cosmogony; from an animistic landscape to a mechanistic one defined by laws operating independently of any supernatural agency. Espousing beliefs that would later be condemned by the Catholic Church, Boehme himself gravitated toward Copernican heliocentrism and the more seductive notion of *creatio ex materia*. This dramatic assertion flows translucently from the pages of *Aurora* (1612) when he postulates: "From what sort of *materia* or force did the grass, vegetation, and trees proceed? What sort of substance and circumstance [*Gelegenheit*] was involved in this creation? The simple person says that God made everything from Nothing; but he does not know this God, and does not know what He is. When he beholds the earth together with the depths above the earth, he thinks 'that is not God, there is not God'. He has formed the notion that God dwells only above the blue heaven of the stars..."[59]

Faith in a divine substance underpinning all created Nature, such as the one just mentioned, had been native to alchemy since late antiquity, and it was to this discipline that Boehme now turned for answers. During the seventeenth century, the corpus of scientific discoveries being made frequently featured nitre, a chemical compound parading nowadays under the label potassium nitrate.[60] Given its prominence in the enterprise of chemistry, a morbid fascination with its uses and properties ended up developing among circles of alchemists and emerging chemists, one that Boehme clearly wasn't exempt from. Boehme married the organic compound and his notion of a divine substance, resulting in an unprecedented hybrid. By drawing the formless yet forming *prima materia* into his theosophy under the name *Salitter* (the German word for nitre), Boehme was allying himself with a Platonic dualism that had dominated Western philosophical thought and furthermore, attempting to comprehend an equivocal Christian model of the universe in organic terms. This early engagement with alchemy appears to have greatly influenced his speculative paradigm.

Boehme describes his philosophy surrounding the nature of *Salitter* as a divine substance in *Aurora* (1612). What exactly was *Salitter* and how could it be grasped by the rational mind? According to Boehme, it was the force of mutual attraction that infused all created matter in the spiritual and material realms with vital life force. It was concomitantly visible and invisible and everywhere present; it was the unconscious origin and determined the *nisus* of all things. In describing its inherent qualities, Boehme posits: "The corporeal drying is to be called in this book the Divine SALITTER. For the seed of the entire Divinity is in it, and it is like a mother which receives the seed and bears the fruit again and again, in accordance with all qualities of the seed."[61] What Boehme is implying is that it existed in the Sphere of the Fixed Stars; in the hydrogen powering the sun; in the planetary motions; in phenomena that enable an illusion of time; in vegetable and tree growth; and in human thought-desires, dreaming cognition, and waking cognition. In fact, it compelled the cosmic animal called Nature to subject her children to the cycles of birth, death, and regeneration. It was the reason for life, self-awareness, and the innate but natural compulsion to want to subdue another extension of Nature or one's own inherent nature. It was quite simply the primary mover behind evolution.

We could probably equate the *Salitter* with a more contemporary idea in quantum physics—for instance, the membrane that underpins the multiverse in modern superstring theory. Just as the splendid sun infuses the entire solar system with its scintillating rays, so too does the *Salitter* permeate an ethereal septenary body of source-spirits named Dry, Sweet, Bitter, Fire, Love, Sound, and *Corpus*.[62] These source-spirits are similar in function to Renaissance planetary daemons, and serve as intermediaries between the spiritual and corporeal realms. Boehme was able to bridge these worlds through differentiation of the divine *Salitter* into an upper exalted spiritual realm of perfection; a lower celestial realm where perceptual discrimination of disparate forces was possible; and last but not least, a lowest material realm plagued by warring sympathies and antipathies that strived for fundamental harmony but were never quite in a state of equilibrium. As a miniature replica of the entire cosmos, the human being assumed the role of a pitiful creature, a fallen angel, and was assigned by Boehme to the debased realm of material existence.

Embedded within a ladder of interconnected dimensions of disparate densities, the individual source-spirits were imagined to arise from the continual contractions of ether or fluid of God's eternal nature. As the *Salitter* was transposed from one source-spirit to the next, it became polarized in composition and identified with either a sensate or animate property. In this way, each manifestation drifted further and further away from God. In *Aurora* (1612), Boehme continuously draws our attention to differences in the humus from whence the celestial and material planes emanate; the first is a child of a pure and translucent form of the divine *Salitter*, while the second child is of a crude, defiled, poisonous, and stinking version full of dissonance.[63] Boehme also suggests that the everlasting angels are by-products of the higher form, while the animal, plant, and mineral kingdoms comprising the material realm are spawn of the lower form. Even though the second Salitter was a debased reflection of the first, it could still mimic divine unadulterated perfection by manifesting in diamonds, gold, persistent mental states of illumination, and other things that appeared incorruptible to the naked eye. The impetus for Boehme's elaboration of a dual conception of *Salitter* is reflected in organic processes whereby saltpetre was purified for commercial use[64]; in the first, the

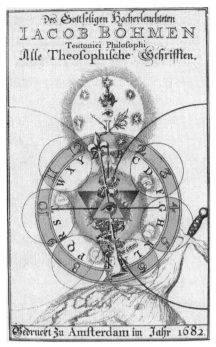

Figure 3-1. Title page to Jacob Boehme's *Alle Theosophische Schrifften* (1682), which was published by Boehme's disciple, Johan Gichtel. As is so often the case with Boehme illustrations, the design centers upon an eye. This is incorporated into a burning triangle, which is overlaid over a triangle symbolic of the element of water—together, the two triangles are not only preparatory to forming the Seal of Solomon, but they also represent the conflict of opposites (fire and water). The full appreciation of the Boehme symbols and designs (especially those drawn by such men as Gichtel or Freher) requires a familiarity with his writings. For example, the numbers on the "clock-face" (as Boehme calls the device) point to time, while the letters of the alphabet concentric to this dial represent space. The letter I (which is equated with the number 1) represents God and Adam. Because it represents Adam, it has not been placed at the top of the radiant circle (a place due to God) but at the bottom, to symbolize the Fall.

celestial version corresponds with the hard, translucent crystals generated when saltpetre is subjected to repeated distillations, whereas the second corporeal form of the substance can be equated with an unrefined brownish filtrate called *sal terrae*, which reeked badly because it was still undergoing purgation from organic animal matter. For all intents and purposes, all converging evidence indicates that the variants of Boehme's *Salitter* are both idealized versions of the chemical compound from whence they take their name.

Salitter is the German word for saltpetre (*sal petrae*), earth salt (*sal terrae*), or sal nitre (*sal nitri*).[65] In Boehme's time, saltpetre was known as a ubiquitous natural compound, making it a pertinent candidate for a theoretical role that had formerly been held by other naturally occurring substances like earth, water, mercury, lead, dew, and menstruum. Saltpetre was also a vital ingredient in the fabrication of chemical explosives like gunpowder. It is not difficult to see how an innovative mind able to perceive creation in an analogical manner might link it with claps of thunder, bolts of lightning, and other spontaneous acts of violence that are qualitatively allied to demiurgic powers. These associations would have been blatantly obvious — claps of thunder and lightning had been construed as portents of divine displeasure since time immemorial. The spontaneous deflagration that nitre suffers when brought into contact with molten rock, black coals, or any other sweltering surface[66] might also be construed as a sign of divine intervention. On the other hand, when the compound is tossed into topsoil it enhances the growth and flourishing of trees, plants, flowers, and all agricultural produce,[67] evoking images of a divine seed able to create and nurture life in even the most noxious and hostile of environments. The parallels are undeniable.

Saltpetre also exhibits other uncanny features reminiscent of Boehme's divine *Salitter*. When calcined in an alchemical retort, it transforms into a matrix of colorless white prisms. These have an astringent texture and are cold to the touch. Courtesy of alchemists like Basil Valentine (c. 1400), we also know that heating an amalgam of common salt and green vitriol produces hydrochloric acid, or the "spirit of common salt." Similarly, the confluence of vitriol (ferrous or cupric sulphate) and saltpetre generates the "fiery spirit" of *aqua fortis* or nitric acid.[68] Mixing these two together spawns an ultimate agent of dissolution in *aqua regia*,[69] named so because of its ability to liquefy the noblest and most incorruptible of all metals—gold. In the sixteenth century, nitric acid, or what the alchemists termed the "dulcified spirit of nitre," was also famed for its propensity to yield ethyl nitrate when combined with ethanol or "the spirit of wine."[70] The amalgamation of the two nullified the corrosive properties of the former and rendered the entire tincture saccharine so that it emanated an intoxicating odor that was at times reminiscent of honey-based fermented infusions like mead and at other times of sweet apples. In the final analysis, many unique qualities of the divine *Salitter* (i.e., transparency and purity of form) as well as the primary characteristics of the septenary source-spirit system sprouting forth from the divine substance (i.e., dry, sweet, bitter, and "hellish fire")[71] must have been heavily influenced by chemical experiments involving saltpetre in a laboratory setting.

The seven source-spirits emanating from the *Salitter* can also be understood from the perspective of the seven major alchemical operations comprising the Magnum Opus. The first, called Dry or *herb* by Boehme, denotes qualities like coldness, hardness, inertia, lamentation, and death and is connected to the Saturnian sphere. Its subordination to the forces of chaos links it to the alchemical *solutio* or *nigredo*, a phase where old forms are annihilated and replaced by newer ones.[72] Following this is Sweet, a fiery, pleasant, and wet condition responsible for

the mysterious and spontaneous generation of life. Mediated by
the Jovian force, its main purpose is to counter the polarized
force set in motion by the Dry principle. His second quality,
Sweet, is synonymous with the active, masculine principle
of the Paracelsian triad called sulphur, which wills itself to
consciousness and corresponds to *calcinatio*,[73] the chemical
reduction of a solid into a fine, granular powder through
the element of fire. The mutual interaction of the Dry and
Wet principles produces the Bitter energy ruled by Mars—a
destructive and choleric force associated with elevation,
penetration, and subjugation. Its inclination to rise upward
links it to the *sublimatio*.[74] a chemical reaction whereby solids
are transformed into gases and vapors without first passing
through liquefaction.

Further action upon the *Salitter* produces a fourth quality
mediated by the sun and moon called Fire or Hot. Boehme
postulates that this force injects the vital life principle into inert
matter and is inexplicably linked with the *nisus* of any object,
substance, or creature. Because it involves the amalgamation
of opposites and their mystical union along with invigoration
and insemination, the fourth principle can be equated to the
lesser *conjunctio*,[75] the conciliatory union of substances in an
alchemical retort usually personified by sulphur and *argent
vive*, the sun and moon, man and woman, and a gamut of other
couplets including male-female pairs of animals. Next along the
chain of divine generation is Love, an extension of the fourth
principle brought about through the concentration of warmth.
According to Boehme, this power generates consciousness
through kinesthesis and sense perception and is facilitated by
the Venusian sphere. A crucial prerequisite for the emergence
of consciousness is the ability to discriminate, separate, and
compartmentalize; to carve out the universe using the "Logos-
cutter" within ourselves. This first occurs at one's birth and

persists until the time of death. We should not then be surprised that Boehme chose the mythological goddess of birth, herself depicted as being born out of a scallop shell on the shores of the froth-filled sea, as sovereign and protector of the fifth quality. In the alchemical cycle, this is the stage of *separatio*,[76] which always follows the lesser *conjunctio*.

Sound, the principle of expression and illumination where incarnating beings receive the gift of semantic language, articulation, and harmony, is the sixth stage. It arises under the auspices of the Mercurial sphere and renders audible to the human ear the mellifluous voices of singing angels. Looking at the alchemical cycle in its entirety, the only time angelic voices could be heard was during the deepest stage of blackening, the *mortificatio*[77]; save for being a period of torture and lamentation, it also represented a psychospiritual state known as the "black sun" in which divine wisdom or Sophia was temporarily shadowed and shackled by the bonds of *physis* [Nature]. What we have here is a qualitative link between Boehme's Sound principle and *mortificatio*. To end, we have the Corpus or Body, an amalgamation of the other six qualities mediated by the earth principle. In alchemy, the act of becoming earth can be equated with *coagulatio* or *fixatio*,[78] a stage defined by the congealing of quicksilver until it acquires a discernible form. There are obvious analogies and interrelationships, but parsing out to what extent operations of alchemical theory and practice influenced the speculative septenary system that Boehme conceived remains excruciatingly difficult. Accessing this information would require seeing the world through the eyes of Boehme, which is obviously not possible. Unfeasible as this endeavor is, we can remain contented knowing that divine *Salitter* and its septenary emanation stand at the intellectual crossroads of Paracelsian occult philosophy and a proto-empirical chemistry, with the latter being a discipline that grew increasingly hostile to the esoteric agenda.

In retrospect, the alchemical leitmotifs constituted a lifelong love affair for the Christian theosopher and featured prominently in his extensive treatise on the transfiguration of the divine Word into Jesus Christ, *De Signatura Rerum* [The Signature of All Things] (1622).[79] The impetus for writing this book was the animistic belief that all created matter— everything from detritus, dust, and unicellular organisms, right up to the most complicated biological systems on the planet, like human beings with their hardwired neurological programming for expressive and receptive language and higher-order consciousness—was infused with a hieroglyphic "signature" that revealed its inner essence and its relational dynamics within the inspirited web of Nature. The *nisus* of the object, substance, or organism was embedded in the respective signature, and these were projected into the creation itself by the sixth ray—Boehme's sixth mercurial source-spirit, which was purportedly responsible for illumination and expression. Here, we should aptly recall that signatures, the notion that everything created under the sun contains a vital life principle that can reveal subtle occult virtues or qualitative properties when properly deciphered, are a Paracelsian importation,[80] and that Boehme deliberately assimilated them into his septenary theosophical system because they complemented and validated his own beliefs about a patterned creation from an ineffable but divine origin.

Another Christian theosopher who was profusely influenced by alchemy was Englishwoman Mary Anne Atwood (maiden name South) (1817–1910). She was, among other things, a leading figure in the resurrection of spiritual alchemy during a Victorian era when every layperson seemed to be captivated by the occult. Mary Anne grew up around her father, Thomas, a wealthy and erudite gentleman who lived at Bury House, Gosport in New Hampshire, and immersed himself in the psychic revolution of the nineteenth century. Thomas was a creative individual with both the aplomb and financial means to pursue metaphysical interests and delve into his own metaphysical postulates. During the formative stages of their partnership, the two joined an occult-oriented secret society called the *Zojese* where they learned about and conducted experiments into hypnotic phenomena.[81] They entertained metaphysical theories about the cosmos that had long been discarded by orthodox science. Thomas and Mary Anne also participated in group therapy sessions involving the alleged polarization of mesmeric fluid in the bodies of ailing individuals through the application of "magnetic" forces, a technique pioneered by Franz Anton Mesmer (1734–1815) late in the preceding century.[82] Both were highly competent in classical studies and their sound knowledge of the Greek and Latin languages was equally commendable.

Before moving onto the crux of the Souths' interpretation, it should also be mentioned that Mary Anne was an active member of James Pierrepont Greaves's theosophical circle[83] and was probably influenced by what she learned there. Greaves was a traditional Behmenist, faithful to the musings of Jacob Boehme, which had been rendered accessible to the general public through translations and annotations made by the English philosopher William Law (1686–1761).[84] Boehme employed an alchemical veneer to explicate his panentheistic vision of the cosmos, particularly in *The Signature of All Things* (1621) where he took the Paracelsian doctrine of signatures a step further by postulating that God worked through the reflective beauty of Sophia to infuse these seals into everything. This makes Boehme an innovative and progressive thinker, at least within the context of Christian theosophy. The inspiration for this thought can be traced back to a single moment in the year 1600 when he was involuntarily flung into what transpersonal psychologists today might call a peak experience. Perusing the reflection of the sun's rays in a pewter dish one day, Boehme suddenly found himself disembodied—he became caught in the waves of a psychedelic trance where the underlying principles of all things stood united under the universal language of geometry and coalesced under the insignia of divine love.[85] The epiphany enabled him to penetrate through the veil of appearances, and experience the interconnectedness and mutual interdependence of all being, the mantle of creation as it stands unfettered by the imposed perceptual sieves and schemas of the human mind. Given her avid participation in Greaves's circles and interest in English theosophy, there's no reason why knowledge of Boehme's visions shouldn't have reached Mary Anne South directly.

After having examined a plethora of primary and secondary sources, the Souths jointly came to the conclusion that alchemy wasn't a proto-chemistry based on false premises, but rather a transcendent and salvific operation through which the practitioner gained knowledge of the soul's immortality. Recent advances in psychical research added credence to their conviction that illumination probably occurred through altered states of consciousness, like hypnotic trance states. The best possible way of understanding Mary Anne's interpretation of alchemy is to examine the contents of her book, titled *A Suggestive Enquiry into the Hermetic Mystery* (1850). In the opening chapter, she presents a series of convincing anecdotes from widely respected figures in alchemy such as Paracelsus (1493–1541), Thomas Vaughan (1621–1666), Basil Valentine (c. 1600), and Raymond Lully (c. 1232–1315) to support the opinion that metallic transmutation is actually possible. She posits that the reason why only a handful of adepts have succeeded in this is because alchemical recipes "have been the means of surrounding many a literal soul with stills, coals, and furnaces, in the hope by such lifeless instruments to sublime the

Spirit of nature, or by salt, sulphur and mercury, or the three combined with antimony, to extract the Form of gold."[86] What she's basically saying is that chemical operations alone aren't enough to get the job done. If the *prima materia* being converted into the *ultima materia* was an intangible "psychic ether" of some kind, and if the human being was the vessel in which distillations occurred and concurrently the substance being distilled (as she herself believed), then success in metallic transmutation must be contingent on the practitioner's competence when it came to pouring his or her own vitality into the crucible.

The Souths definitely regarded the alchemical secret to be magical in nature. While some basic alchemical experiments, like maceration and decoction, could be performed in a laboratory by almost anyone, success in what is termed the Greater Work (i.e., synthesis of the "red stone") required a sophisticated understanding of psychic energy and its effect on matter along with knowledge about the individual stages of the alchemical opus. To fabricate the splendor of eternal gold, the practitioner had to emit and project a spurt of mental energy into the base matter at a specific moment during the circulation. The energy would seep into volatile mass and effect changes at the subatomic and electronic levels. Mary Anne admits to the probability of such when she says: "It is not... that the Spirit is free from material bondage, or able to range the universe of her own sphere, that guarantees the truth of her revealments, or helps the consciousness on to subjective experience; for this a concentrative energy is needed, and an intellect penetrating into other spheres."[87]

South's ambiguous statement makes complete sense in light of the formative influences that were dear to her. Peering through these kaleidoscopes, we see that in Victorian times altered states of consciousness were believed to magnify the existing powers of the human mind—an unfettered exchange of mesmeric fluid between the microcosm and the Universal Mind was deemed entirely possible. By collecting magnetic fluid from the Universal Mind in the way that artificial solar panels harness energy from the sun, the conscious mind could then turn imagination and thought-desires into matter, or as Mary Anne puts it: "move with demiurgic power and grace."[88] Hence, the line between transience and immortality blurred when one plunged into mesmeric trance states, allowing humans to enact Herculean god-like feats and to make royal gold of detritus and dust.

Endnotes

52   Nicholas Goodrick-Clarke, *The Western Esoteric Traditions: A Historical Introduction* (New York, NY: Oxford University Press, 2008), p. 87.

53   Antoine Faivre, 'Christian Theosophy', in *Dictionary of Gnosis and Western Esotericism*, ed. by Wouter J. Hanegraaff et al., two vols (Leiden: Brill, 2005), II, p. 259.

54   Goodrick-Clarke, p. 89.

55   Florian Ebeling, *The Secret History of Hermes Trismegistus: Hermeticism from Ancient to Modern Times*, trans. by David Lorton (London, UK: Cornell University Press, 2007), p. 90.

56   Pierre Deghaye, 'Jacob Boehme and His Followers', in *Modern Esoteric Spirituality*, ed. by Wouter J. Hanegraaff et al., two vols (Leiden: Brill, 2005), II, p. 211.

57   Ernst Koch, 'Moscowiter in der Oberlausitz und M. Bartolomaus in Gorlitz', in *Neues Lausitzisches Magazin* (Berlin, Germany: 1907), pp. 83–86.

58   Henry Guerlac, 'John Mayow and the Aerial Nitre', in *Actes du Septieme Congres International d'Histoire des Sciences* (Jerusalem, Israel: 1953), pp. 332–349.

59   Jacob Boehme, 'Morgenröte im Aufgang (Aurora)', in *Samtliche Schriften*, vol. 1, ed. by Will-Erich Peukert (Stuttgart, Germany: 1955), p. 308.

60   Andrew Weeks, 'Jacob Boehme', in *Dictionary of Gnosis and Western Esotericism*, ed. by Wouter J. Hanegraaff et al., two vols (Leiden: Brill, 2005), II, p. 188.

61   Jacob Boehme, p. 137.

62   Jacob Behmen, *Works of Jacob Behmen: The Teutonic Philosopher V1* (Whitefish, Montana: Kessinger Publishing, 2010), p. 73.

63   Boehme, p. 55.

64   Please see Alan Williams, 'The Production of Saltpeter in the Middle Ages' in *Ambix* (London, UK: Maney Publishing, 1975), 22, pp. 125–133.

65   Weeks, p. 188.

66   G. Starkey, 'The Chymistry of Isaac Newton', *Alchemy Laboratory Notebooks and Correspondence* (2004), http://webapp1.dlib.indiana.edu/newton/reference/glossary.do [Accessed November 23, 2012].

67   Boehme, p. 55.

68   Starkey.

69   Ibid.

70   Jon Eklund, 'Incompleat Chymiste: Being an Essay on the Eighteenth-Century Chemist in his Laboratory, with a Dictionary of Obsolete Chemical Terms of the Period', in *Smithsonian Studies in History and Technology* (Washington DC, USA: Smithsonian Institution Press, 1975), 33, p. 18.

71   Boehme, pp. 85–88.

72   Edward Edinger, *Anatomy of the Psyche: Alchemical Symbolism in Psychotherapy* (Chicago, Illinois: Open Court, 1994), p. 47.

73   Ibid, p. 17.

74   Ibid, p. 117.

75   Ibid, p. 154.

76   Ibid, pp. 187–188.

77   Ibid, p. 158.

78   Ibid, pp. 83–85.

79   Lawrence M. Principe and William R. Newman, 'Some Problems with the Historiography of Alchemy', in *Secrets of Nature: Astrology and Alchemy in Early Modern Europe*, ed. by William R. Newman and Anthony Grafton (London, UK: MIT Press, 2006), p. 387.

80   For more on Paracelsian signatures, see Lindy Abraham, *A Dictionary of Alchemical Imagery* (Cambridge, UK: Cambridge University Press, 1998), p. 57.

81   Wouter Hanegraaff, *New Age Religion and Western Culture: Esotericism in the Mirror of Secular Thought* (Albany, NY: State University of New York Press, 1998), p. 511.

82   Harvey J. Irwin and Caroline A. Watt, *An Introduction to Parapsychology* (London, UK: McFarland & Company Inc., 2007), p. 12.

83   Wouter Hanegraaff, p. 511.

84   Arthur Versluis, 'William Law', in *Dictionary of Gnosis and Western Esotericism*, ed. by Wouter J. Hanegraaff et al., two vols (Leiden: Brill, 2005), II, pp. 677–679.

85   Goodrick-Clarke, p. 91.

86   Lawrence M. Principe and William R. Newman, p. 390.

87   Mary Anne Atwood, *A Suggestive Inquiry into the Hermetic Mystery* (Classic Reprint), (Central, Hong Kong: Forgotten Books, 2012), p. 203.

88   Ibid, p. 38.

Chapter 4

Carl Jung and Alchemical Symbolism

Carl Gustav Jung (1875–1961) was a major interpreter of the Western esoteric tradition—most notably alchemy, astrology, and the Gnostic sects of antiquity. Running somewhat contrary to popular belief, Jung was himself influenced by the diverse cluster of rich philosophical ideas that were circulating among the literati during the nineteenth and twentieth centuries. It may come as a surprise to many, but he was not the first person in the annals of psychology to promulgate a psychological interpretation of alchemical symbolism. Twenty years prior, Herbert Silberer (1882–1923) of Zurich, a reputed Freemason and psychoanalyst, had scrupulously juxtaposed dream leitmotifs belonging to his patients and alchemical symbols and in doing so made the introspective leap. Silberer contended that "elementary types," that is, psychic prototypes that might cogently be described as inherited forms or concepts of a transpersonal nature, could in fact be parsed out from dreaming cognition that was more personal in scope and from characters in dreaming cognition. These, he argued, had "insinuated themselves into the body of the alchemical hieroglyphs" as the spiritual alchemists "struggled to gain a mastery of the physico-chemical facts by means of thoughts."[89]

In layman's terms, what Silberer is saying is that the chemico-operative processes described in medieval alchemical manuscripts for the synthesis of the Philosopher's Stone and innumerable other laboratory recipes are, in fact, projections of archetypal content irrupting from the unconscious of the individual alchemist. In Silberer's opinion, the alchemists were compelled to engineer concrete representations and offer feasible descriptions of these "elementary types" as a potential way of understanding and making sense out of the stable mental processes that underpinned and gave rise to them. However, the degree to which they succeeded in this endeavor is questionable.

Compellingly, the idea that alchemical symbols primarily reflected unconscious projections of the ego-self axis as it gradually oriented toward self-actualization (or individuation) was the central thesis in his *Problem der Mystik und ihrer Symbolik* [Problems of Mysticism and its Symbolism] (1914). In addition to its masterful exposition of alchemical symbols in the context of mythological narrative, Silberer's work suggested that these "elementary types" were both identifiable and subject to psychoanalytic interpretation. Desperate to make the "discovery" himself, Jung dismissed Silberer's proto-psychological attempts at explicating alchemical symbols as "too primitive and still too much wrapped up in personalistic assumptions."[90] This shouldn't really surprise us, given the salient impunity that many established intellectuals display when it comes to crediting pertinent sources for ideas, which at first blush seem unprecedented and novel but are actually borrowed wholesale. Obviously, attempting to garner credibility, awe, and admiration through dishonest claims of originality or a direct oversight of pertinent references didn't start, nor did it end, with the father of analytical psychology. It has existed since the advent of writing.

Silberer's own work is thematically consistent with the spiritual breed of alchemy wrought during the eighteenth- and nineteenth-century Victorian fascination with the occult. During this time, the Enlightenment denunciation of animism caused applied alchemy and its quest for the Philosopher's Stone to fall into universal disrepute, but by the same virtue the Romantic disenchantment with deterministic and reductionist perspectives introduced by Sir Isaac Newton (1642–1727) and his *Philosophiae Naturalis Principia Mathematica* (1687) spawned a cultural countermovement involving a Renaissance-style fusion of alchemy with astrology, theurgy, and natural magic. As a consequence, an array of interpretative schools for putative esoteric spirituality were born. The most popular of these was the occultist tradition, which viewed the allegories and symbols in alchemical treatises as cryptic veneers and disguises for inner psychospiritual processes latent in the soul of each human being. There was a plethora of esoteric writers and secret circles with obligatory oaths of silence that took up this interpretation: Albert Pike, American Freemason Ethan Allan Hitchcock (1798–1870), Mary Anne Atwood (1817–1910), Arthur Edward Waite (1857–1842), the Pietists of Germany and the United States, the *Gold- und Rosencrantz*, *L'Association Alchimique de France*, and a Parisian Masonic order called 'The Convent of the Philalethes,'[91] to name a few.

The Freemasonic circles, in particular, favored the adoption of alchemical symbols — everything from the ubiquitous dragon, the black sun, the salamander, the hermaphrodite, and the copulating king and queen, to the inner transfiguration of a human psyche seeking illumination, conscience, and *unio mystica* with the godhead.[92] The aforementioned Hitchcock, whose father was responsible for incorporating masonic heraldry into the green-rich seal of Vermont, offers a chiefly spiritual interpretation of alchemy based on a consummate moral life. In Hitchcock's *Remarks upon Alchemy and the Alchemists* (1857), he writes: "Man was the subject of Alchemy; and that the object of the Art was the perfection, or at least the improvement, of Man."[93] Moreover, an insightful comment made in the preface, namely that "alchemical works stand related to moral and intellectual geography, somewhat as the skeletons of ichthyosauri and plesiosauri are related to geology"[94] seems to foreshadow Jung's notion of a collective unconscious—the functional stratum of the human psyche encompassing the everlasting archetypal forms that possess, seize, overwhelm, and work through each of us in ambiguous and mysterious ways.

Silberer, who we've dealt with already, was also a Freemason. He acquainted himself with Hitchcock's work before writing his personal exposition on alchemy. Silberer's philosophical position was probably colored by a Protestant soteriology seeing in alchemical symbolism a psychospiritual pursuit toward salvific illumination, and nowhere else is it more transparent and obvious than in his *Probleme der Mystik und ihrer Symbolik*. The first blushes of this idea appear in a "parabola" now correctly attributed to *Guldener Tractat vom Philosophischen Steine*, a medieval treatise concerned with natural philosophy and composed by the alchemist Johannes Grasshoff (c. 1560–1623). As the chief inspiration and driving force behind Silberer's work, the "parabola" defers to the Christian determination of self-knowledge, self-mastery, and self-improvement of a truth-seeker who is both an initiate of the mysteries and an alchemist, and in doing so invokes the "physical mysticism" of Waite. Before his chivalrous renunciation of Victorian occultism in favor of 1920s positivism, Waite was of the humble opinion that the Hermetic Art was truly a dual pursuit of metallic transmutation and spiritual transcendence. He expounds upon this viewpoint considerably in *Azoth* (1893) where he declares "alchemical literature deals primarily at least with the conscious intelligence of man, and with the unevolved possibilities of the body and mind of humanity."[95]

This sounds remarkably like the Jungian approach, which emphasizes interpretations pertaining to the transformation of the psyche and concomitantly deemphasizes chemico-operative processes of transmutation. The similarities between Waite's and Jung's views on alchemical transmutation are brought to our attention in a paper by Lawrence M. Principe and William R. Newman titled, 'Some Problems with the Historiography of Alchemy.' In this eye-opening paper, the authors reveal that Waite's earliest treatises had been disseminated to members of an eclectic Jungian circle in Zurich long before Jung had propounded his psychological importation of alchemical symbology. At best, the exposition reveals the scope of Jung's preoccupation with Victorian occultism; at worst, it suggests an unacknowledged pirating that was, to all intents and purposes, conveniently oversighted.

Some 20 years after the circulation of Waite's texts, the Sinologist Richard Wilhelm (1873–1930) sent Jung a cryptic Chinese Taoist treatise called *The Secret of the Golden Flower*.[96] As he perused the text, Jung was struck by the ample use of mandala symbolism—the wheel of life or magic circle— which cropped up repeatedly in his patients' own dreams and reveries, including those of his eccentric maternal cousin Helene Preiswerk (1881–1911). The mandala had even manifested in his own "confrontation with the unconscious" in the years between 1912 and 1917, a period of creative disorder that precipitated monumental revelations about the dynamics and nature of the human psyche. During this intense period of immersion, a self-induced psychosis if you will, Jung's prolific conversations with an inner daemon named Philemon convinced him that the psyche is quintessentially teleological; two conflicting psychic forces within—the conscious and the unconscious—are in perpetual opposition. When they coexisted in fundamental harmony, the inner kingdom was prosperous, regulated, gratified, and integrated; on the other hand, disconnect between the two spawned discord, a "dark night of the soul" that displaced one's conscious life from its moorings in the nourishing unconscious, and galvanized the kind of psychological fragmentation and splitting we see in psychoses and psychosomatic illnesses.

By virtue of this logic, the chief goal of psychotherapy, then, was to heal the rift between conscious and unconscious and auspiciously place the ailing individual back on an individual yet transformative path of self-discovery, equanimity, and flourishing. Jung's perspective was no doubt conditioned by the demographic he served as a practicing psychiatrist. The clientele who sought his professional services weren't suffering from fulminant psychopathologies — they were, more often than not, of affluent sociocultural status and beleaguered by deplorable feelings of existential dread (i.e., worthlessness and emptiness): "About a third of my cases are not suffering from any clinically definable neurosis, but from the senselessness and aimlessness of their lives."[97]

In his discourses, Wilhelm concedes that *The Secret of the Golden Flower* had been in circulation within esoteric circles in China since the seventeenth century. Written by an unknown author, the central thesis of the text appears in a section named *Hui Ming Ching* [Book of Consciousness and Life], where an overarching instruction is given: "If thou wouldst complete the diamond body with no outflowing, diligently heat the roots of consciousness and life. Kindle light in the blessed country close at hand, and there hidden, let thy true self always dwell."[98] What might we make of this equivocal message? Which hermeneutic is apropos for translation as to render it comprehensible and accessible to Eurocentric audiences? An interpretation that remains respectful of and faithful to the cultural context from which the text sprung is the single best interpretation; hence, what is being alluded to here is spiritual integration through meditative instruction.

With this in mind, let's attempt to decipher the cryptic message of the *Golden Flower*. The Chinese signs *hun* and *p'o* are in essence metaphysical symbols for a higher-soul remaining temporarily active after death and a body-soul disintegrating at death. These are translated by Wilhelm as *animus* and *anima*,[99] respectively. Wilhelm's interpretations were profoundly influenced by the pictograms that accompany the Chinese hieroglyphs for the psychic structures; the first was a masculine cloud demon, the second a corporeal white ghost. Jung's understanding of these concepts was overly contingent upon Wilhelm's "objective" descriptions; however, making them commensurate with his own "psychology of the unconscious" would have necessitated stripping them of their metaphysical associations and dressing them in purely psychological jargon. In this way, we get an *animus* understood as a masculine Logos-cutter innate to the personality of a woman and an *anima* assumed to refer to the feminine Eros-glue predominant in the personality of a man.[100]

Using this transcultural interpretation as a map of Chinese ontological terrain, Jung made revelation after revelation: "the roots of consciousness and life" and "the blessed country close at hand" were analogies for the unconscious mind; the indestructible "diamond body" was a figurative way of describing the birth of the archetypal Self from the combat between the conscious and unconscious aspects of the mind; and the "circulation of light" was the simultaneous activation of all intrapsychic forces using psychodynamic methods like active imagination and guided fantasy. In his comprehensive annotations, Jung argues that the generation of the "diamond body" is none other than "superior personality"[101] born from a reconnection with transpersonal aspects of oneself that are immune to desirousness, attachment, and illusion, along with the shackles of pain and suffering they can create. As acknowledged by Jung himself, the *Golden Flower* was something of a harbinger for his analytical psychology as a whole for it offered up the intellectual blueprints through which a tripartite division of the human psyche—the unconscious, the psychological archetypes, and the process of individuating tendencies—could develop.[102] Ironically, Eastern spirituality provided Jung with incentives to exhume and resuscitate a legitimate hypothesis that he'd prematurely consigned to the intellectual dustbin some time ago.

After exhausting speculative exploration of the *Golden Flower*, Jung shifted his attention to medieval alchemy. He commissioned a Munich bookseller who specialized in nuanced out-of-print works to locate as many alchemical treatises as possible. Attempting to make sense out of confusing visual narratives punctuated by winged dragons, tail-swallowing serpents, and copulating couples in these works would have been overwhelming, if not exasperating. Fortunately, Jung was able to unravel this Gordian knot with the aid of earlier insights into mythical folkloristic literature offered by Silberer and Freud. Through analogical deduction he gauged that if mythological narratives were epiphenomena of collective dreams, then the multiplicity of alchemical symbols alluding to the *prima materia* (i.e., mercury, water, menstruum, Mother Ocean, lead, earth, salt, and so forth) were intrapersonal expressions of autonomous psychic content projected unconsciously onto outer reality.[103] Stated another way, the *prima materia* had been credited with many names simply because the specificity of projective material was different for each individual.

Jung attempted to bring alchemy back from the bin of obsolete disciplines by interpreting all alchemical symbols within an analytical context. The alchemical hermaphrodite, for instance, represented the serial couplings of ego-conscious and the unconscious, a mystery facilitated by fires of suffering and experience, which eventually produced vital changes in the ego-self axis.[104] Jung stipulates that the exalted state of self-actualization can be attained with or without the intercession of an analyst, but complete submission to an alchemistic cycle both threefold and sevenfold in nature cannot be avoided. These stages include: *calcinatio*, a reduction of ego complexes; *solutio*, the subjection of questionable ego attitudes to intense scrutiny; *coagulatio*, the promotion of objective ego building; *sublimatio*, the acquisition of metacognitive insight most imperative to day-to-day problem-solving; *mortificatio*, becoming aware of the Shadow or disenfranchised aspects of one's personality; *separatio*, awareness of what qualifies as subjective and objective in reality; and *coniunctio*, an awareness of the Self generated through conciliation of conflicting psychic forces.[105] Jung then connected the *nigredo* or blackening with *calcinatio, solutio*, and *mortificatio; albedo* or whitening with the culmination of *calcinatio;* and *rubedo* or reddening with the greater *coniunctio*.[106] The last of these, a stage associated with the Philosopher's Stone and the prolongation of human life, was an anthropomorphic allegory of humankind's deepest truth and destiny—the plight to become an actualized Self with conscious and unconscious aspects of mind standing alongside one another as equal partners in a marriage. So too was the central figure of Christianity, Jesus Christ.

Despite speculative moorings, Jung's psychological yet ahistorical position attracted minimal criticism and influenced innumerable clinicians, academics, artists, and writers; alchemists were purportedly projecting the same unconscious contents onto laboratory operations that contemporary psychotherapists make conscious through methods like active imagination and guided fantasy—nothing more, nothing less. The profound correspondence between alchemical motifs and dream imagery marking a time of transformative crisis for a dreamer was first presented in its entirety in Jung's *Psychology and Alchemy* (1944) and then further elaborated upon in *Alchemical Studies* (1968), a heterogeneous collection of prior essays on alchemy, and the compelling *Mysterium Coniunctionis* (1956). Together, the three aforementioned tomes comprise the final instalments of his *Collected Works* and absorbed him entirely until his death in 1961.

Psychology and Alchemy, in particular, conveys a fundamental kernel of his belief system: "that the soul possesses by nature a religious function."[107] The religious function is directly influenced by cultural myths, which in turn determine the sociopolitical attitudes of a particular epoch. Jung describes the influence of the Catholic Church as adverse and detrimental to the collective human psyche. Quite simply, it inadvertently contributed to the arrest of collective human development from a rudimentary state to one of perfection, or spiritual gold, by way of its austere judgment, sanctimony, and rigid moral boundaries. Since its inception and swift rise to hegemony, the Christian patriarchy always emphasized the significance of the aesthetic masculine consciousness, the *animus* of mankind as a whole, and glorified the domination, subjugation, multiplication, and quantification of Nature. Could there be space for acknowledging, if not honoring, the bonds of unity, mutuality, and interconnectedness intimated by the creative fountainhead of all life, the unconscious, in a sociocultural milieu of empire-building, ownership, distinction, independence, and compartmentalization? The answer, sadly, is a resounding "no." Nonetheless, amid the throes of such an unbalanced situation, the attenuated power—in this case the aesthetic feminine consciousness or *anima* of mankind as a whole—will somehow compensate for the egregious distortion. Jung understood this psychosocial phenomenon and identified the palpable tension between the exoteric, orthodox form of Christianity and the esoteric counterculture embodied by alchemy as a historical reflection of this psychological disharmony: "It [alchemy] is to this surface as the dream is to consciousness, and just as the dream compensates the conflicts of the conscious mind, so alchemy endeavours to fill in the gaps left open by the Christian tension of opposites."[108]

The epic implications of this "discovery," or dare we say "rediscovery," were stressed in his memoirs titled *Mysteries, Dreams, Reflections*:

> My encounter with alchemy was decisive for me, as it provided me with the historical basis which I had hitherto lacked... As far as I could see, the tradition that might have connected Gnosis with the present seemed to have been severed, and for a long time it proved impossible to find any bridge that led from Gnosticism — or Neo-Platonism — to the contemporary world. But when I began to understand alchemy, I realized that it represented the historical link with Gnosticism, and that a continuity therefore existed between past and present. Grounded in the natural philosophy of the Middle Ages, alchemy formed the bridge on the one hand into the past, to Gnosticism, and on the other into the future, to the modern psychology of the unconscious.
>
> When I pored over these old texts everything fell into place: the fantasy-images, the empirical material I had gathered in my practice, and the conclusions I had drawn from it. I now began to understand what these psychic contents meant when seen in historical perspective. My understanding of their typical character, which had already begun with my investigation of myths, was deepened. The primordial images and the nature of the archetype took a central place in my researches, and it became clear to me that without history there can be no psychology, and certainly no psychology of the unconscious.[109]

The second part of *Psychology and Alchemy* contains the fruits of a 10-month labor that involved the examination of 59 dreams and visionary experiences belonging to Nobel prize-winning physicist Wolfgang Pauli with whom Jung had pioneered the synchronicity principle. The collaboration produced favorable outcomes for both; Pauli, who was experiencing bouts of depression at the time, could be treated by a reputable psychotherapist, while Jung could use his therapeutic acumen to treat a member of the intellectual elite and at the same time seek empirical validation for his "psychology of the unconscious." Uniform across the entire sequence of dream leitmotifs was the *anima*; she initially appears as a veiled woman seated on a stair [dream segment 6] before uncovering her face so that it emanates a scintillating light [dream segment 7] and then dominates the heterogenous dreamscape. Like a chameleon, the *anima's* colors alter to reflect the ever-fluctuating dynamic between conscious and unconscious aspects of Pauli's mind: in her third appearance, she is a psychopomp lighting the way for him [dream segment 10]; in the fourth, she assumes the form of his own mother and sister [dream 15]; and in the fifth, she transforms into a woman's head emitting light [dream segment 19].

The trend continues into a second series of emblems emphasizing the mandala symbol. Here, she is a gruesome foe and assailant [dream 6, series 2], yet she also transforms into an overly zealous woman contending for her lover's attention [dream 7, series 2]; she expresses herself as the subject of a portrait painted by the dreamer [dream 23, series 2], yet she also appeals to him through an articulately written letter as a woman with excruciating pains in her uterus [dream 32, series 2]; she is the spirit guide showing him the mooring post around which all perambulations occur [dream 40, series 2], the wicked witch facilitating a ceremonial dance with Lilliputians [dream 44, series 2], and the solemn priestess engaged in a ritual to commemorate the summer solstice [dream 56, series 2]. These fragments are accompanied by a compelling visual representation of an unknown woman balancing on a globe and worshipping the Sun, a leitmotif almost identical to the fourth plate of woodcut images belonging to Solomon Trismosin's famed *Splendor Solis* (1532–1535).[110]

Jung resorted to psychological types (the quaternary) in his psychoanalysis of Pauli's depression. He noticed an overidentification with sensation and thinking, characteristics of the aesthetic masculine consciousness, as the root of the problem. Pauli's choice of profession and discipline—quantum physicist in the theoretical sciences—corroborated this sentiment; the sacralization of the masculine and suppression of the feminine, the latter epitomized by aesthetic feminine qualities of feeling and intuition, had a tumultuous internal tension, which sublimated into a disturbing set of lucid dreams. The recurring dream images of the chthonic feminine— tail-swallowing serpents, fountains, seas, and a plethora of anonymous women—all attest to the disaggregation of Pauli's psyche, an inner disharmony caused by an overexpression of one psychic energy type at the expense of another.

Mysterium Coniunctionis offers a lucid depiction of Jung's position on alchemical symbolism, and identifies the *coniunctio oppositorium* [conjunction of opposites] between egocentric conscious principle and the unconscious as the chief concern of the alchemical opus. Referring explicitly to Gerard Dorn's (c. 1530–1584) attempts at harnessing a *substantia coelestis* [spirit of wine], Jung posits that "no amount of incineration, sublimation, and centrifuging of the vinous residue can ever produce an 'air-coloured' quintessence."[111] In layman's terms, Jung is affirming that descriptions of laboratory operations offered by alchemists are allegories for a process of individual growth predicated on crisis, conflict, and change—the process of "individuation." Jung viewed the dogmatic premises that medieval alchemists never questioned from this ahistorical position; for instance, men like Morienus, Gerard Dorn, and Michael Maier (1568–1622)

Figure 4-1. The fourth plate of Solomon Trismosin's *Splendor Solis* depicting the Solar King with the Lunar Queen.

espoused a crude and inchoate understanding of the association between *nigredo* and psychical danger but could not fully grasp and appreciate a phenomenon that was quite patently to Jung an encounter with dark and disenfranchised shards of their own personalities.[112] They were also oblivious to the fact that resolution of the internal conflict could be deliberately pursued through active imagination.

And what is *active imagination*? Basically, it is a therapeutic adjunct pioneered by Jung in the 1910s aiming to (re)integrate disconnected fragments of the personality with the ego-self. Described in some detail in *Mysterium Coniunctionis*, it involves fixating upon "a spontaneous fantasy, dream, an irrational mood, an affect or something of the kind"[113] while in a relaxed state. Through concentration and meditation, the fantasy content takes on a life of its own, evolving into a narrative with mythopoetic characters that are latent projections of psychological archetypes like the *anima*, *animus*, and shadow, and thus re-establish lines of communication with the unconscious mind. The technique, according to Jungians, is a legitimate way of gaining insight into an individual's current intrapsychic conflict.

Without a doubt, Jung's historiography and interpretation of alchemy was convivial and intellectually attractive when it was first presented, but in the aftermath weaknesses in his arguments became apparent. Outspoken polemicists like ex-Jungian Richard Noll (1959–), for instance, have drawn attention to characterological vices and his interest in parapsychology as a way of discrediting him and casting doubt around his legacy as a legitimate interpreter of the Western esoteric tradition — the paucity of empirical objectivity and rigor when it came to scrutinizing his own theories, the clinical transgressions (i.e., sleeping with his patients), and the adoption of a political stance for furthering one's professional aspirations (i.e., that he was a Nazi sympathizer and wasn't bothered by the public burning of Freud's works), to name but a few.

For all his ingenuity, Jung was inept at recognizing the paradox inherent in his own historiographical analysis; how might certain views elucidated in the *Paracelsica*[114] — for example, the deliberate application of cipher codes for the sake of disguising a mystical enterprise and hence eschewing a vituperative attack at the behest of a Christian patriarchy — actually be reconciled with an unconscious projection of archetypal projections onto laboratory operations? Enforcing an either-or-logic in this instance is mandatory — both can't be veridical. Moreover, some of the ideas intending to bring analytical psychology into line with a psychological rendition of alchemy are sketchy, at best; in *Psychology and Alchemy*, Jung equates his four psychological functions—thinking, feeling, sensation, and intuition—with the four elements, the four stages of the alchemical opus, and the four arms of the mystical cross without any plausible explanation as to why these associations should have been made at all. Here, Jung is overly reliant upon the neo-Pythagorean "axiom of Maria Prophetissa"[115] to justify the associations. Traceable all the way back to the 53rd chapter of a European alchemical tractate called *Turba Philosophorum* (c. CE 900), this idiom speaks to the central importance of four in the creative process: for Jung, the "one" is the uroboric autarchy of paradisal perfection; the "two" is differentiation into the functional strata of the individual human psyche; the "three" is the *coniunctio* that produces the transcendental function; and the "four" is the psychological totality mediated by the archetypal Self. Of course, basing an epistemological foundation chiefly on numerical relations constitutes what many would describe as the proverbial non sequitur, a mistake that even his disciple and commentator Aniela Jaffe inevitably acknowledged: "There was no particular book that he valued above all others. He would single out one or another according to its applicability to the theme he was interested in... at the moment."[116]

Till now, equally concerning for the fort of analytical psychology is the complete dearth of scientific evidence from theoretical and clinical disciplines like the neurosciences that might corroborate arguments for the existence of a transpersonal entity like a collective unconscious. The observations that enabled Jung to make that theoretical leap are tenuous, at best. They derive from Swiss patients who were more often than not apathetic, well-integrated, and endowed with above-average intelligence. His scope of clinical practice, which served a specific demographic, did not permit the attitude to make overarching generalizations and premature extrapolations about the entire population, but that is what he did—if you weren't neurotic and asymptomatic, you were suffering from a fundamental disconnection with the unconscious. For Jung, the clinical label a patient received—manic-depressive, psychotic, dissociative— was superficial and irrelevant; signs of any disturbance or abnormality were, in his opinion, creative impasses or arrests in the dynamic process of individuation. The blockage occurred in a place beyond the persona and the masks buttressing superficial social cohesion, perhaps at the deepest point in the human psyche. Was there someone able to shed light upon this phenomenon or entity?

Incidentally, a pivotal piece of the puzzle was offered up by one of Jung's schizophrenic patients. This patient was plagued by florid hallucinations, including a very vivid and carnal one of a sun endowed with a flexible phallus, one that would have undoubtedly resembled an elephant trunk. According to the patient, the four winds were generated by the motion of the prehensile phallus. Strange as it was, the images offered up for observation were strikingly similar to descriptions of a Mithraic liturgy found in an unpublicized Greek papyrus, where a phallic tube suspended from the bottom of the solar nimbus embodied the aerial forces.[117] Jung claimed that the patient lacked foreknowledge of the manuscript and that the phenomenon only made sense in the context of a telepathic projection—this was clear evidence in support of an unconscious seat of primordial symbols of transpersonal character that manifest in dreams and psychoses universally and found in mythologems. Attempts to discredit "the psychology of the unconscious," such as those initiated by ex-Jungian Richard Noll, have depended upon casting dark veils of suspicion over the experiential legitimacy of this "Solar Phallus Man." Noll, in particular, has argued that both English and German translations of the Mithraic text were in circulation before the patient's hallucination came to pass,[118] insinuating that cryptomnesia is a much more feasible explanation for this phenomenon. Deferring to the transpersonal, or the unbridled expression of a psychological archetype from the collective unconscious, is apparently unnecessary.

In recent years, the Jungian school has also had to contend and compete with a growing gamut of interpretive scholars seeking to demonstrate alchemy's importance in the transition from Renaissance vitalism to post-Enlightenment mechanistic philosophy. For instance, Isaac Newton's lifelong interest in chemico-operative alchemy and the extent to which it stimulated conjectures that led to the birth of classical mechanics is illuminated by Betty Jo Teeter Dobbs (1930–1994) in her book *The Foundations of Newton's Alchemy* (1991). A similar argument is promulgated in Lawrence Principe's book *The Aspiring Adept: Robert Boyle and His Alchemical Quest* (2018) about a man who is more often than not regarded as the founding father of modern chemistry. On the other hand, the French historian of science Barbara Obrist (1950–) has sought to purge late medieval and Renaissance alchemical literature of psychospiritual interpretations inspired by nineteenth-century Victorian occultism by asserting that the religiously-flavored metaphors exploited by the authors are merely rhetorical devices and should not be misrepresented academically as an indication of religious or spiritual orientation. We find enumerated arguments against the presentist approach in her extensive reading of *Aurora Consurgens*, an emblematic fifteenth-century text that Jung frequently used as a psychoanalytic hermeneutic; its core narrative, Obrist claims, appears more lucid and coherent when one resists construal through the kaleidoscope of analytical psychology.[119]

Obrist also argues that Jung's "historical vision" gave rise to sweeping generalizations about the ethos of all individuals who self-styled as alchemists in the medieval period. The misperception resulted in a fundamental error in that Jung envisioned these individuals as progressive inheritors of an ancient soteriological quest for selfhood within a religious, fervent, and vitalistic milieu, which operated on a collective scale as an outright defiance of church dogma. It is clear from descriptions of the *lapis*-Christ parallel offered up in Chapter Five of *Psychology and Alchemy* that Jung perceived the dissemination of Christological leitmotifs among medieval alchemists as a pictorial masquerade for the individuation process. He argues that this same process enjoyed unhindered expression under the Gnostic doctrine of the Anthropos (i.e., the *Visions of Zosimos*) at a time when the religious climate was far more liberal. Obrist dismisses this impression outright:

> In the texts attributed to Arnold [of Villanova], the metaphor of Christ appears amongst others which are used as examples, helping to demonstrate chemical processes that are difficult to understand. They are metaphors like the others, and nothing but metaphors, a fact which Arnold and the authors who follow in his tradition explain extremely well, and which also applies to the illustrations of such treatises. Nothing allows us to speculate on the religiosity of an author when he uses a consciously rhetorical process.[120]

The resolve of historians of science like Obrist and Principe in demonstrating coherence and continuity between alchemy and the emergence of the modern scientific method underscores the importance of intimately acquainting oneself with the sociopolitical conditions of the epoch one wishes to study before prematurely imposing one's own psychological frame of reference onto it. In 'Some Problems with the Historiography of Alchemy,' Lawrence Principe and William Newman identify twentieth-century figures like Jung, the psychoanalyst; Mircea Eliade (1907–1986), the scholar of comparative religion; Helene Mertzger (1886–1944), a popular historian of chemistry; and the writers Carolyn Merchant (1936–) and Evelyn Fox Keller (1936–) as advocates of "presentist" interpretations that either devalue the philosophical or scientific aspects and value of the Great Work, or dismiss it outright as a "hair-raising chemical fantasy." The crux of their argument is that the same alchemical symbols used by Jung to progress his psychological rendition are contrived *Decknamen* [codenames] for chemicals and minerals bearing no association whatsoever with nascent unconscious content. If the symbols were products of unconscious projection, then the "possibility of working backwards from them to decipher such images into actual, valid laboratory practice" would be impossible.[121]

Never at any stage do the authors entertain the possibility of a dual interpretation; why do the symbols have to be relegated to either a chemical or a psychological context? Isn't it the nature of a symbol to embrace multiple meanings? After all, Western alchemy has always been a theoretical powerhouse for a plethora of religious and mystical ideas about the universe in the manner that the cosmopolitan Alexandria of late antiquity was the receptacle and melting pot for knowledge arriving from the four corners of the world in the guise of books. *The Emerald Tablet*, otherwise known as the *Tabula Smaragdina* in Latin, is a condensed and apocryphal summa of Hermetic and alchemical tenets that was reintroduced to the Latin West sometime during the thirteenth century. In it, Hermes Trismegistus prudently declares that the alchemical work delineates the processes of *all* creation. That would include every theory about the mechanics of the cosmos that has existed, exists, or shall come into existence in the future—scientific, speculative, or otherwise. Might the recent germination of panpsychism and intelligent design, then, be an unconscious bid to unclog a *univers imaginaires* and counteract the determinism, materialism, and dogmatic scientism that has monopolized what gets to define itself as science since the publication of Newton's *Philosophiae Naturalis Principia Mathematica* (1687)? Or would this be too Jungian of an idea and thus not credible?

Endnotes

89 Hereward Tilton, *The Quest for the Phoenix: Spiritual Alchemy and Rosicrucianism in the Work of Count Michael Maier (1569–1622)* (Berlin: de Gruyter, 2003), p. 24.

90 Ibid, p. 25.

91 Lawrence M. Principe and William R. Newman, 'Some Problems with the Historiography of Alchemy', in *Secrets of Nature: Astrology and Alchemy in Early Modern Europe*, ed. by William R. Newman and Anthony Grafton (London, UK: MIT Press, 2006), p. 387.

92 Arthur Edward Waite, *Azoth, or the Star in the East, embracing the first matter of the Magnum Opus, the evolution of the Aphrodite-Urania, the supernatural generation of the son of the sun, and the alchemical transfiguration of humanity* (Whitefish, MT: Kessinger Publishing, 1994), p. 44.

93 Lawrence M. Principe and William R. Newman, pp. 392.

94 Ethan Allen Hitchcock, *Remarks Upon Alchemy and the Alchemists, Indicating a Method of Discovering the True Nature of Hermetic Philosophy; and Showing That the Search after the Philosopher's Stone Had Not for Its Object the Discovery of an Agent for the Transmutation of Metals: Being Also an Attempt to Rescue from Undeserved Opprobrium the Reputation of a Class of Extraordinary Thinkers in Past Ages* (Boston, MA: Crosby, Nichols, and Company, 1857), p. iii.

95 Arthur Edward Waite, pp. 54, 58, and 60.

96   Richard Wilhelm (trans.), *The Secret of the Golden Flower: A Chinese Book of Life*, with a Foreword by Carl Jung (Orlando, FL: Harcourt Brace & Company, 1961), pp. xiii–xv.

97   David Sedgewick, *Introduction to Jungian Psychotherapy: The Therapeutic Relationship* (London, UK: Routledge, 2013), p. 23.

98   Wilhelm, p. 69.

99   Ibid, pp. 14–15.

100 Henri F. Ellenberger, *The Discovery of the Unconscious: The History and Evolution of Dynamic Psychiatry* (New York, USA: Basic Books, 1970), pp. 708–709.

101 Wilhelm, p. 124.

102 Ibid, p. xiv.

103 Carl Gustav Jung, *Psychology and Alchemy, Collected Works*, vol. 12 (Princeton: Princeton University Press, 1968), p. 317.

104 Ibid, pp. 202, 205, 232.

105 Edward Edinger, *Anatomy of the Psyche: Alchemical Symbolism in Psychotherapy* (Chicago, Illinois: Open Court, 1994), pp. 21–22, 56–57, 83, 117–118, 149, 187–188, 218–220.

106 Ibid, pp. 147–148.

107 Carl Gustav Jung, *Mysteries, Dreams, Reflections* (London: Routledge & Kegan Paul, 1963; Fontana, 1977), p. x.

108 Carl Gustav Jung, *Psychology and Alchemy, Collected Works*, vol. 12 (Princeton: Princeton University Press, 1968), p. 23.

109 Carl Gustav Jung, *Mysteries, Dreams, Reflections* (London: Routledge & Kegan Paul, 1963; Fontana, 1977), pp. 226–227, 231–232.

110 Carl Gustav Jung, *Psychology and Alchemy, Collected Works*, vol. 12 (Princeton: Princeton University Press, 1968), p. 86.

111 Carl Gustav Jung, *Mysterium Coniunctionis, Collected Works*, vol. 14 (Princeton: Princeton University Press, 1968), p. 526.

112 Ibid, p. 521.

113 Ibid, p. 526.

114 Carl Gustav Jung, *Alchemical Studies, Collected Works*, vol. 13 (Princeton: Princeton University Press, 1968), p. 171.

115 Carl Gustav Jung, *Psychology and Alchemy, Collected Works*, vol. 12 (Princeton: Princeton University Press, 1968), pp. 23, 26.

116 Aniela Jaffe, *Jung's Last Years and Other Essays* (New Orleans, LA: Spring Publications, 1984), p. 54.

117 Ellenberger, p. 705.

118 Richard Noll, *The Aryan Christ: The Secret Life of Carl Jung* (New York: Random House, 1997), pp. 22–52, 98–119.

119 Lawrence M. Principe and William R. Newman, 'Some Problems with the Historiography of Alchemy', in *Secrets of Nature: Astrology and Alchemy in Early Modern Europe*, ed. by William R. Newman and Anthony Grafton (London, UK: MIT Press, 2006), p. 406.

120 Hereward Tilton, *The Quest for the Phoenix: Spiritual Alchemy and Rosicrucianism in the Work of Count Michael Maier (1569–1622)* (Berlin: de Gruyter, 2003), p. 10.

121 Ibid, p. 14.

Part II: Processes of the Mind

Chapter 5

The Black Sun: A Symbol of Transformation

Figure 5-1. The black sun (or dark sun) from the *Splendor Solis* plates by Solomon Trismosin.

The black sun is one of the most compelling and awe-inspiring images that crops up in alchemical manuscripts. For those unacquainted with alchemical symbolism, the pairing of the words "black" and "sun" may seem bizarre and to some degree discordant. How can a source of omnipresent light, which sustains organic life on Planet Earth, be linked to the color black or to the concept of darkness in general? Answering this question entails looking at the nuanced and near-perfect conditions that must subsist on our planet for life to take root. These, as we all recognize, are contingent on the relative position of Planet Earth to the proximal source of heat in our solar system, the sun. Veering too close would scorch its surface and reduce everything to cinders. Alternatively, venturing too far would spur a detrimental drop in global temperature as to coat it in thick layers of inimical ice. The hostile and extreme environments of our two closest neighbors—Mars and Venus—corroborate this theory. We also know that anomalous activity on the spotted surface of the sun generates bursts of radiation (i.e., solar flares) that kill off life forms that can only flourish in nuanced and relatively stable environmental conditions. The deadly potential latent in the autogenerator of life, the sun, is also a psychological phenomenon embodied by the alchemical image of a black sun in Jung's analytical psychology and is discussed at length by Stanton Marlon in his wonderful book *The Black Sun: The Alchemy and Art of Darkness.*

Closely allied to the black sun are the *nigredo* and the *caput corvi* phases of the alchemical opus, both processes that are intimately connected with darkness, pain, torment, and death. *Nigredo*, as we should recall from the chapters on the history of alchemy, is all about an unprecedented, sometimes fearsome encounter with those unconscious, disenfranchised, and dystonic facets of being that exist within the concentric sphere of the Self. Jung branded these aspects of the human personality one's "shadow." Confronting one's shadow is usually a frightening experience. Just as an excess of heat may extirpate life, or cause an alchemical vessel holding the matter to be worked on to burst and shatter into shards, so too does an absolute identification with only the contents of conscious awareness activate transpersonal forces within as to overturn the existing order and plunge the inner kingdom into discord. When this happens, one might feel like a mortal hero or heroine being seared alive by the fiery breath of a green dragon; an Egyptian Osiris being dismembered by the hands of his evil brother, Seth; an intoxicated Dionysus being torn to shreds by a group of Maenads intoxicated by mead and deaf to reason and order; or a Christ bearing the collective burdens of humanity by electing the path of suffering and subsequent death by crucifixion. What these mythological tropes are telling us is that in Nature there can be no congelation of a new form without a preceding dissolution, no birth of a new light without the enveloping darkness, no new creation without the necessary precursor of deconstruction, no victory and celebration without first suffering the excruciating pain of defeat, and no form without the preexistence of a formless *prima materia*. Something can't come from nothing.

Understood from a psychological perspective, the *nigredo* is imminent when the ego-self cannot contain the intrusion of transpersonal forces into conscious awareness, and when a growing number of phenomena and facts can no longer be explained away or reconciled with one's epistemic paradigms and cognitive schemas for consensus reality. This occurs innumerable times over the course of one's lifetime; there is no limit to the number of cycles of *nigredo* one might endure during their plight to maximize their innate creative potential and become the best version of themselves they can be. During the alchemical *nigredo*, the fundamental unity of our personality, our sense of Oneness, is undermined and we are reduced to the sum of our parts. Some of these parts will enter into transient dialogue with one another and manifest in conscious awareness as equivocal feelings. The ebbs and flows of transpersonal forces (i.e., the psychological archetypes) can be so overwhelming and discombobulating at this time as to convince one that they are losing their grip on reality. Fortunately, the psychospiritual process is mediated by hope, an omnipresent source of wisdom and metacognitive insight reminding one that any plunge into somnolent darkness is temporary and will be superseded by fundamental harmony in time. One remains well insulated from confusion, paranoia, anxiety, pain, or any other guise of psychological distress precipitated by the *nigredo* phase when faith in the healing power of the Self has not been forsaken. This makes any shade of suffering all the more bearable.

The image of the black sun can also be connected with death and defeat in the Narcissus myth. Psychologically speaking, the handsome youth Narcissus personifies an inflated ego-self—an overabundance of qualities like omniscience, omnipotent control, arrogance, and self-pride. A powerful imbalance between the archetypal forces at war within the psyche will automatically self-correct. As expounded in the classical tale, this inner titration does not come from transpersonal forces that exist somewhere outside the individual; nobody, not even the beautiful water nymphs, can trigger such a powerful thought-desire within the young man as to dissolve his core self. Narcissus, it appears, remains unmoved, uninspired, and unmotivated by anything from the social environment that is not cut from the same inner fabric as he is. In the end, the corrosive agent that dissolves his "narcissism" comes from within, from intercourse with his own self. Peering into the surface of a calm, limpid lake one day, he catches sight of his own reflection and becomes enamored of it. Desire and lust for physical forms can overpower someone to the degree that they lose control and engage in dystonic behaviors (i.e., doing things that are incongruent with one's established identity and self-image). For the unfortunate Narcissus, a momentary impulse to get up close and personal with his own likeness was irresistible and cost him his life; he plunges into the water and drowns while kneeling over for a meticulous examination of his own physiognomy. Looking at the tale through the lens of analytical psychology, we might say that the burgeoning narcissism triggered a *nigredo* that dissolved the myopic ego-self, allowing for a more sophisticated and refined version of the self to emerge from the charred cinders. The narcissistic youth had to die for the introspective scholar, the progressive artist, and the valiant hero to be born.

From what we know about different states of consciousness, the unconscious aspects of the human psyche seek expression through leitmotifs or symbols that are natural and organic in nature. They may be nested into a highly nuanced, nonverbal language unique to the genetic-environmental footprint of each individual. A stream of visual images irrupting from the unconscious psyche, either through mechanisms of dreaming cognition or hallucinatory processes, relinquish veridical information about existing problems and issues. They are existential commentaries about our present life situation. Any other hermeneutic that one might subscribe to in understanding their ultimate significance or meaning is purely speculative. For instance, surreptitiously stealing the property of a relative in a dream could connote an unconventional solution to a current creative—or in more literal terms, a hitherto undisclosed—desire for vengeance against the relative for their transgression. The interpretation or narrative extrapolation is informed by interpersonal and social context and much of that context is known only by the dreamer. This is why the dream interpretation most likely to be true is best formulated by the dreamer themselves. Who knows the dreamer better than they know themselves, right?

There are also certain images that are intraculturally homologous, meaning they carry identical or equivalent meanings for individuals belonging to the same culture. One of the most dreaded, according to Carl Jung, is the black sun. Disturbingly vivid and highly convoluted dreams are sometimes harbingers of the black sun, and may manifest in dreaming cognition either as literal renditions of a black sun in the diurnal sky or with more subtlety as metaphors involving feces, foul and putrid odors, death, and earth-shattering lamentation for a living or deceased relative. Images of decaying flesh, graves, overflowing toilets, and the presence of worms and other organisms involved in the decomposition of organic matter are also signs that the black sun has risen. In his book, Marlon professes that the appearance of the black sun in dreams often precedes a major life transition, such as a change in health, socioeconomic, or psychospiritual status. In this way, it acts like the great star Sirius whose heliacal rising in the east may be construed as a loud announcement of a new dawn.

One of the most striking depictions of the alchemical black sun can be found on the second plate of the third sequence of illuminating paintings known as the *Splendor Solis* (c. 1532–1535). Here, the black sun is portrayed as a black orb with a corona of emanating golden-orange rays. It is in the process of ascending over a picturesque town couched within a beautiful countryside with the latter divided into three dunes. The sun's rays pierce both the rose-tinted wisps of cloud above and the earth layers, nourishing the vegetative and mineral kingdoms. The burning flame enabling life comes from the heart-centers of the solar system and the earth. This dual fire suggests that inner and outer, above and below, are one reality. Perusing proximal areas of the aurora, one can see that the terrain is semitranslucent; the shape of the sun's orb is clearly illuminated behind the meandering path, which connects the horizon to the adjacent mounds of the countryside. A more scrupulous perusal of the image reveals an underlying paradox; the green hills and meadows proximal to the horizon, paragons of fecundity and fruitfulness, are juxtaposed by a foreground dominated by a desiccated watercourse. A source of further confusion is that a bed of young shrubs and plants has miraculously sprouted from amid the dust. Finally, a cluster of dead tree stumps sprout from a mound near the bank of the dry watercourse; these remind the observer that the ancient land on which they once thrived is periodically sieged by natural cataclysms and upheavals.

So, what are the inferences in this image? In many ways, the entire plate is an emblematic reminder that order and growth are dependent upon cyclical periods of chaos and crisis in self-esteem. Indeed, birth, death, and regeneration are indivisible aspects of creation. This unshakable law pertains to more than just the psychological level; it's one that defines all processes of creation. If we examined the evolution of life on Planet Earth, for instance, we see that major advances in biological complexity are preceded by an extinction event. Loss of diversity in the ecosystem equates to gains in complexity. How? First, some guise of habitat disruption occurs at the behest of a global cataclysmic disaster (i.e., a paroxysmic eruption of a supervolcano, or the impact of an asteroid striking the earth), relegating innumerable species to the extinct class. More resistant strains are adversely impacted by cumulative environmental stress, spurring radical increases in mutation rates from whence a plethora of new body plans and modes of life appear. Those that are most efficient and demonstrate stealthy competence in appropriating the remaining natural resources in a milieu with reduced biodiversity will survive, reproduce, and successfully transmit their genetic traits to subsequent generations. These traits and characteristics are bound to be functionally more complex, sophisticated, and resilient than those that perished or served as predecessors. Yes, loss of diversity is sometimes commensurate with a gain in complexity.

The same is patently true for the process of individual growth, or individuation as Jung labeled it; when the existing schemas and epistemic frameworks of the self become too dissonant with the status quo reflected by the outer world and cannot be adequately assimilated, fragmentation of the individual psyche ensues. The process of fragmentation and the concurrent activation of transpersonal forces within an individual is also intimately connected with a surplus of thought-desires or psychological projections. Change comes about when the existing form of the personality is dismantled, existing psychological projections are withdrawn, and the personal shadow—in other words, disenfranchised aspects of self experienced as ego-dystonic—is resurrected, acknowledged, and finally integrated with the recognized, syntonic aspects. Our new illumined and exalted self-state is a coveted product of the relentless friction between, on one hand, our own mental processes and subjective inner world, and on the other, the social environment—a child of the Great Above and the Great Below.

The black sun plate of the *Splendor Solis* celebrates the interconnectedness and mutual interdependence of all things, living and inanimate, by illuminating their obedience to the same cosmic law, pattern, and cycle. Separation may be an illusion of the senses and a necessity for survival imposed by the evolutionary process. Ignorance, arrogance, and narcissism are just some of the thought-desires that keep us shackled to our self-imposed limitations and delusions, removed from the participatory nature of reality and creation, and hopelessly blind to the majesty of the universe as a whole. The tendency to describe life and all forms of development as a dynamic process of gaining traction and moving forward only after several regressive steps have been made seems somewhat counterintuitive and bizarre. The concurrent representation of disparate states (i.e., flourishing and languishing vegetation) in the picture reflect the fundamental truth that past and present are in perpetual coexistence, and that their perceived temporal and spatial dimensions are simply a necessary construction of the human mind to eschew internal disorganization. Just as the earth contains within all its prior incarnations in the guise of fossils within subterranean strata, so too do we humans carry the mercurial and sometimes fossilized memories of prior developmental stages within our consciousness until death. The black sun is given anthropic features—a reference, perhaps, to intelligent design or a creative esemplastic power at work in the cosmos?

Chapter 6

Child's Play: A Key to Transformation

Figure 6-1. The children's play scene from the *Splendor Solis* plates by Solomon Trismosin. The illustration shows children at play, some with hobbyhorses and windmills, in a large room with a mother nursing her baby, and birds, flowers, and butterflies in the border.

The second illustration of the third and final collection of *Splendor Solis* plates is both puzzling and mysterious. It depicts

10 children involved in light-hearted play. The first thing that becomes apparent here is the capaciousness of the room and the slivers of sunlight emanating through the windows. There's also a gargantuan tiled stove in the background. These features are very reminiscent of the alchemical vessel in which dross matter is sealed in and subjected to a gradually intensifying and controlled fire for the purpose of purification. A woman decked in a black-collared red dress and a white headscarf is seated magnanimously in front of the stove. Incidentally, black, white, and red are the tutelary colors of the alchemical process—*nigredo*, *albedo*, and *rubedo*. The woman's central roles as benevolent guide and competent caregiver are inferred; she's cradling a small infant who sits complacent on her lap and simultaneously tends to a needy toddler tugging on her dress. A lustration bath or washbowl is depicted on the floor beside them. To their right stands an open doorway; the wooden arch above it supports two stoppered flasks containing the same yellow solution, a not-so-subtle reference to an intermediary alchemical phase called *citrinitas* or *xanthosis*. Beyond the opening, one can see another female figure holding a minuscule lustration bath in the somnolent darkness.

On the opposite side, one sees a solemn child clad in blue who physically assists a younger peer to climb onto a wooden bench. Proximal to this subplot is another pair of carefree children engaged in fantastical role-play; the younger of the two, a naked boy, rides a toy horse and holds a toy pinwheel, while the other boy who is decked in a blue outfit vies for his attention by waving around another toy pinwheel. In the space directly between the interacting couplets is a black bird, probably a crow or jackdaw, with its wings partially outstretched. This is a powerful symbol of the omnipresent *prima materia*. In the foreground of the plate, a passive observer will see five other children pretending to be charioteers and passengers; two older children, one robed in a cobalt-blue garment and the other in a sunflower-yellow one, are providing essential mechanical support for a nude toddler lying on an opulent red cushion. The cushion has been converted into a sledge or chariot and is being drawn around the room by two naked drivers who appear self-absorbed; one is delicately stroking the head of the other and admiring him. All primary colors—red, yellow, and blue—and the fourfold composition of matter conceived in Aristotelian terms—water, fire, air (inferred by the wings of the black bird), and earth—are present, indicating that some kind of transformative process is underway.

To which psychospiritual stage of development, if any, does this plate allude to? Perhaps the best way of answering this question is by looking at the plate in its entirety, as an integrated whole. A group of vivacious children who are either modeling behaviors they've observed in adults or are in the process of trying out social costumes, identities, and roles may indicate that stages connected with undifferentiation, Oneness, and the complete absence of an ego-self have been superseded. Under the auspices of Carl Jung's analytical psychology, conditions like emptiness, immobility, inertia, and unconsciousness are equivalent with the *pleromatic* (i.e., state of being before birth) and the condition of partial differentiation from the ambient background of the social environment synonymous with the *uroboric* (i.e., state of being inside the womb). These are not the stages embodied by the effervescent, rambunctious children. The relative positions of two specific figures in the plate—the black bird, a symbol of the *prima materia*, and the maternal caregiver, an embodiment of carnal drives and the gratification of physiological needs—corroborates this view. Their proximity to the robust children aptly reminds one that any existing phase of psychological development is predicated upon the successful navigation of and graduation from more foundational levels.

Progress is vacillatory and nonlinear, and an individual can either progress to a more exalted, sophisticated stage or regress to a more rudimentary one at any time.

Now, let's shift our attention toward the children. The interacting family of children can be divided into three distinct subgroups: the naked toddlers, the older children bejeweled in beautiful blue garments, and a single child dressed in yellow. The first of these personify a state that the transpersonal theorist Ken Wilber (1949–) called *body ego* [consciousness] and Pierre Janet (1859–1947) called the *sensorimotor* [stage of development]. This formative stage is all about adjusting to the condition of embodiment and experiencing the social environment through the rapidly maturing sensory organs. From birth, toddlers are equipped with a gustatory acuity able to differentiate the saccharine from the bitter and can parse out pungent odors from those more pleasurable. They are highly sensitive to nociceptive pain and are even proficient at localizing the source of auditory frequencies. Relative to the other senses, vision, our dominant sense, develops much more slowly. Visual acuity, for instance, doesn't reach full maturity until 4–6 years of age. The newborn's perceptual interface with the environment is increasingly refined as different neural systems begin to wire together through synaptogenesis, axonal projection, and myelination—object recognition, and control of head and eye movements is possible at 3 months, grasping for objects is possible at 6 months, visual control of locomotion is possible at 6 months, and formulation of speech is possible at 18 months. The maturation and attunement of the sensory organs to the environment corresponds well with the emergence of a *body ego*, an incipient and very nebulous sense of self as an embodied thing-in-itself.

This stage is also about emulation, the reproduction of behaviors that are instinctively purposive, and the formation of internal representations that enable him or her to move backward and forward in time. A toddler exposed to a face of a clown baring teeth will emulate that particular facial expression. Witnessing a caregiver or guardian figure striding about with a limp will elicit the same behavior in the toddler. Expletives heard arbitrarily or by accident may join their growing shortlist of rudimentary words. All observations are assimilated into an existing schema. In short, the toddler's mental space is a *tabula rasa* unsullied by the shades of sociocultural conditioning, a world of eternal feasibilities that is coming-into-being and is ready to be impressed and shaped by causal relationships existing somewhere "out there" through make-believe (symbolic) play. The unsullied condition, the state of unadulterated purity, is mirrored by the six toddlers who are stark naked. Dressing oneself or the act of being dressed is synonymous with the manufacture of a social persona informed by interlacing micro- and macro-scale networks in the environment. Toddlers are like little dark moons, waiting for the slivers of light to give them color, shape, and texture.

The next group of children, the ones decked in blue, are slightly older in age and represent a stage of development that Wilber called the *membership-self*. This equates with Piaget's *preoperational* stage of cognitive development under the orthodox model of psychology. Just as the term itself suggests, a key characteristic of this stage is identification in the context of group membership. There is bound to be heightened sensitivity to social context and relationship to others when redirecting one's conscious awareness "outward." Moreover, a critical window of opportunity exists here for the establishment of a coherent, stable, and positive self-image by observing social roles and adopting those that are congruent with the child's dispositional dowry and fulfill the innate desire for validation. During this stage, direct observation of adults is something of a double-edged sword: it is a powerful vehicle for a child's own self-expression but also the progenitor of their own egocentricity, narcissism, and a developmentally appropriate inability to de-identify from their own perspective.

Scampering about with their elaborate silk garments, these children are learning and problem-solving with the aid of semantic language, mental representations, and other symbols. Still with limited intellectual powers, children in this stage view the world through the lens of precausal (transductive) reasoning—there are supernatural explanations for natural phenomena that subsist in a universe where inanimate objects are humanized, and eternal feasibilities are physical laws and not anomalous exceptions. In this stage, there may be copious use of the pronouns "I" and "me," revealing a clear differentiation from the maternal uroboros. The *membership-self* also has a fairly superficial and proto-scientific understanding of causality—it focuses and fixates upon the gestalt of an object, disregarding any intricate detail and believes in the finality of actions once they are carried out. Perhaps the most compelling feature of this stage is the intermittent switching between two paradoxical methods of information processing—a fluid intercourse between the monosemantic, chronological, and linear processes of the dominant hemisphere, which enable participation in consensus reality, and the holistic, analogical, and nonverbal processes of the dominant hemisphere, which underpin imagination and self-determination, and maintain an internal locus of control.

The third subgroup consists of a single individual, a slightly older boy: he wears sunflower yellow, the color of illumination, rides a toy horse, and assists a toddler reclined on a red cushion. Interestingly, the stoic image of horse and rider has been used by many psychological schools as an allegory describing the union of the ego-self, the inner mental world, with consensual reality, the "external" world. This successive stage is characterized by the appearance of more sophisticated mental operations and bursts of intellectual activity: nomothetic rules for the transformation, manipulation, and internalization of information; semantic clustering; conservation of number, length, weight, and displacement volume; computational proficiency; and some capacity to inhibit and control impulses. Inhibition processing is sometimes symbolized by the horse and its rider; just as the rider is the master of his or her animal and can control it at will, so too is the human intellect the executive control center that can downregulate the volatile sea of emotions and maintain titration.

Ken Wilber's nonhierarchical map designates the appearance of these capacities to *mental ego* consciousness. The equivalent in Janetian terms would be the *concrete operations* and *formal operations* stages of development. At this time, parents may also bear witness to abstraction (i.e., symbolic thinking, deductive reasoning), more complex forms of problem-solving (i.e., solving class inclusion problems), and exercising willpower. The growth of these cognitive powers is complemented by growing narcissism and egocentricity, and children in this stage may find it virtually impossible to separate the intentional states of others from their own (i.e., no theory of mind). Moreover, their inflated sense of self-importance fuels specious personal narratives about their own uniqueness and importance in the world, and they may act with impunity and with little to no regard for the feelings and welfare of their peers. When describing themselves, they mostly subscribe to binary systems.

To give a more tangible example, a child who has entered this phase might say, "My name is Axel. My dad is a doctor and my mother a teacher. My best friend's name is Jack. I like chocolate milk and white-chocolate raspberry ice-cream. I believe in ghosts. I don't like playing sports. I think there's a pink hippopotamus on my roof that comes out at night and makes funny noises. When I grow up, I want to become a pilot." The *mental ego* stage is solemnly solipsistic in comparison with the preceding stages, which are punctuated by fluidity and an inchoate, nebulous sense of self. Powerful psychological automatisms preside over paradigm-building and subscription to idiosyncratic belief systems during this stage, with the child perceiving both themselves and others through a black-and-white, either/or binary sieve; there is no bandwidth for shades of gray and little to no tolerance for ambiguity. Something is either black or white, right or wrong. There is no room for, or appreciation of, the contextual nuances introduced by conflicts between the law, personal ethics and sentiments, and social etiquette.

In review, it appears the second illustration of the third series of plates that comprise the *Splendor Solis* alludes to three stages of development described by Ken Wilber as the *body ego*, the *membership-self*, and the *mental ego*. Germane correlations to Wilber's stages exist in the orthodox disciplines of cognitive and development psychology. Collectively, these states are a fundamental key to the transformation of human consciousness, and the modus operandi enabling that transformation is inquisitive play and make-believe. When children play, they are actively internalizing relational blueprints through inductive reasoning, expressing and refining their intrinsic traits and creative potential, and moving toward self-definition. Unfettered by the imposed protocols of etiquette and free of the sociocultural conditioning that encumbers expressions of candidness and authenticity, they are also mindfully present. It is much easier to remain grounded in the here and now when there is no pre-recorded white or pink noise in the ambient background of fields offering running social commentaries and pontificating about what you should think, how you should feel, and how you should behave. Under such ideal circumstances, one can enter into a relational dyad and just be themselves without fearing ridicule or judgment. Without operative cognitive schemas to consign the information gleaned from our sensorium to specific semantic categories, each simulation of a world event—even the exact same event—becomes an inimitable, sublime experience able to enhance, elaborate, and add meaning to our personal narratives. Social conditioning and habitual responses to stimuli hinder and sometimes decimate the expression of extraordinary creative potential dormant in the human spirit. Perhaps this is what the Apostle Matthew had in mind when he said: "Truly, I tell you, unless you change and become like little children, you will never enter the kingdom of heaven."[122] Entering heaven may be synonymous with seeing through the eyes of a newborn.

Children create visual images in their mind's eye and put them into action without ever doubting their feasibility. Nothing is ever unreasonable or too farfetched in their wondrous eyes. One minute they're princes and princesses stuck in medieval towers; the next they're transforming into dreadful witches and magicians intending to cast spells on the rude lady next door; and a little while after that they're fluffy white rabbits trying to jump out of Willy Wonka's top hat! This self-imposed and natural freedom to pretend, to act, to be what one wishes to be, and to do as one pleases is a source of empowerment for children; it's a chance to learn from trial-and-error within a safe and controlled environment while concurrently wielding a kind of unbridled power that is nonexistent under the more regimented and supervised structure of their day-to-day lives. Being allowed to think and act for oneself is imperative for survival, and make-believe play renders that possible during one's formative stages of development.

We could make other extrapolations about the illustration based on the abovementioned associations. Is it alluding to the importance of competent perspective-taking in psychospiritual development? Or perhaps to the role that worldview deconstruction and the withdrawal of psychological projections plays in the process? Alternatively, the illustration could be a reminder of how to manifest something in consensus reality through the sustained conjuring of mental images, or a reminder of the formative powers of the placebo (the belief effect) and self-fulfilling prophecies. Who hasn't heard the axiom, "Be careful what you wish for, because you may just get it"? Indeed, a picture is worth a thousand words but which words abound will be of the author's choosing.

Endnotes
122   *English Standard Version Bible* (2001), Matthew 18:3.

Chapter 7

Women's Work: Mechanisms of Consciousness

Figure 7-1. The women's work scene from the *Splendor Solis* plates by Solomon Trismosin. The illustration depicts women washing laundry.

The third illustration from the third series of plates belonging to the *Splendor Solis* collection initiates a dramatic departure from both the alchemical images of *sol niger* [the black or dark sun] and the equanimous children at play. Gone are the harrowing and mysterious visions of death and decomposition and the light-hearted playfulness we see when young children are interacting with one another in playpens, playrooms, or playgrounds. Instead, we see a coterie of women actively engaged in domestic duties, which many would describe as ordinary and mundane—the washing, rinsing, and drying of white linen. At first glance, it's a scene that might strike a casual observer as an oddity, somewhat misplaced and unprecedented; what connection, if any, could there be between washing fabric and bringing oneself into harmonious alignment with the governing psychophysical principles of Nature as alluded to by the alchemical process?

To untangle this conundrum, one must take a closer look at the nature of transformation itself. Major life transitions are periods of emotional turmoil and unrest, but they are preceded and superseded by states of quiescence where the individual has assumed an imposed, obligatory role of societal convention and is engaged in tasks commonly associated with that role. Remaining in an ossified condition for an indeterminate time is a necessary evil, for it allows tensions to develop between the persona, a chameleon contrived to navigate the social world, and the true self, the part of ourselves that works tirelessly in service of our own empowerment, contentment, and creative potential. The relentless friction builds into a prodromal disequilibrium and foreshadows the proverbial crises of self-esteem. Motifs of women washing, cooking, and completing other quotidian tasks of living frequently appear in alchemical manuscripts. On the third emblem of Michael Maier's *Atalanta Fugiens*, there's an inscription below an illustration of a woman tilting over a washing tub that reads, "Go to the woman who washes the sheets and do as she does."[123] The instruction may be drawing one's attention to the common denominator of chemical processes like *solutio* (i.e., when solid becomes liquid) and *sublimatio* (i.e., when solid becomes gas), the ostensibly disparate processes of liquefaction and evaporation—the concealed element of fire. This is why master alchemists would instruct their protégées to: "Go and look at the women who are employed over the washing and fulling of linen: see what they do, and do what they are doing." One should judiciously observe Nature's operations and acquire first-hand knowledge of her handiwork—in this case, the rotation of the elements through the mysterious receptacle of heat—before endeavoring to replicate and accelerate those processes in artificial settings.

The illustration itself is strongly evocative of work-in-progress. Its centerpiece is a winding waterway cleaving through a beautiful courtyard adorned by immaculate green lawns. It's impossible to discern its source and destination. There's vigorous activity in the foreground. On the extreme left-hand side, an assortment of black pitchers and a cauldron are being scorched by a robust fire. Adjacent is a group of three working women. They are piously preoccupied in their work and don't seem to be alarmed by a fire that could under more lamentable circumstances become uncontained and noxious. One washes linen in a shallow wooden basin; the other two purge the linen of excess water. They are all dressed in tricolored attire. The first one on the left is decked in white, black, and blue; the second one in the middle wears white, black, and red; and the third one on the right is in white, black, and gold. An incandescent black garment, perhaps made of exquisite silk, has been draped over a wooden barrel behind them. Another woman balancing a basket atop her head can be seen venturing toward them in the background; the position of her arms is reminiscent of the ritual gesture of epiphany.

There are two women in the middle ground, one wearing a blue dress and the other a cherry-colored one; the latter has ventured into the stream to wash linen, while the former pegs freshly washed linen onto the clothesline to dry. In the area beyond, an observer may bear witness to three women with red dresses and vaguely defined physiognomies covering lawns over with rectangular pieces of linen. The linen pieces have been strategically positioned horizontally or vertically along the ground as to aid ventilation. In the distance, a man standing near the bank of the waterway can be seen pouring water from a container onto a piece of linen. A different man is perusing something occluded from the observer's view in a courtyard on the opposite side. The space beyond is filled by two blue-domed cathedrals, an unpaved meandering footpath leading to the arched entrance of a fortified town, and a precipitous, jagged peak jutting into a thick layer of ominous-looking cumulonimbus clouds. Inklings of a golden hue can be seen near the horizon. Analogous to the family of interacting children, the five colors depicted by people present in this illustration are the same colors that circumscribe the pivotal qualitative changes in the Great Work: black for *nigredo*, the stage of putrefaction and corruption; blue (or blue-green) for *cauda pavonis*, the stage of multiplication; white for *albedo*, the stage of purification; yellow for *citrinitas*, a stage of illumination; and red for *rubedo*, a stage embodying the culmination of the entire process. The quaternary of fire, water, air, and earth, elements required for the synthesis of the Philosopher's Stone, are also present in the illustration.

What might this plate reveal about the nature of transformation? First and foremost, there is an explicit reference to *solutio* and *sublimatio*. Strongly connected with the water element, *solutio* may be understood as the fragmentation or degradation of an organic system or inanimate object into its basic components. In simpler and mechanistic terms, it is the reduction of an integrated whole into its discrete units. The act of submerging something into water, especially a soluble agent like salt or atenolol, could serve as a symbol for *accommodation*, a psychological phenomenon described by Piaget involving the deconstruction and reconstruction of personal narratives to incorporate new knowledge and jettison cognitive dissonance. Modifying one's existing schemas and hence the manner in which they interact with the phenomena around them is contingent on cumulative encounters with the micro- and macro-systems (either individuals or groups) of one's own sociohistorical milieu. For a developing individual, this may take the guise of coming into the orbit of a sophisticated intellectual or mystic, an esoteric society or school, a political faction, a cultural league, or a cult of religious zealots. The systems themselves are beguiling and attractive because they project an irradiating aura of omnipotence—explanatory powers, a scope of influence, and an inner locus of control— perceived by the individual as superior to their own. For one reason or another, comparative psychological worldviews appraised as internally cohesive and coherent, intellectually attractive, functionally refined, and aesthetically pleasing can precipitate the *solutio*.

Solutio is also an experience that forces a developing individual into an encounter with their own shadow, to put it in Jungian terms. Ken Wilber called it *vision-logic*, describing it as a by-product of *centaur* consciousness—a stage of development focused almost exclusively on vigorous activity and responsibility. Those who enter this phase will retain a strong sense of accountability and responsibility to others (i.e., family, occupation, circle of friends, etc.) but will not cede to social pressures in ways that encumber them from leading authentic lives. They flourish in their chosen environments and can readily tap into internal resources to surmount psychosocial stressors. Moreover, their inner locus of control remains intact, and they believe they can exert a quantifiable influence on the world. These sentiments correspond with what seems to be transpiring in the illustration. The women are all patently industrious and conscientiously collaborate in the service of a communal goal, but we can also see that the type of engagement and labor is different for each one—some wash, some rinse, some dry, and so forth. There is fundamental harmony, coordination, and natural flow within and between them, both in the intrapsychic and interpersonal space. The scope of influence is always greater when individuals aggregate and form a "group mind."

The idea of a "group mind" exerting influence isn't just psychological conjecture or pseudoscientific riffraff. Several research studies with sound methodological designs have, in fact, examined whether nonphysical energies can be harnessed under collective volition. Conducted in the 1980s, the first of these ambitious experiments examined the role of prayer on patients in need of coronary care and involved 393 patients, a considerable number for any prospective study. Of these, 192 were randomized into a treatment group and the rest into a control group, with the former receiving long-distance prescriptions of prayer from affiliates of the Catholic and Protestant churches. Scrutiny of clinical notes revealed that there were common medical denominators linking the participants, meaning that severity levels of the ailment, its known time length, symptomologies, and the prescribed medications were comparable across the participants prior to their experimental engagement. Byrd, the experimenter, juxtaposed the two groups following the allotted set of treatments and discovered that patients in the treatment group had benefited somewhat from the long-distance prayer. In all, the prevalence of detrimental epiphenomena like congestive heart failure, cardiac arrest, and pneumonia was lower in prayer patients ($p<0.03$, $p<0.02$, and $p<0.03$, respectively), which naturally meant that they were less likely to necessitate the assistance of artificial ventilators ($p<0.002$), antibiotics ($p<0.005$), or diuretics ($p<0.05$).[124]

Later, a researcher by the name of Daniel Worth used the same rigorous protocols as Byrd in designing an experiment to examine the tangible effect of therapeutic touch on biopsy wounding. The empirical validity of Worth's methodology was amplified with the deliberate use of deception so that participants remained oblivious of the true nature of the study, thus thwarting experimental confounds over which the experimenter has no control, as with the placebo effect. Again, the study yielded significant results, with the treatment group displaying a statistically verifiable increase in the rate of healing roughly eight days after being punctured ($p<0.001$). Consequently, the majority of patients in the treatment group returned to healthy functioning much faster than those in the control group and were completely healed by the 16-day mark ($p<0.001$).[125] Worth's significant findings seem to vouch for the idea that nonphysical mechanisms other than the placebo phenomenon play a role in anomalous healing.

A third experiment investigating the effect of distant healing on individuals with HIV infection was conducted in San Francisco, CA. To strengthen the quality of the experimental design and eradicate possible compromise by way of observer and subject-expectancy effects, the patients, doctors, and research associates were kept in the dark as to which groups each participant was assigned to. Initially, all prospective volunteers underwent stringent and comprehensive clinical assessments involving blood work and psychometric testing, enabling research staff to pair match according to significant variables like illness phase, nutrition, and general lifestyle. The volunteers were then randomly assigned to treatment and control groups, with the former receiving a well-rounded prescription of distance healing and clinical care. Conversely, the control group only received conventional medical care, as is the norm in the industrialized West.

The experimental trials lasted 10 weeks. When the progress of the two groups was merged into a blind medical chart, it became apparent that AIDS-related conditions, ailment severity, the frequency of required medical attention, the frequency and number of hospitalizations, and the experience of undesirable emotions were all statistically lower in the treatment group (p=0.04, p=0.03, p=0.01, p=0.04, p=0.04, and p=0.02).[126] Despite these heartening developments, the tangible markers of HIV progression—that is, the CD4 and T lymphocyte counts per cubic millimeter of human blood—remained statistically insignificant throughout the duration of the study. Perhaps the scope of psychophysical influence that a "group mind" can exert has demarcations and limitations, or maybe a more salient manipulation of the gross material necessitates a kind of cognitive control (i.e., powers of focused attention and imagination) that only Buddhist monks develop and attain mastery over. Clarification of these conditional nuances is obviously contingent on further research.

Sublimatio, on the other hand, can be seen in ventilation of the white linen on the lawns of the country estate. The predominant quality of this stage is one of rising upward, an urgent and rapid ascent. The frenetic nature of this stage is epitomized in the chemical process that circumvents liquefaction completely and involves the transformation of a solid straight into a gaseous vapor. Under more organic conditions, moisture, like dew or from bodies of freshwater, is evaporated by the sun's heat during the diurnal hours. Transposed to the psychological domain, rising upward could imply transcendence over our emotional tempests. Separation from the conditions of our own lives is impossible except in retrospect, and so it is not uncommon to become overidentified with our own projections— idealizations of colleagues and public figures, covetous feelings toward lovers, and gaping disappointment when friends and acquaintances don't subscribe or live up to our own standards and expectations. These may overwhelm, seize, and even possess us if allowed to proliferate unchecked. They grow to be much larger than us, take on a life of their own, and throw us off our homeostatic orbit in the process.

Fusing with the cumulative content of the mind as self-as-content—thoughts, feelings, sensations, and social roles—is a recipe for pain, suffering, and a self-imposed limitation on one's degrees of personal freedom. On the other hand, developing an awareness and understanding of self-as-context, a coherent observing quintessence that cleaves a fiery path through the space–time continuum without identifying too closely with snowballing scripts and histories, is a definitive hallmark of psychospiritual growth. The merged content of our life experiences must not be the sole criterion by which our identity is defined, but rather one way of discovering the limitations and farthest reaches of the human condition. To give a concrete example, somebody with a conceptual myopia, entombed within a self-as-content perspective, may profess, "I am an aerospace engineer who works for NASA." However, a more sophisticated individual who embodies the third-person observer or self-as-context perspective will resist compartmentalization and rebel against that kind of rigid labeling: "I am an aerospace engineer working for NASA, and I am also an astronaut, teacher, and philosopher, among other things." When self-identity becomes commensurate with the crucible, container, or vessel encompassing the mental content, the *albedo* has arrived.

The aforementioned ideas—a group mind's convalescing powers and extant scope of influence, the idealized state of nonattachment, and the wisdom and perspicacity associated with acquiring a third-person observer perspective of one's own life path—are all cleverly woven into this straightforward and unremarkable portrayal of domestic activity. Alchemy is, without any doubt, a discipline that deeply honors multiple levels of interpretation.

Endnotes

123 Meredith K. Ray, *Daughters of Alchemy: Women and Scientific Culture in Early Modern Italy* (Cambridge, MA: Harvard University Press, 2015), p. 7.

124 Pamela Rae Health, *Mind-Matter Interaction: A Review of Historical Reports, Theory and Research* (Jefferson, North Carolina: McFarland & Company, 2011), p. 106.

125 Ibid, p. 106.

126 Ibid, p. 107

Chapter 8

The Spiritual Sun: Disidentification from Convention

Figure 8-1. The splendid sun scene from the *Splendor Solis* plates by Solomon Trismosin. The illustration depicts the sun rising over the city.

The final plate of the *Splendor Solis* series is also the most allegorically profound and cryptic. It mimics the inaugural one with the dark sun in that the observational trajectory has been transposed to the macro-scale and the third-person observer is once again some distance outside the walls of an anonymous city. The interpersonal narratives unfolding within—the rambunctious children at play, the conscientious women at work—are once again shrouded from view. Everything personal and intimate has once again been occluded from view and replaced by a supernal panorama of the fortified town and the surrounding countryside. The town's remote distancing from the third-person observer is deeply redolent of qualities like objectivity and nonattachment.

The town itself is blanketed by a nebulous veil of gray mist. For reasons unknown, the unfettered solar rays are unable to completely irradiate the surface of the earth. In the foreground, a cluster of ghastly tree stumps protrude from a carpet of grass-green vegetation, reminding us of the perpetual natural cycle of birth, death, and regeneration. There are nomothetic laws existing outside the scope of human control and influence that facilitate our psychophysical development and at the same time impose limitations on our potential. The centerpiece of this illustration, the splendid sun, has just emerged from the eastern horizon and will soon trace its routine diurnal arc across the cerulean sky. Or is it setting and in the inaugural stages of descent into the western horizon? While it is true that parsing out dawn and dusk in artistic renditions can be problematic, the relative position of this plate as the culminating aspect of the alchemical opus gives it away. An aurora always succeeds a dark night of the soul; it is never a predecessor. The light spindles emanating from the anthropomorphic sun epitomize a propitious but unexpected illumination, a revelation, an epiphany; its human features may be an implicit allusion to intelligent design and perhaps blueprints of creation being quintessentially nonrandom in nature.

The axiom "the devil is in the detail" certainly rings true for this illustration. Observation and investigation of intricate details, subtleties, nuances, and anomalies may reveal things about human nature that have been hitherto outrageously oversighted. The transpersonal theorist Ken Wilber would equate this more sophisticated way of encountering reality to his *subtle* consciousness stage of development. Acquisition of this psychological perspicacity requires a turning inward as to parse out the self from the non-self, or to separate the dross (i.e., dogmatic schemas and conventional beliefs imposed onto the individual by the sociocultural milieu) from the subtle (i.e., truths deeply rooted in and informed by experience). It necessitates courage, chivalry, and a high tolerance for ambiguity. To discover and chart new territories, one must meekly relinquish the known world and assumptive worldview, the past prejudices, and sometimes memory itself. To enter the kingdom of heaven, one must become like an inquisitive child who is constantly awe-inspired and tickled by the phenomena around them, a child who is perpetually asking intrepid questions and intrepidly questioning everything. Children are all individuals though they share specific *subtle* qualities when interacting and co-constructing narratives: feelings of mutuality, heightened awareness, and peak playfulness; the willful suspension of intellect and disbelief; trust in the unfolding process; and a nonjudgmental openness to experience. They are expressions of unconditional love. A child is an exemplar par excellence of a scientist, or at least what the disposition of a scientist might look like if it were not contaminated by agendas, biases, and axes to grind.

The *subtle* reminds us that the whole is greater than the sum of its parts and our self-imposed limitations. For instance, once an individual is operating on the *subtle* level, they may awaken to the truth that every epoch has constructivist paradigms for medicine and disease, and that prognostic impressions, orthodox treatment strategies, and protocols are informed by internalized and largely unconscious assumptions about the way the "external" world *is*. Thanks to seventeenth-century Cartesian philosophical discourse, the laurels of orthodox medical science—what little there has been—rest on the unchallenged postulate that biological systems are divisible, reducible, and transposable.

The repercussions of such rigid convergent thinking are there for all to see. We poison pathogens with pharmacological agents; we kill neoplasms with gamma rays and radiation; we carve out necrotic tissue with surgical blades; we replace worn or damaged ligaments and bones with artificial ones; and we hope that by driving shifts in brain chemistry, patients will spontaneously "feel better" about their lives. In many ways, our medical science of best practices, with its emphasis on validated efficacy through the rigorous criteria of randomized controlled trial design, is a dramatic improvement on the blind-sighted trial-and-error philosophies used by medical practitioners in bygone ages and in other ways not.

For reasons to do with sociocultural conditioning and the prevailing hegemony of the Western biomedical model, dynamic inner mental processes or the mind, if we prefer, is all too often left out of the clinical picture and not factored in when clinicians formulate their prognostic impressions. How long will it be before Naomi, a nonfunctional traumatic brain injury (TBI) patient with penetrating brain trauma, can reintegrate into society, clinicians ask? How long will it be before Samuel, another patient with a malignant tumor metastasizing in his body, takes a downward plunge and capitulates? What about Tanya and Jeremy, patients just diagnosed with Alzheimer's and vascular dementia? How long before they forget their names? What doesn't get factored in and should—the proverbial elephant in the room—is the personality styles and temperaments themselves.

Much to the embarrassment of orthodox health practitioners, healing has and does occur in the absence of evidence-based treatments. In medical parlance, the terminology most frequently used to describe it is "spontaneous remission." All too often, elucidations offered for the latter are ambiguous and it is left to the patient's own understanding to make sense of the phenomenon in question. We don't really hear about these cases because they are retrospectively attributed to some clinical misapprehension and/or because they never make it into peer-reviewed scientific journals. Perhaps the closest anomalous healing investigation ever got to the purview of orthodox medicine was when Benjamin Franklin and the French Royal Commission initiated an official inquiry into the efficacy of Mesmer's animal magnetism and quite ironically attributed its potent effects to the human imagination.

On closer inspection, it seems so bizarre that Franklin and his associates should forget that the human imagination, a world of eternal feasibilities, can move mountains and seas, a sentiment that had been allegorically echoed by the great Stagirite Aristotle more than two millennia ago when he decreed, "A vivid imagination compels the whole body to obey it."[127] A concrete example of that adage is the placebo effect. Healing studies employing double- and triple-blind protocols consistently demonstrate that participants duped into believing that they're receiving genuine medical intervention show marked improvements in health, sometimes as much as, if not more than, the group receiving the actual treatment.[128] Moreover, it appears improvements may occur in either the psychological or organic domains of functioning, adding weight to the postulate that mind and body are interdependent and not mutually exclusive. In their most orthodox form as water-based sugar pills, placebos trump psychotropic drugs when it comes to coupling beneficial psychosomatic interactions with the enduring Hippocratic ethical code of "do no harm"; they're efficient, energy-based, environmentally friendly, free of insidious side effects, and most importantly, they're absolutely free. Now here's a treatment worth its weight in gold!

Some anomalous healings have drawn attention because they appear to violate the conventional physical and biological laws. For myself, an exceptional case of a teenage boy suffering from fish-skin disease, a condition whereby black warts and horny skin are omnipresent on the body, comes to mind.[129] After successive skin grafts had failed to yield improvements to the horny skin texture, the treating physician referred him to an anesthetist, a certain Dr. Albert A. Mason, in the hope that hypnotherapy might help where surgery had failed. Mason had successfully cured warts and other skin conditions before, so there was no reason to believe that this specific case should be any different. After placing the young chap in a hypnotic trance, Mason suggested that the leathery skin on his left arm would drop off in a few days, which it did. Mason's triumph was met with an incredulous stare by the surgeon, who had recently discovered that the boy was suffering from a rare genetic disorder called *ichthyosiform erythrodermia*. If the diagnosis was correct, and sources suggest it was, then any treatment method was hopeless.

How could the horny coat resembling an arachnid's exoskeleton soften and fall off to reveal a layer of soft, pink-colored skin beneath when the oil-forming glands responsible for it were absent? It was supposed to be impossible, and yet Mason succeeded in dissipating the vast majority of the grotesque body warts and improving the boy's physical appearance. Being able to venture out in public worked wonders for the boy's confidence and self-image, and he even scored a job as an electrician's assistant! The hypnotic cure was nothing short of a miracle.

Published in the *British Medical Journal* (BMJ) in 1952, Mason's results spurred a medical furor. Individuals suffering from fish-skin disease, something long decreed by traditional medicine to be both rare and lethal, suddenly found themselves grasping at the straws of a visible lifeline again. They began turning up at his doorstep, demanding that he administer treatment. At this stage, Mason was shrewd enough to realize that ceding to their requests was a formidable way of maintaining professional integrity and virtue, and he swiftly set about trying to program suggestions into his patients' minds through hypnotic induction. In retrospect, this case is characterized by the fundamental alignment of intentions unfettered by internalized schemas of what is and isn't feasible, a phenomenon most scarce in our post-post-postmodern world where scientific data is easily downloadable and accessible through electronic mediums.

Another anomalous healing case that remains deeply etched in the author's memory involves a young girl suffering from a tumorous growth on her back. According to Arnold Mindell, multiple surgical interventions aimed at clearing out the cancerous tissue were unsuccessful, and it seemed almost certain the girl would die. With the case relegated to the hopeless or "too challenging" basket, the treating physician saw no harm in having a clinical psychologist step in and try his hand at eliciting some kind of sanguine response in what was evidently an overly despondent and depressed child. After the therapist succeeded in gaining her trust, the child opened up with a dramatic narration of an ominous dream in which her small hands relinquished their hold on the security fence guarding her lithe body from a deathly plunge into a deep lake.

Then came the expression of an unconscious wish; she prostrated herself on the floor, spreading her arms out to creatively simulate the act of flying. Mindell expedited her inner process by engaging in the fantasy play with appropriate dramatizations able to reduce even the most cold-hearted and detached of sentient observers to tears. Together, they soared into the azure blue of the heavens, weaved their way through a bulbous army of cotton-textured clouds, and took turns ascending into the highest striations of the atmosphere, close to outer space. Before long, she enunciated the earnest desire to explore the greater cosmos: "I'm going away to another world, a beautiful world where there are strange planets."[130]

Somewhat perturbed by the implications of this symbolic admission, Mindell assured her that the decision was solely hers to make: she may *choose* to fly away and explore the mystical dominions of space, or she may *choose* to descend and rejoin the other earthlings in the only world she knows. Initially, she chose the first, but subsequent cogitation of the bond she'd just forged with a paternal figure cast a serious element of doubt in her mind. Now, there was a social synapse on the horizon able to tap into the levitational wonders of altruistic and unconditional love, connectivity, and security where previously there had been none; now, there was a reason to survive. Mindell believes it was this meaningful event that precipitated her convalescence.

These anecdotal cases illustrate the notion that there are nonphysical energies at work in healing; it's something more than a blind and mechanistic biological process. Also, the average layperson is mostly ignorant of an existing body of experimental research supporting the idea that mental imagery, imagination, positive thinking, call it what you will, can alter the trajectory of a disease. Some of these studies were described in the prior chapter. What is there to make of all these "rogue" anecdotes and controlled experiments? How do these fit into the reductionistic biomedical agenda? Clearly, they don't, which is why they've been overlooked, often denounced as fraudulent, and excluded from scientific debates revolving around evidence-based medicine. Do they relinquish clues and puzzle pieces pertaining to the ineffable psychophysical principles underlying Nature of which healing is a dynamic part? Probably. The phenomenal experience of meaning-making, of having something to live for, is clearly a crucial factor in healing. On the other hand, sociohistorical appraisals made by the collective prerogative of what adversity can and cannot overcome trickle down to the ailing individual, and have either devastating or auspicious consequences. Whether it be person, microculture, or global community, the whole has, is, and will always be greater than the sum of its parts.

Shifting into the *subtle* stage of psychospiritual development can mean full-blown contact with the "deepest" stratum of the human mind, an obscure Stygian region that is not amenable to empirical investigation at the present time; it is the locus of supranormal activity and contact, hinting at a relationship between the inner and outer worlds that is concealed from our cognitive workspace, along with the leaps of human understanding and foresight predicating those discoveries and inventions that expert judges might appraise as ingenious and historically novel. The latter requires an absolute immersion, receptivity, and unconditional surrender to the fundamental harmony of the universe, and is determined in part by the level of intensity and in part by the individual's qualities and personality structure.

For reasons that currently elude us, altered states of consciousness such as hallucinatory episodes appear to be especially conducive to spiritual encounters, or meetings with denizens of the paraphysical worlds. Typically, the spirit will impart knowledge of its own individuality and separateness from the percipient by providing temporary access and knowledge of veridical phenomena (i.e., persons, places, and events) that are ordinarily unavailable to that percipient through the conventional sensorium. The spontaneous nature of the spirit contact and of the information shared can be immensely frightening, disorienting, and internally fragmenting, especially when it is incommensurate with and counterintuitive to the percipient's internalized schemas and world paradigm.

One of the most intriguing anomalous cases involving a "psychotic decompensation" pervaded by spirit contact was published in the BMJ by a consultant psychiatrist in England, Dr. Ikechukwu Obialo Azuonye.[131] It involves an ordinary woman in good health who began hearing distinct voices informing her to seek medical counsel for a proliferating brain tumor. Typical neurological symptoms associated with a cortical neoplasm (i.e., migraine headaches, seizures) were absent; nevertheless, the psychiatrist ordered a brain scan to reassure his client. A meningioma was subsequently identified and surgically removed. The neurosurgeon who operated on her reported: "A large left frontal bone flap extending across the midline was turned following a bifrontal skin flap incision. Meningioma about 2.5 [inches] by 1.5 [inches] in size arose from the falx and extended through to the right side. A small area of tumour appeared on the medial surface of the brain. The tumour was dissected out and removed completely along with its origins in the falx."[132]

The patient reported that once she recovered consciousness, the voices, who had previously identified themselves as employees of the Children's Hospital on Great Ormond Street, expressed earnest gratitude for being able to help her and mysteriously disappeared. The scoffers and doubting Thomases of *psi* phenomena have tried to discredit cases like these as either outlandish fabrications, or where scant evidence corroborating the case exists, as instances of cryptomnesia. A more likely explanation is that it was a transient psychic opening.

Hallucinatory phenomena have been under empirical investigation for roughly 150 years now. Unfortunately, we subsist in an epoch that idealizes and overvalues the biomedical model of mental illness. The emphasis on treating emergent hallucinations and delusionary beliefs in patients with antipsychotic medications that block D-2 receptors in the limbic system usually leaves no room for curious ventures into their phenomenology. Doctors aren't really interested in the content per se. They simply want to eradicate these nuisance phenomena from their patients' perceptual interface with the world. In doing so, the doctors deprive themselves of useful information pertaining to their patients' unconscious wishes, desires, and motivations. On a macro-scale, we, the aggregates, are deprived of an enhanced and more sophisticated understanding of the hallucinatory process and deeper philosophical musings on what constitutes self versus non-self, among other things.

Working with the mentally ill at Mendocino State Hospital in California for some 17 years, the clinical psychologist Wilson Van Dusen conducted a comprehensive investigation into the nature of his patients' hallucinations. He found that many were intimately bound up with extrasensory perception. Van Dusen describes one individual whose nexus of idiosyncratic perceptual experiences involved witnessing a giant crystal punch bowl descend from the ceiling, which he later saw at a dance.[133] Similarly, a woman who was due to embark on a pilgrimage to southern California to stand trial for murdering her husband was informed by a spirit who self-identified as the Virgin Mary that two earthquakes would occur, one when she left and one when she arrived at her destination. Both came to pass.[134]

Another more captivating case involves an elementary-educated gas pipefitter with schizophrenia. According to Van Dusen, this patient was languishing and a spirited Lilliputian lady who went by the epithet "An Emanation of the Feminine Aspect of the Divine" came to offer temporary relief.[135] Using the gas pipefitter as an intercessor, Van Dusen was granted transient access to a world of universal symbols and archetypes, some of which pertained to ancient myths. This Lilliputian woman was a paragon of wisdom, knowledge, and virtue; she was able to compellingly describe the spiritual and psychological truths encoded in mythopoetic narrative, and was more perspicacious than Van Dusen himself in understanding their implications.

Moreover, she espoused extrasensory powers. Working as a plumber's assistant, the patient was dumbfounded as to why water from a specific drinking fountain was at times cold and at other times hot. The woman later disclosed that a bypass valve, differential pressure, and a shower on the opposite side of the wall was behind the unusual variances in water temperature coming from that fountain. In the final analysis, Van Dusen admits there was no way that an individual of the gas pipefitter's intellectual aptitude could ever orchestrate such a "hallucination," not unless some external agency was involved.

These cases elude any logical explanation that might be offered by a philosopher or scientist operating under the assumptions of the Cartesian-Kantian epistemological box. They should not exist, according to the dominant philosophical attitudes and scientific intelligibilities of our time, yet here they are. Some children, eccentrics, and mystics, a very small proportion of the psychiatric demographic (i.e., those with genetic vulnerability to psychosis), and select individuals who resist conditioning and sometimes carry a genetic loading for enhanced creative cognition can readily tap into these extraordinary phenomena. This is the nebulous and unplumbed realm of the *subtle*, and it can be cultivated through diligent inner work and harmonious alignment with judgment-independent truths (i.e., truths that exist in an objective sense and are not necessary inventions or fabrications for fluid and efficient functioning of human perception, consciousness, and social relationships), like mutuality and attraction. Those audacious enough to explore and to found a proto-cartography for nonphysical wavelengths of the human mind will trigger a set of unprecedented discoveries, which in a cumulative sense will shed light upon the farthest limits of human potential and then some.

Endnotes

127 Anees A. Sheikh (ed.), *Imagination and Healing* (Oxfordshire, UK: Routledge, 1984), p. 5.

128 Pamela Rae Health, *Mind-Matter Interaction: A Review of Historical Reports, Theory and Research* (Jefferson, North Carolina: McFarland & Company, 2011), pp. 108–109.

129 Albert A. Mason, 'A Case of Congenital Ichthyosiform Erythrodermia of Brocq Treated by Hypnosis,' *British Medical Journal*, 30 (1952): 442–443.

130 Arnold Mindell, *Working with the Dreaming Body* (Portland, OR: LaoTsePress, 2002), p. 9.

131 Ikechukwu Obialo Azuonye, 'A Difficult Case: Diagnosis Made by Hallucinatory Voices,' *British Medical Journal*, 315 (1997): 1685–1686.

132 Ibid, p. 1685.

133 Wilson Van Dusen, *The Natural Depth in Man* (New York, NY: Swedenborg Foundation, 1981), p. 155.

134 Ibid, p. 153.

135 Ibid, p. 151.

Chapter 9

Remembering the Self: An Integrated Theory

Figure 9-1. My personal insignia depicting an integrated theory of personal development.

What we term the "self" cannot be completely divested from personality and personal growth, and the two are not mutually exclusive terms. What we recognize as an integrated and unremitting sense of self is in fact the product of an ephemeral interaction between that something which invigorates us, the vital life force, and an ambient background of fields called the external world or environment. The unique psychological worldview, the internal guidance and appraisal system, and the perceptual interface of every living human is decisively manifested, fashioned, modified, and obliterated by contingencies (i.e., time and place) not amenable to direct control and impermeable to conscious will. Coming to the sobering conclusion that we are all helpless beings unable to select the parents we are born to, the social and cultural programs we will be conditioned by, and liable to suffer the exact same existential crises, it then becomes easier to see others as extensions of "self" rather than entirely discrete entities; we are all but the same vital life force subjected to a set of different experiences.

What makes our identities different is the personal history associated with our specific configuration of animated matter. Our personal histories are shaped in part by the familial environment, the institutions to which we belong, and the societal standards, values, and ethical sensibilities of the time. On the other hand, there is also an impersonal aspect to our identities—the nonphysical, enlivening, inspirited energy that animates our physical bodies and imbues it with the characteristics of movement and heat; the conscious awareness that can intermingle with the space–time continuum, learn, and encode memories into the mysterious web-like forms of neural architecture; and the higher "solar" intelligence within us able to make choices or veto a conglomeration of unconscious processes from reaching fruition. This phenomenon, too, may be defined as my or your "self."

As one might surmise from the aforementioned, the author espouses a very integrative approach to human and personal development and the manifestation of personality. There is, more often than not, veridicality and legitimacy to the epistemological assumptions of developmental theories in psychology, irrespective of whether or not they are corroborated by collateral clinical and experimental evidence. These only become limiting or problematic when they circumscribe development in a strictly linear fashion and within regimented temporal parameters, or when a cadre of proselytes or faithful followers (i.e., Freudians, Jungians, Adlerians) equate theoretical assumptions with gospel and disregard phenomena incompatible with their worldview.

First and foremost, genetic loading and polygenetic linkages are not something imagined by the collective scientific prerogative. Inheriting specific mutations will make you more susceptible to experiencing certain states of consciousness, emotional hyperarousal, psychotic processes, and dementing diseases, providing the pertinent environmental risk factors are present.[136] If you carry a specific promoter polymorphism of the neuroregulin 1 gene (NRG-1) on chromosome 8, it is very possible that you will develop an affinity for creative pursuits and express honorary eminence in creative achievement, but lamentably you will also be vulnerable to psychosis and schizospectrum disorders, lower working memory capacity, decreased activation of frontotemporal neural networks during cognitive processing, and hypersensitivity to harsh criticism.[137] Inheritance of this gene is something of a double-edged sword; you would be blessed and cursed at the same time.

Interestingly, the more reductive or total-equals-the-sum-of-its-parts perspective is embodied by evolutionary psychology. In *The Righteous Mind* (2012), the social psychologist Jonathan Haidt argues that members of the human species are confined to the evolutionary prison of selfish and "groupish" behavior. Long before the advent of a shared intentionality able to forge cultural innovations, trait selection in *Homo sapiens* was profoundly skewed in favor of self-interest. Only the most reflexive, responsive, and dexterous in outmaneuvering other primates and organisms competing for the same natural resources would survive long enough to reproduce and pass their traits onto subsequent generations. Such an unrefined and unscrupulous mode of being, one would think. There can be no doubt that "hivish" nature is etched into our genetic and mimetic memory, and that it serves the most noble purpose: to unite us into a phenomenal superorganism. There can be no doubt that the jealousy which balloons and swells from somewhere deep within each time we see our friend's Lotus has, from an evolutionary standpoint, a motivational purpose so that we may acquire the same or better and render ourselves into desirable and eligible mates for procreation.

Pitched at the macro level of analysis, the social school hypothesizes that behavioral outcomes are habitually motivated by a continuum of evolutionary pressures acting upon and eternally shaping the individual.[138] These include cognitive-based needs (i.e., understanding, belonging, and orientation within a seemingly chaotic world) related to the acquisition of purpose and stability, as well as more emotionally driven ones like self-esteem and trust. One doesn't want to displease or spur disaffection in an authority figure whose decisions may determine the fate of the collective, as Milgram found out.

Then there's cross-cultural psychology with its emphasis on the dynamic role of cultural processes in human development. According to this lens, there is a bidirectional flow of information between the individual, the immediate environment, and the sociocultural framework encompassing certain roles and practices—three interdependent variables contained within a mutually consisting process, which is in and of itself in a state of ongoing transmutation. An overarching tenet of this subdiscipline of psychological inquiry is that the developing individual cannot be separated from the sociocultural milieu, which she influences and is influenced by throughout her life. If my mother enjoyed contemplating and adhering to the morals intricately woven into the fabric of Greek mythology, she will expose me to the same narratives and allow my own moral conscience to be shaped accordingly.

Let's consider some Eurocentric lenses. Maslow's hierarchy of needs deems satisfaction of physiological and instinctual drives to take precedence over ego transcendence and self-actualization.[139] My grandmother, who was from rustic Greece, would always tout: "Esoteric philosophies are for the financially privileged. When you're poor with no stable source of income, the only thing you think about is how you're going to feed your children." According to Piaget, children in a developmental phase he called the "concrete operational" stage (7–10 years) can "think" before engaging in social interaction.[140] At the age of eight, I had the gumption to switch the deteriorating batteries of my train set with newer ones belonging to my dear cousin when nobody was looking; at nine, I was unwrapping Christmas presents bought for the entire family by relatives, picking out the most interesting and appealing ones, and then claiming them as my own; and at 10, I was threatening to shift the gearstick of my dad's thrifty Kingswood from parking to reverse if my cousins capitulated to a frivolous ruse.

Prevalent in my early and mid-twenties were intermittent acts of sexual deviance and disinhibition, reflecting a superficial mind aground on the reefs of hedonism. Everything I did back then—joining fee-based websites for online dating, organizing spontaneous rendezvous with acquaintances, and forging new interpersonal connections—was motivated by the promise of sexual gratification. It just so happens that during these periods my dreams were punctuated with surreal, albeit traumatic, experiences of losing my prehensile phallus. Sometimes it would drop to the ground while I was meandering about naked, at others it would snap off while I was urinating, and at others still it would crumble in my hands. The dreams would culminate with frantic attempts to reattach it, and I would frequently awake awash in perspiration and frozen in terror. Looking back, this literal case of castration anxiety is explicable as an unconscious reaction to sexual desires deemed taboo by my social conditioning and higher conscience (Freud's punitive superego). Erupting from the unconscious was the warning that many sexual transgressions come at a cost, and so it may be better to repress these rather than placidly submit and humiliate oneself in the process. Freud decrees castration anxiety to be a salient hallmark of the Phallic Stage (3–6 years) in his model of psychosexual development,[141] but in truth it could probably crop up at any time.

One other phenomenon that is often sidestepped and deserves a brief mention is the role of narrative in the role of personality development and personal growth. Narrative is a ubiquitous phenomenon, transcending epoch, place, sex, religious and spiritual orientation, and sociocultural milieu. Long before the emergence of Indo-European semantic languages, our ancestors congregated about fireplaces to listen to, to feel, and to perform engaging narratives about mass migration, the far-reaching consequences of the world flood, and the seemingly insurmountable quest of a heroic ancestor to undermine the forces of evil. Their preeminence in our phylogenetic history is explicable within both cultural and neural contexts: they contribute to the co-construction and transmission of culture from generation to generation while concurrently fashioning and maintaining sophisticated integration of the left-right hemisphere and cortical-subcortical neural circuitry.[142] Narratives ground our experience in ways that allow for goal-directed action and progression to self-definition; they link our individual selves into a group mind, like beaded pearls of a beautiful necklace; and they support the complexity and self-organization of brain function.[143] A multilevel function of narrative, then, is to facilitate neural connectivity in the brain, emotional stability, psychological flexibility, and psychosomatic health.

Dan Siegel has much to say about the notion of narrative emerging, in part as a mechanism of neural integration and coordination between the left and right hemispheres of the brain.[144] The integrative neural processes occurring during formative periods of development can be vertical, dorso-ventral, or interhemispheric.[145] The importance of the latter, according to Trevarthen, cannot be overstated because the anterior commissures and corpus callosum combined is "the only pathway through which the higher functions of perception and cognition, learning and voluntary motor coordination can be unified."[146] Associational neurons in the frontal, temporal, and parietal lobes are the modus operandi, linking intricate representational processes of the hemispheres together.[147]

From this bottom-up perspective, the persistence of disparaging and punitive messages about "self" precipitates failed neural integration, which in turn releases the valves for the temporal manifestation of psychiatric disorders.[148] Moreover, it just may be that the functional specialization of the two hemispheres and their different modes of processing information—with one excelling in monosemantic, linear, and intellectual processes; and the other in processes of holistic, musical, artistic propensities, spatial perception, and sensory discrimination—is somehow transposed into irreconcilable and perpetual conflicts between so-called opposites like cognition and emotion, self and other, or masculine and feminine in the spotlight of conscious awareness. We probably spend inordinate periods contemplating these philosophical impasses because we're programmed to do so. The healthier and more adjusted among us may find constructive ways of coping with and compensating for the tragic limitations and flaws of our neurocognitive hardwiring, but the vast majority just end up running over the same ground and digging themselves into deeper trenches. It's the Gordian knot that no real-life hero can unknot, a riddle of the Theban Sphinx that no Oedipus can solve.

In any case, any personality theory needs to take into account genetically programmed differences between the sexes, aspects of behavior that are hardwired into our nervous systems and not learned from social cues. Male development is controlled in part by testosterone while female development is mediated in part by estrogen and progesterone. These hormones function differently in boys and girls.[149] There's a disparity between the sexes in the context of sexual development, with girls entering puberty as early as nine or ten and boys not moving into this stage until several years afterward. Sequence and tempo of brain maturation differs in males and females also; temporal gray matter, areas which underpin visuospatial perception and the identification of visual objects in space, appears to develop slightly faster in boys, while parietal gray matter, areas involved in sensory integration, proprioception, and stereognosis, develops faster in girls.[150] In general, the proliferation of gray matter occurs quicker and earlier in girls, intimating that they are developmentally ready for the acquisition of certain skills and behaviors before boys are. Information processing is also different, with connectivity in male brains especially wired for visuo-constructional and visuomotor tasks, while female brains tend to be adroit in balancing analytical and intuitive modes of cognition.[151] There are obvious sociocultural implications here.

Then there's our private inner stage with subjective thought content that others aren't privy to. We live with one foot in consensus reality and one in an internal private theater of shadows, dreams, and artificial worlds. Though ignored, beleaguered, and disparaged by the modern science of eliminative materialism, the internal world and its compass do have a significant hand in shaping our development and life trajectory. Thinkers of the intellectual caliber of Emanuel

Swedenborg, Carl Gustav Jung, and Wilson Van Dusen were all influential in mapping an inner mental world, which was once an exclusive dominion of the mystic and the seer. Swedenborg, for instance, intimated that orders of existence, from the spiritual and mental to the molecular and subatomic, represent a stepping down or lapsing of the One into symbolic and literal representations to form increasingly limited orders of existence.[152]

Jung spoke about a repository of collective primordial images, the psychological archetypes, which exist, express themselves through human interactions, and fuel the enactment of certain tropes and narrative blueprints across time. These allegorical and symbolic images, the language of the collective unconscious, were particularly abundant in altered states and inspired Jung to make further ontological elaborations, claiming that the collective unconscious is "not a person, but something like an unceasing stream or perhaps ocean of images and figures which drift into consciousness in our dreams or in abnormal states of mind."[153] One such image that continually crops up in alchemical manuscripts and is mentioned by Jung as a potent catalyst of transformation is the *sol niger*, the black sun.[154] Several years ago, I had a very vivid dream featuring just that image; the sun looked more like a black hole with spokes spinning across the sky rather than the supernal golden disc we're all familiar with. A few days after having this dream, I came up with an original and radical idea for a work of fiction.

Wilson Van Dusen's clinical findings seem to further strengthen the case for psychological archetypes and the collective unconscious. Working with the mentally ill at Mendocino State Hospital in California for some 17 years, he conducted a comprehensive phenomenological investigation into the nature of his patients' hallucinations.[155] In his clinical appraisal, Van Dusen stated that about 20% of psychotic experiences contained higher-order content, while about 80% contained lower-order content. The first he defined as sensory experiences that were highly feeling-related, nonverbal, and symbolic; more often than not, he found that experiences of this type possessed intellectual, instructive, and creative merit, far surpassing the understanding and IQ level of the patient through which they'd manifested. These hallucinations expressed the utmost respect for personal conscience and conation and usually broadened the patient's values. On the other hand, the lower-order experiences were critical and malicious voices with mutable qualities, and a crude and unsophisticated vocabulary, and expressed themselves as running critiques that undermined, ridiculed, threatened, and beleaguered the patient.

In *The Natural Depth in Man* (1981), Van Dusen describes a higher-order hallucination experienced by an elementary-educated gas pipefitter, which appeared in the form of a spritely female Lilliputian. Communicating through the gas pipefitter, who had no understanding of mythical, religious, and historical contexts, Van Dusen stresses that his multiple dealings with the beautiful lady who went by the epithet of "An Emanation of the Feminine Aspect of the Divine" went far in convincing him that she was, without any reasonable doubt, a master of hermeneutics; she frequently produced cosmic images, letters, and universal symbols from within herself, and described the implications of archetypal myths that were unknown to both the gas pipefitter and the clinical psychologist. Van Dusen claims that she possessed extrasensory powers and demonstrated them when she revealed, quite casually, that a bypass valve and differential pressure were behind unusual variances in the temperature of water coming from the drinking fountain. According to Van Dusen, there was simply no way that an individual of the gas pipefitter's level of intelligence and cognitive capacity could ever engender or conjure such a "hallucination," not unless some external agency was involved.

One's natural inclination is to be suspicious and skeptical of such radical assertions, unless, of course, he or she experiences something uncannily similar. Several years ago, I encountered a woman from Greece with a very clear psychic opening. A male entity named Lucas would appear in what can only be described as dreams of preternatural clarity and disclose veracious information unbeknown to her about people she knew. Her way of dealing with the powerful psychic opening, or at least her way of seeking validation for her supranormal experiences, was to openly disclose private details bequeathed by Lucas to the pertinent individuals and then scry their verbal output and nonverbal behaviors for confirming or disconfirming evidence. At one stage, Lucas started to tell her things about my own trials and tribulations. They were far too specific and detailed to be coincidental or arbitrary. In one of her visionary dreams, he and another "spirit guide" performed a puppet play about two "soulmates" —a good "soulmate" and a "not so good soulmate." She described the narrative to me exactly as it had unfolded in dreamtime. It left me somewhat awestruck, discombobulated, and in serious doubt of my own sanity. In the space of a few minutes, the two entities managed to accurately capture and convey the emotional trajectory of a five-year romantic relationship I'd had that ended in heartbreak, and it was done in the most imaginative way. It smelled of creative intelligence.

As an aspiring alchemist, I am of the sturdy opinion that there's something, some kind of primordial creative power, that stands separate from us and yet suffuses our very being and influences us in ways that elude our intellectual understanding. This power evades the circumscription of our logical operative cognition and its inchoate scientific tools. That's the dimension of existence acknowledged and circumnavigated by transpersonal psychology, a discipline that is informed by the Eastern and Western esoteric traditions and formed as a subversive counterreaction to behaviorism and psychoanalysis in the 1950s. Going beyond traditional ego psychology and honoring transpersonal elements of development, it may be described as nascent, promising, and coming-to-be.

In hindsight, it appears we are all marionettes recapitulating the same circular motions within linear, co-created narratives across expanses of time. Only on rare occasions do we peer upward and become aware of the prehensile forces to which we are attached with strings, the pressurized gravity of the past, and rarer still do we mobilize internal resources and twitch so that a specific self-action can thwart an imminent interaction from commencing or being carried to completion. Contingent on timing, this minor amendment to the theatrical act may have far-reaching consequences for the scene, the crescendos and diminuendos within particular scenes and acts, and sometimes the entire play and the nature of its closure. Even though we can't quite fully comprehend who or what might be pulling the strings, the partial simulation of the world theater we experience is lucid and detailed enough to incriminate the existence of something sublime and majestic manifesting and expressing itself in innumerable ways. In the final analysis, perhaps the ultimate developmental milestone in one's life is to awaken to the memory of who we really are, and to start clearing with one's bare hands the paved yellow brick road coursing back to the Emerald City, or better to say the Immortal City.

Endnotes

136 Robert Plomin, John C. DeFries, Valerie S. Knopik, and Jenae M. Neiderhiser, 'Top 10 Replicated Findings from Behavioral Genetics,' *Perspectives on Psychological Science* 11, no. 1 (2016): 3–23.

137 Szabolcs Kéri, 'Genes for Psychosis and Creativity: A Promoter Polymorphism of the Neuregulin 1 Gene is Related to Creativity in People with High Intellectual Achievement,' *Psychological Science* 20, no. 9 (2009): 1070–1073.

138 Richard J. Crisp, *Social Psychology: A Very Short Introduction* (Oxford, UK: Oxford University Press, 2015).

139 Abraham Maslow, *A Theory of Human Motivation* (Reprint of 1943 Edition) (Eastford, CT: Martino Fine Books, 2013).

140 Gerald Young, *Development and Causality: Neo-Piagetian Perspectives* (New York, NY: Springer Science & Business Media, 2011).

141 Patricia H. Miller, *Theories of Developmental Psychology* (New York, NY: Worth Publishers, 2016).

142 Ernest Lawrence Rossi, *The Psychobiology of Mind-Body Healing: New Concept of Therapeutic Hypnosis* (New York, NY: WW Norton & Company, 1993).

143 Lewis Mehl-Madrona, *Healing the Mind Through the Power of Story: The Promise of Narrative Psychiatry* (Rochester, VT: Inner Traditions/Bear & Co, 2010).

144 Louis Cozolino, *The Neuroscience of Psychotherapy: Healing the Social Brain (Norton Series on Interpersonal Neurobiology)* (New York, NY: WW Norton & Company, 2010).

145 Daniel J. Siegel, *The Developing Mind: How Relationships and the Brain Interact to Shape Who We Are* (New York, NY: Guilford Press, 2012).

146 Ibid, p. 341.

147 Cozolino.

148 Gerald M. Edelman and Giulio Tononi, *A Universe of Consciousness: How Matter Becomes Imagination* (New York, USA: Basic Books, 2000).

149 Leonard Sax, *Boys Adrift: The Five Factors Driving the Growing Epidemic of Unmotivated Boys and Underachieving Young Men* (New York, NY: Basic Books, 2016).

150 Ibid.

151 Ibid.

152 Emanuel Swedenborg, *Arcana Coelestia: The Heavenly Arcana Contained in the Holy Scriptures or Word of the Lord Unfolded Beginning with the Book of Genesis Together with Wonderful Things Seen in the World of Spirits and in the Heaven of Angels.* Translated from the Latin (Vol. 9) (American Swedenborg Printing and Publishing Society, 1870).

153 David Tacey, *The Jung Reader* (New York, NY: Routledge, 2012), p. 55.

154 Stanton Marlon, *The Black Sun: The Alchemy and Art of Darkness* (Texas, USA: Texas A&M University Press, 2008).

155 Wilson Van Dusen, 'Hallucinations as a World of Spirits,' *Psychedelic Review* 11 (1970): 60–69.

Chapter 10

Allegory and the Authorship of the World

Figure 10-1. *The Birth of Venus* by Watson, George Spencer (1869–1934) © Russell-Cotes Art Gallery and Museum, Bournemouth, UK/The Bridgeman Art Library.

At the heart-center of each human is a fiery imagination wishing to make sense out of no-sense and paint the self in the best possible light. Sentience, wherever and whenever it manifests, peers into the mirror like a young Narcissus and asks itself the following questions: Who am I? How did I come to be? Do I live in a world of eternal feasibilities, or am I shackled by gross limitations? What are the social, moral, and ethical codes of conduct that govern behavior and society as a whole?

What are the consequences of law-making and law-breaking, of conformity and dissention?

As we are expelled from the life-bestowing womb, we come not into a cogent world of limitations, demarcations, frontiers, compartments, and conditioned responses, but rather a nebulous, protean, and raw *prima materia*, a primordial synaptic swamp where all is possible and nothing is regimented and absolute. The scaffolds that are integral to human development and concurrently guide the psychophysical and psychospiritual trajectory each individual will cleave into the ambient background of fields are mentally transmitted through both oral and literary devices called narratives. Narratives are evolutionary precursors of semantic language, civilized societies, and the current form of the human brain. They predate Newtonian science, property rights, medicine, consumer societies birthed by the Industrial Revolution, the religious work ethic, and anything else of worth ever invented by the human species. They represent our greatest collective failures and successes... everything we have been, are, aspire to be, and will be.

Myth is one discrete and powerful form of narrative. The function of myth has been a topic of contentious and polemical debate. Are they proto-scientific accounts of historical phenomena? Or quasi-scientific attempts to understand psychological processes and spiritual truths? Distorted memories of the past? Transmitters of magico-religious ceremonies? Did they emerge, in part, as a mechanism of neural integration and coordination between the dominant and nondominant hemispheres of the brain? All we can offer are educated guesses, but in truth we don't really know. What we do know is that they ground lived experience in a linear, sequential framework; they serve as blueprints for emotional regulation, problem-solving, behavior, and identity; and they provide frameworks for goal attainment and movement to self-definition. In this capacity, they are the most valuable, exquisite thing we'll ever know—worth their weight in gold. Through myths, we create and recreate, and we construct, deconstruct, and reconstruct ourselves, personally and collectively, generationally and intergenerationally, athwart different sociohistorical milieus.

And despite being temporally and culturally bound, they speak to us and play with our heartstrings in an impartial and indiscriminate manner. The antediluvian allegory of Atlantis, for instance, cleverly implies that the destruction of the old precedes generation of the new. In a time before this, King Minos of Crete imprisoned the Minotaur, the theriomorphic son of Queen Pasiphae, in a subterranean labyrinth; we, too, imprison our instinctual drives, our sadomasochistic and destructive impulses, within a socially mediated patina that can restrict self-definition and self-expression. Jason, the legendary Greek hero, once embarked on a dangerous quest to Colchis to capture a priceless treasure known as the Golden Fleece; is this not a figurative expression of the intrinsic rewards that come from risk-taking behavior and having the chutzpah to venture beyond one's own comfort zone or mapped territory? The Egyptian Isis is inexorable in her plight to gather the scattered parts of her dismembered brother-husband, Osiris; like Isis, life equips us with ample opportunities to become whole again by gathering back dismembered parts of ourselves that weren't mirrored, validated, or celebrated.

Not all our stories are benign or noble, though. Like the vengeful sorceress Circe, we can direct the full brunt of our jealousy at a lover when we are no longer the preferred object of their desirousness. King Midas underscores the idea that some people are harbingers of serendipity; however, what good can come of wishing if it is barren of common sense? We can be furtive and disingenuous in pursuit of our selfish agendas—disguised as a femme fatale, Isis confronts her brother Seth on an island, and tells him that a stranger entered her life after the death of her husband intent on stealing domestic possessions and banishing her young son from the household. Without thinking, Seth reproaches the foreigner for the same injustice that he was attempting to commit against little Horus, and in doing so unwittingly confesses his own depravity. Knowledge, my friends, is power, and we are perpetually conflicted as to whether we should use it for personal gain or altruistic ventures beneficial to society as a whole; a long time ago, Isis blackmailed the sun god, Re, by poisoning him with a serpent made from his own spittle and then agreeing to heal him on condition that he reveal his secret name to her. These are the dark, less-than-honorable shadows pervading the human spirit.

Finally, we do not have omnipotent control over the environment, nor are we impermeable to calamity. Like Icarus, whose wings were melted by the sun's heat because his father's reasoning fell on deaf ears, our lofty ambitions and hubris may be leveled at any moment. The universe punishes grandiosity and shatters illusions of cosmic supremacy. In a Coptic version of the Gnostic myth of Pistis-Sophia, the goddess appears before her arrogant son Yaldabaoth and utters a spine-chilling prophecy: "There is an immortal man of light who has been in existence before you and who will appear among your modelled forms; he will trample you to scorn just as the potter's clay is pounded. And you will descend to your mother, the abyss, along with those that belong to you."[156] Arrogance, it seems, is not aligned with the fundamental harmony of the universe.

On a different note, tragic sociopolitical consequences can ensue from mythographical detail. Eve, according to the biblical account of Genesis, is fashioned by Jehovah-Elohim from the rib of Adam. She is a second and inferior creation, and it is she who tempted Adam to taste of the forbidden fruit. Similarly, in the Christian tradition, the Virgin Mary gives birth to the divine son, the Christ, but is not herself divine. This patriarchal bias and appreciation of the masculine gender over the feminine crops up in both semantic language and in societal conventions that have underpinned Eurocentric consciousness for millennia. In the wake of the twenty-first century, our most empowering myths have receded from view, caught in an occult backwash caused by the post-Reformation waves. And what have these waves brought us but school after school of dogmatic approaches to absolute knowledge: Newtonian mechanics, Darwinian natural selection, evolutionary psychology, behaviorism with its controversial agenda of reducing all human interactions to the level of basic reflexes and conditioned responses, biological psychiatry with its aim to identify biomarkers for mental illness, and cognitive neuroscience with its embodied mind hypothesis.

Myths preserving memories of human divinity and giftedness, the unharnessed powers of will and belief, and a Mother Nature enchanted and inspirited have been forgotten or relegated to the dustbin of pseudoscience. This disenchantment with Nature has saturated the clinical disciplines and consequently, most ailments, organic and psychiatric, aren't treated in the context of the whole: instead of treating the patient from within a holistic framework—as an active, dynamic member of a sociocultural system replete with an assumptive worldview, conflicting motivations, and psychospiritual leanings— clinicians adopt unconscious philosophical attitudes where the central premise is that what's walked into the room is a bundle of psychobiological impulses with defects that must be "fixed" with surgery, somatic-based therapies, and polypharmacy.

Perhaps the way forward is illuminated by the Gnostic text "On the Origin of the World" wherein Pistis-Zoe, daughter of the goddess Pistis-Sophia, stumbles upon the lifeless carcass of Adam. Overwhelmed by grief and pity for her male counterpart, she breaths the divine spark into him with the help of her mother. "Adam!" she shrieks. "Become alive! Rise upon the earth!" The divine element moves with him like a slithering serpent and imbues him with life. Perhaps, then, for a modern myth to nurture and actualize human potential it must retain an unconditional positive regard for the aesthetically feminine: mutuality, trust, vulnerability, playfulness, and curiosity, all integral foundations of true love; pluralism; intentionality; intellectual synergy; intuition; egalitarianism; and a humble, modest Gaea-based empiricism. It must promote deepest meaning-making and remain diametrically opposed to judgment, separation, and hierarchy. These are the qualities that move mountains and occasionally create them. Despite being far from that promised land, we cannot lose hope; yes, we must remain resolute and undaunted in our plight to get there—remember, no good has ever come of doubting, either.

We, the mortal children of Pistis-Sophia (whose name means *Faith-Wisdom* in Greek), have been tasked with this sacred duty.

Endnotes

156 Bentley Layton (ed.), *Nag Hammadi Codex II, 2–7, Together with XIII, 2* Brit. Lib. Or. 4926 (1) and P. Oxy. 1, 654, 655: I. Gospel According to Thomas, Gospel According to Philip, Hypostasis of the Archons, Indexes. II. On the Origin of the World, Expository Treatise on the Soul, Book of Thomas the Contender* (Leiden, Netherlands: Brill, 2020), p. 41.

Part III: The Noetic Science

Chapter 11

Ars Aurifica: Metallic Transmutation

Figure 11-1. An illustration from a 1674 alchemical treatise *by Joh. Janssonius van Waesberge* titled *De Groene Leeuw of Het Licht der Philosophen.* It showcases the major alchemical symbols and a labyrinth symbolizing the personal quest for the Philosopher's Stone.

Alchemy's ambition to perfect Nature, to make gold of detritus and dust, has certainly contributed to its quixotic appeal. Curiosity and inquisition are innate to the human condition— we are perpetually trying to parse out the feasible from the impossible and separate self-imposed limitations from absolute and veridical ones. What are the farthest reaches of human potential? Is the science fiction we immerse ourselves in today a double-edged blessing and curse of the morrow? Can we manifest all that is conjured by the esemplastic powers of the human imagination? And even if we can, should we? These questions have never been the prerogative of any particular discipline, culture, or epoch. They are ubiquitous, transcultural, and cross-generational; they have manifested through the dominant ontological-epistemic framework of any one era and have been addressed in ways that do not egregiously violate the incumbent ethical sensibilities and moral codes of the aggregates.

Without doubt, these profound philosophical questions also served as unconscious catalysts for chemico-operative pursuits that first appeared in China during the fourth century BCE under the guise of a quest for an elusive herbal medicine that prolongs life or grants life eternal—the so-called Elixir of Life. This original Chinese quest was later inherited by the Egypto-Hellenic, Arabic, and medieval alchemists who did everything zealously possible to manifest the scarce and coveted Elixir. The Elixir of Life could not only cure diseases and prolong human life, but also do other miraculous things like turn base metals into a supernal and splendid gold. The Western alchemists emphasized its powers of transmutation over its healing properties, and warned all who dedicated themselves to the plight that the path to making it was fraught with complications and setbacks. Nevertheless, there was always a handful of tenacious and obstinate practitioners whose gusto and resolve kept them from abandoning the alchemical quest prematurely. Inevitably, these individuals would all reach a forked road presided over by a Theban sphinx, which articulated the same questions: "Can base metals like lead and mercury be transmuted into silver and gold? Does the Elixir of Life or Philosopher's Stone, that elusive red powder with magical powers of projection and the ability to heal ailments, actually exist?"

Answering these questions in any satisfactory and compelling manner is contingent on the absolute clarification of two conjectures, which are interconnected: (1) is there empirical truth in any of the esoteric principles described by alchemical practitioners of the past, and (2) what are the exact properties or characteristics of the Stone? Both must be answered before a verdict on the Stone can be sanctioned; if the theoretical assumptions upon which the creation of the Stone is predicated are indeed fallacious, and if there is no general consensus among alchemists regarding the nature of the Stone, then the viability of metallic transmutation crumbles in the manner that Atlantis was leveled to the ground before sinking to the bottom of the ocean in the recesses of Plato's own mind, some 2,000 years ago.

There is no mention of the Philosopher's Stone in the revelatory visions, parables, and recipes comprising the early Alexandrian literature on alchemy. In fact, the earliest known reference to it comes from instructional texts written in Arabic between the seventh and ninth centuries and attributed to such legendary figures as Jabir ibn Hayyan (721–815) and Balinas, the Pseudo-Apollonius of Tyana (c. 500). Through their engagement with Egypto-Hellenistic alchemy in Alexandria and other intellectual centers, these pioneers of the Arab alchemical tradition produced notable works such as *The Second Book of the Elements of Foundation* and *The Book of the Secret of Creation and the Art of Nature* which preserve the earliest known fragments of the *Tabula Smaragdina* [Emerald Tablet], a cosmological-philosophical text that achieved widespread circulation in the fourteenth century and was celebrated as the Bible of all medieval alchemists. In this condensed summa of alchemical knowledge, we learn that the Stone's father is the solar orb (also fire or philosophical sulphur) and its mother the lunar orb (also water or philosophical *argent vive*). The wind, on the other hand, is implicated as the womb that carried it and the volatile, moist humus that is earth is cast in the presiding role of wet nurse. This description is rather abstruse, for the most part, and it isn't really until the advent of the "transmutational" history, a genre of literature that arose as a knee-jerk reaction to the growing fame of alchemy in the early modern period, that we have a more concrete description of the Philosopher's Stone.

While discrepancies do exist among primary sources that offer descriptions of the Stone's form and color, there is also a degree of unanimity about its quintessential features. The alchemists describe it as a refined and delicate powder, usually quite hefty, that emits a potent odor and coruscates when held up toward a light source, like shards of broken glass. Intrinsic to the Stone was a scarlet red color, although other colors like gold, auburn red, orange red, emerald green, and cobalt blue have also been promulgated. The Flemish chemist and physician Jon Baptiste van Helmont (1579–1644) was convinced that it possessed a saffron color and sparkled, whereas the alchemist Beregard asserted that it emanated a vibrant hue like that of a wild poppy and gave off the moist odor of sea salt. Differences of opinion also extend to its powers of projection, perhaps due to the seasonal fluctuations in Mother Nature's generative powers. Anything from a hundred to a million times the projection of its own weight in pure silver or gold has been proposed, specifically from authorities like Arnaldus de Villa Nova (1235–1311), Isaac of Holland (c. 1600), and Roger Bacon (1214–1294).

Following the integrated and consistent description of the Stone were a plethora of eyewitness accounts describing the transmutational feats of renowned alchemists. The most captivating and extraordinary of these is the Flamel legend, a quasi-historical narrative pertaining to the life of a Parisian notary by the name of Nicolas Flamel. He dreamed of and then acquired an enigmatic and wonderfully illustrated manuscript titled *The Book of Abraham the Jew*.[157] For Flamel, this book was a source of splendor and wonder, and paradoxically also a source of consternation and frustration; he knew that the sequence of pictograms in the book were ciphers for the creation of the Stone, but try as he might, all his conscientious attempts at deciphering them were futile. Later, he traveled abroad with the intention of finding an adept who might be able to help with the translation. While sojourning in Leon, Spain, he met Master Canches, a Jewish merchant and physician who bequeathed to him requisite knowledge for a precise decoding of the book's strange characters. The narrative specifies that Canches died suddenly and never made it back to Paris with Flamel. Three more years of failed experiments followed before Flamel met with triumph. The momentous moment occurred at around midday on Monday January 17, 1382, when half a pound of red mercury was morphed into silver. The serendipitous and propitious turn of events didn't stop there. On April 25 of the same year, at about 5 p.m., Flamel used the red powder to transmute another half a pound of mercury into alchemical gold, which was familiar "by the strong scent and odour thereof" and "better assuredly than common gold, more soft and more pliable."[158] The proceedings were all witnessed by his closest and best-beloved confidante, his wife, Perrenelle. A further three successful transmutations took place between 1382 and 1413. Nicolas and Perrenelle were magnanimous and philanthropic individuals, and the swift accumulation of wealth connected with these lucrative endeavors enabled the founding and building of 14 hospitals, seven churches, and three chapels in Paris and Boulogne.

Roughly two centuries afterward, at around 4 p.m. on March 13, 1602, the charismatic Scottish alchemist Alexander Seton stunned a Dutch seafarer at a modest dwelling in Enkhuysen just outside Amsterdam by transmuting minute quantities of lead into gold. Seton was quite like a protean god and evanescent light, meandering across Europe and performing metallic transmutations in public places without imparting secrets of the Stone's synthesis to anybody. Legend has it that his sojourns were brief as to deter inquisitive individuals from prying or asking. On January 15, 1648, exactly 46 years after Seton's transmutation, the alchemist Richthausen of Vienna sprinkled granules of a mysterious red powder onto three pounds of mercury in front of Emperor Ferdinand III at his Imperial Court in Prague. The miraculous transformation of mercury into gold so mesmerized the Emperor that he proceeded to knight Richthausen immediately and had a medal struck to commemorate the event. James Price, a member of the Fellow of the Royal Society in England, conducted a public demonstration of transmutation at his personal laboratory in Guildford on Saturday May 25, 1782. During the conjuring, he cast an alchemical powder called "red earth" or the "powder of projection" into a crucible of heated mercury before taking a backward step to watch the incredulous facial expressions of those present as it morphed into gold. The members remained incredulous and forced Price into surrendering the product to two independent examiners, an assay-master and an Oxford goldsmith, for closer scrutiny. Both testimonials were favorable; the alchemical product, they decreed, was authentic. The Oxford goldsmith went so far as to suggest that it was superior to English gold. Reports of the acquisition or manufacture of similar transmutational powders, real or imagined, are woven into the biographies of monks like Wenzel Seiler (1648–1681) and John Dastin (1288–1334), as well as seventeenth-century scientists of the caliber of Robert Boyle (1627–1691) and Sir Isaac Newton (1642–1727). The contemporaries Boyle and Newton were to some degree deceptive when it came to their personal feelings and attitudes; they vehemently decried alchemical theory and practice as a fraudulent enterprise, writing contemptuously of the art to please the literati while surreptitiously formulating and partaking in alchemical pursuits of their own.

Taken at face value, these accounts suggest that there may very well be an alchemical powder of projection, and that knowledge of its synthesis is known by adepts operating under obligatory oaths of secrecy. But the legitimacy of the transmutational accounts themselves are suspect on several grounds. Most were transcribed and disseminated before the advent of the printing press in 1440; hence, there's no way of determining whether they are veridical events, exaggerations, or mythologizations of quasi-historical persons and events, or absolute fabrications made by charlatans intending to convince the ignorant and credulous majority that metallic transmutation was possible. Incidentally, descriptions of master alchemists are made with no mention of their actual birthdates; is this explicable in the context of their mercurial and mysterious nature and the necessity of using pseudonyms for anonymity, or is it because these characters and their associated narratives are fictitious in nature? On the other hand, how could an enterprise predicated on erroneous philosophical assumptions about the universe and reality have survived as long as it did without suffering redundancy and being challenged or replaced by some other equally flawed practice in due course? How did it enchant the most sagacious minds of the era, including some of the most illustrious intellectuals in recorded history, like Sir Isaac Newton and Robert Boyle?

This conundrum is epitomized by the Atlantis myth. If Atlantis were nothing more than a plot device conjured by Plato's vivid imagination, then the enthusiastic modern-day crypto-archaeologists who bide their time searching for the lost city's architectural remnants are doomed to failure. While, during their lifelong quest, they may end up disinterring items of archaeological significance belonging to some long-lost civilization, none of those items will be from the ill-fated Atlantis. Fact. Similarly, if the laboratory operations described in ancient and medieval alchemical texts are nothing but symbolic transcriptions of inner psychospiritual truths, then any aspiring young alchemist who engages the craft for the sole purpose of synthesizing a fine powder of projection called "red earth" is bound for absolute disappointment, if not demoralization. Fact. One way of disentangling this Gordian knot, of separating "the subtle from the gross" and the wheat from the chaff, if you like, is to temporarily jettison our deep-rooted epistemic biases and determine whether the esoteric correspondences hold up to empirical scrutiny.

According to esoteric lore, each planet exerts some kind of influence over base matter in an alchemical retort. Saturn, Jupiter, and the moon are all active during the Lesser Work, which gravitates around the creation of the "white stone." Alternatively, Venus, Mars, and the sun are galvanized into action during the Greater Work, whereby a subsequent set of processes act on the "white stone" to furnish the "red stone." The time an alchemist elects to commence the work is also of critical importance and can be a decisive factor in determining the degree of success or failure. The most auspicious period to begin is during the spring equinox (i.e., between March and May), a time when the generative forces of Mother Nature are proliferating and mimic a gathering storm. Traditionally, any successful transmutations of red mercury into gold are presided over by a conjunction of their celestial counterparts in the sky — in this case, the planet Mercury and the sun.

The author of Hermeticism, Nick Kollostrum, examined this exact phenomenon in his book *The Metal-Planet Relationship: A Study of Celestial Influence* (1993). He found that in five out of the seven astrological charts he examined depicting the precise moment a master alchemist transmuted a small quantity of a base substance into gold, the planet Mercury and the sun were within five degrees of one another. In four of the astrological charts that Kollostrum examined, the base metal used was red mercury. The other two were lead and silver, the metals of Saturn and the moon. Predictably then, the astrological charts immortalizing these epic transmutations of lead into gold and silver into gold should clearly depict a celestial situation where there is no more than five degrees of separation between Saturn and the sun, and the moon and the sun, respectively. Kollostrum's findings indicate that Earth's seasonal rotation and the astrological movement are key players in metallic transmutation. It's exactly as the Hermetic tenet decrees: that which is above exerts a subtle but necessary influence on that which is below. And what of the esoteric correspondences? Does a qualitative, empirically verifiable connection between lead and Saturn, quicksilver and Mercury, silver and the moon, and gold and the sun actually exist as to render the planetary conjunction-affects-metals hypothesis viable, or somewhat viable even? Were our ancient ancestors on to something or were they barking up the wrong tree?

Skeptics and scoffers who remain fiercely faithful to the hegemony of orthodox science with its myopic focus on eliminative materialism, quantitative analysis, and the established nomothetic laws may dismiss these claims as too progressive and radical, or worse still, as iconoclastic and sacrilegious. The conceptual chasm separating them from the curious eyes and rational minds of those who are perpetually informed by the dominant scientific paradigm is just too wide to inspire awe and galvanize inquiry in an impartial and systematic way. Hope of examining phenomena impartially and approaching contentious issues with an open mind necessitates the temporary suspension of disbelief and a necessary suppression of rigid beliefs. All extraterrestrial bodies and the earth are like magnets, emit gravitational forces, and encompass potential when it comes to pulling other celestial bodies into their orbits. This is an acknowledged and undisputed physical law. The moon's own gravitational pull on the earth generates the ocean tides, which we observe and experience. This, too, is an established fact. Up to 60% of the human body is composed of water. This, too, is a biological truth. If the moon can facilitate terrestrial rhythms like the ocean tides, then wouldn't it also have some degree of control over the human body, and by association some of its neurophysiological and functional systems (i.e., higher-order consciousness, emotional valence, memory). There is a positive correlation between general admissions to psychiatric units in hospitals and the full moon, apparently. Further, if the moon can affect organic matter like the human body, which is literally stardust, then wouldn't it also be able to potentially exert some kind of influence over inanimate elements, like metals? This isn't magical thinking; it's the perspicacious application of inductive reasoning.

Unbeknown to many, a series of groundbreaking experiments investigating the planet–metal relationships were conducted by Lily Kolisko, a student of the anthroposophist Rudolph Steiner (1861–1925). She developed a chromatographical method using filter papers to detect chemical changes that might be occurring in specific metal-salt solutions (i.e., silver nitrate, gold chloride) as the respective planetary bodies (i.e., moon, sun) were entering into conjunctions and oppositions with one another. Then came the plethora of experiments. Under strictly controlled conditions in a laboratory-style setting, Kolisko was able to demonstrate that the images produced by silver-salt solutions exhibited a striking resemblance to the crater-ravaged surface of the moon, and that certain idiosyncratic patterns manifested on the filter papers at the inception of each lunar phase, particularly the full and new moons.

Some of her most arresting work explored the connection between the sun and gold. To discern whether there was an esoteric correspondence between the two, she meticulously observed filter papers dipped in metallic-salt solutions of gold chloride before, during, and in the aftermath of a total eclipse. In the dark room, gold chloride typically manifested scarlet reds, bright yellows, royal purples, and other auric colors onto filter paper films. The solar eclipse of June 29, 1927, furnished some very unusual filter paper results; in place of the customary vibrant colors was an agglomeration of filthy reddish and purple-browns, as if an invisible hand had somehow reached out and smudged them over with a paintbrush before dotting them over with black specks. At this time, the gold chloride had also lost its capacity to rise along the full length of the filter papers. Following the eclipse, the gold chloride contained in the filter paper films began producing vibrant colors again. The implications were, for all intents and purposes, sweeping and trailblazing—corporeal gold was somehow "programmed" to synchronize with, match, and reflect the state, condition, or behavior of the sun. The two were in harmonious attunement with one another. From the 1920s up until the 1960s, Kolisko investigated the effects of total solar eclipses on filter papers dipped in reagents of gold chloride and silver nitrate. She discovered that the filter paper films, usually a stonewashed violet color before the eclipse, turned a muddy black as the lunar disc passed over and shrouded the sun temporarily. As above, so below.

Agnes Fyfe, a researcher from a cancer clinic at Arlesheim in Switzerland followed in Kolisko's footsteps. Fyfe initiated a temporary departure from the investigation of planet–metal relationships, deciding instead to focus on planet–plant correspondences. Her decision may have been informed in part by the conjecture that living matter like plant sap might react more robustly to celestial phenomena than metallic salts, and in part by the realization that mercury bichloride, the substance she wanted to work with, was colorless and not very acquiescent to being tracked with the naked eye. Her research question pertained to conjunctions of the sun and Mercury, and whether these had any quantifiable effect on a reagent of diluted plant sap from mistletoe (which traditionally falls under the guardianship of the sun) and iris (which traditionally falls under the guardianship of Mars). In the end, the decision to use plant sap was hasty and ill-advised because it introduced several confounds into the procedure and allowed her chief detractors, namely sycophants of the orthodox scientific community, to tactfully discredit her findings by attacking the study's internal validity.

In 1978, Fyfe turned her attention to the esoteric correspondence between Venus, the planet known to the ancients as the *Eosphoros* [Dawn-Bringer] and the *Hesperos* [Star of the Evening], and copper. She used Kolisko's filter-paper method to determine whether the planet's annual movements had any effect on 1% copper acetate solutions placed inside plant sap. Results indicated that metallic reactions were strongest when Venus was in celestial regions unobstructed by the sun. Equally astonishing were Kolisko's earlier experiments that tracked conjunctions of Venus and the sun using reagents of gold chloride and copper salt; a light-green precipitate would appear on the plastic filter-paper films each time Venus reached its zenith.

Fyfe, in particular, was very astute and diligent in her observations, noting that reaction rates varied with seasonal rotation. Reaction strength was attenuated during the months of December and January (winter solstice) and exaggerated between the months of March and May (spring equinox). Save for being the equinoctial marker for spring and the resurrection of Nature's generative powers, the spring equinox was frequently touted by alchemists as the most auspicious moment for the commencement of the Great Work. Astrologically speaking, it is a period wherein the sun rises in the constellation of Taurus and Venus is in an exalted state. The alchemical pursuit is in many ways the quintessential aesthetically feminine operation. The occult connections are plentiful.

Many of Kolisko's original experiments, especially those tracking the Mars–Saturn conjunction, were replicated in 1949 by Theodore Schwenck and in 1964 by Dr. Karl Voss of Hamburg. Analogous results to Kolisko's were furnished in both instances, and these were dutifully published in various astrology journals in an attempt to generate scientific interest in the study of astrochemistry and occult correspondences. Not surprisingly, the outcome was egregious. Instead of piquing curiosity and stimulating intellectual discourse, they were overlooked by the mainstream scientific community and swiftly faded into obscurity. In time, they were forgotten completely.

The same fate was to befall Thomas Charles Lethbridge (1901–1971) and his life's work. Lethbridge was a shrewd, conscientious, and open-minded man who believed that all knowing begins with scrupulous observation. In hindsight, he was a progressive and original thinker with a natural proclivity for breaking with established tradition, rather than conforming with or remaining faithful to it. He initiated a departure from the family custom of attending Oxford University and matriculated at Harvard instead, where he devoted himself to the study of archaeology and became the Keeper of Anglo-Saxon Antiquities at the Archaeology Museum. During his time there, he met Margaret Murray, an eccentric woman who found his innate curiosity and unconventional ideas about history most endearing and fascinating. Inspired by their manifold discussions and by the chance discovery of a statue of Matrona, the Celtic Great Mother Goddess, near an Iron Age fort called Wandlebury Camp in Cambridgeshire, UK, Lethbridge wrote and released a very thought-provoking book called *Gogmagog: The Buried Gods* (1975), which entertained the hypothesis that a nature-based wicca religion had thrived on the British Isles before the coming of the Christian dispensation. Predictably, the book displeased the Cambridge literati, the "academic trade unionists," because it was blatantly incongruent with the conventional wisdom vis-à-vis historical lore. But Lethbridge wasn't in the least bit interested in pandering to their whims nor bothered by their disdain; he severed ties with Cambridge and moved to Hole House in Devon, where he continued his unorthodox investigations and stumbled upon an inexplicable phenomenon in the process.

His detective work led to many unprecedented discoveries, the most intriguing of which involved a pendulum. One day, while attempting to ascertain what string length was most efficient and appropriate for dowsing, he ran into a fascinating phenomenon: the pendulum would gyrate at different lengths for specific objects and substances. A specific measurement in inches (which he called a "rate") was obtained for each object of interest by standing perpendicular to it and unwinding a ball of string until the gyration began. Soon, it became apparent that several items reacted to the same rate with the only way of differentiating between them being to count the number of individual gyrations. Had Lethbridge run into a specific design intrinsic to the natural world, which had escaped quantitative scientific analysis? Only time would tell. In the years that followed, he tested innumerable items, both material and immaterial. Lethbridge saw that even qualities like human feelings and emotions had rates, impelling his personal conviction that everything existing in the cosmos must be composed of discrete vibrations or densities. This philosophy is definitely congruent with the contemporaneous tenets of M-theory, which aim to reconcile quantum mechanics and general relativity. Proposed by Edward Witten of the Institute for Advanced Study, it aims to define quarks, electrons, and the fundamental forces of the cosmos in the context of one-dimensional oscillating strings that permeate 11 separate dimensions.

In any case, the reaction rates all ranged from 1 to 40, so Lethbridge proceeded to plot them onto the inner rim of a 360-degree rose compass divided into 40 sections. Objects, substances, and concepts that might be described as lackluster, inert, and "dead" were associated with higher values, while those of a more effervescent and inspirited nature were correlated with lower values. Most could be found clustered around the four main pillars of the rose compass: the 40-inch, 30-inch, 20-inch, and 10-inch rates. The shade of black, the cardinal direction of north, the element of air, and thoughts associated with any of the just mentioned all reacted to the 40-inch rate; the color green, the cardinal direction of west, the element of water, the moon, and the thought of these responded to the 30-inch rate; the shade of white, the cardinal direction of south, the quality of heat, and thoughts pertaining to any of these responded to the 20-inch rate; and, finally, the color red, the cardinal direction of east, the element of fire, the sun, and thoughts pertaining to these all reacted to the 10-inch rate.

As anticipated, light and dark were diametrically opposed on the compass; the first responded to the 10-inch rate and the second to the 40-inch rate. The same was true for life and death, with the first responding to the 20-inch rate and the second to the 40-inch rate. Contrary to widespread belief, the male and female genders were not conceptual opposites and could be found at the 24-inch rate and 29-inch rate, respectively. The highly revered metal gold shared the 29-inch rate with females. Concerning the other ancient metals, mercury could be found at 12.5 inches, lead and silver at 22, tin at 29, copper at 30.5, and iron at 32. Substances or objects sharing the same rate could be distinguished from one another by counting the exact number of revolutions. In the case of lead and silver, for instance, these happen to be 16 and 22, respectively. What this enterprise revealed to Lethbridge was that all created forms, mental or physical, possessed a unique footprint in the cosmos. Further, these footprints could be exposed and substantiated through measurement (i.e., gyration rate and number of revolutions) with a basic pendulum device.

We encounter the idea of an occult signature in the esoteric literature. The doctrine of signatures formed a vital component of Pythagorean mysticism, Platonic metaphysics, and the holistic theories of Renaissance physician and alchemist Paracelsus of Hohenheim (1493–1541). More specifically, it was widely accepted among practitioners of the occult arts — the Neo-Platonic magus, theurgist, or Renaissance alchemist — that before one could bend Nature to their will, they had to discover the occult signature(s) of the very thing(s) they wished to manipulate. To give an example, the root of the kava kava plant induces intoxicating effects like euphoria and narcosis once ingested. Its agency is inextricably bound up with the facilitation of dreams, reflection, introspection, and retrospection in humans. Hence, kava kava's occult virtue — in other words, its intrinsic nature — is quintessentially lunar and its gyration rate is probably going to reflect that (i.e., kava kava root will most likely respond to the rate for the moon, the 30-inch rate). Direct knowledge of this occult virtue or planet–plant esoteric correspondence is in a practical sense most invaluable; by grinding sun-dried kava kava roots into a fine powder, mixing it with mead, and then consuming it, a practitioner could potentially augment or wield these powerful lunar influences within himself. Even the most skeptical and suspicious of the doubting Thomases should find this philosophically coherent and feasible. In the end, there's something deeply compelling and nomothetic about idiosyncratic systems of knowledge that crop up in autonomous fashion and either complement, correspond with, or corroborate other existing paradigms. Prudent, on this occasion, are questions pertaining to uncanny similarities between the two alternative systems of knowledge. Are the pendulum rates that Lethbridge serendipitously stumbled upon and the Paracelsian occult signature two sides of the same coin? Moreover, are the four main pillars (10 inch, 20 inch, 30 inch, and 40 inch) of his rose compass one and the same with philosophical fire, earth, water, and air, and is there a connection with the alchemical stages of *nigredo*, *cauda pavonis*, *albedo*, and *rubedo*? In all probability, yes.

Another interesting discovery was made at the Iron Age hill fort of Pilsdon Pen in Dorset, UK, with the assistance of Lethbridge's wife, Mina. During one visit, it dawned upon him that he should examine some of the pebbles around the fort with his pendulum. Predictably, they reacted to the rate for silica, but they also responded to the rates for the male gender (24 inches) and thought (27 inches). That was bizarre; why were they reacting to multiple rates? The most likely answer was that the rates had somehow been impressed upon the stones, perhaps by events that had transpired hundreds, if not thousands, of years ago. Further investigations confirmed this hypothesis. Pebbles handled with gloves and tongs from a nearby beach only reacted to the 14-inch rate for silica. When grappled with the bare hand, they also reacted to the rate for thought. Subsequently, Lethbridge discovered that when pebbles were thrown against a wall with brute force, they reacted to an additional rate for male sex or gender (24 inches). As absurd as it sounded, the pebbles could somehow identify the gender of the individual who had handled them; those hurled by Lethbridge responded to the rate for male gender (24 inches) and those hurled by Mina responded to the rate for female gender (29 inches).

Anyone who didn't know that an experiential approach was used to uncover this hidden system of knowledge would obviously think the idea was nothing more than a fanciful delusion or absurdity. Yet, here it is! Where the naked human eye and the tools of orthodox science either fail or remain silent, the pendulum succeeds in piecing together an alternative narrative for creation that is able to make sense out of nonsense and give coherent form to an ostensible disorder. If there is any legitimacy to Lethbridge's findings, then there must be an exchange of energies occurring perpetually between the constituents of Nature on a subtle and undetectable level, and many existing signatures or unique cosmic blueprints can be intrinsically modified under specific conditions (i.e., violence or the use of external force). The more powerful the force, the more profound and lasting the changes. If inanimate things like rocks could still resonate with rates for the male gender and for thought centuries after they were thrown in battle by men, as Lethbridge was able to show, then why shouldn't a very focused and directed burst of mental energy emanating from the human mind be able to affect or alter the internal composition of its intended recipient during a time supposed to be astrologically auspicious? A successful transmutation could in theory occur if red mercury, the base metal with an occult signature or rate of 12.5 inches, was impressed with the 29-inch rate for gold and then purged of its original blueprint. Such a transformation would, both literally and metaphorically speaking, be gold.

Lethbridge's vibratory rates would have definitely found a faithful ally in the teachings of Albert Richard Riedel (1911–1984). Riedel, also known as Frater Albertus, was instrumental in the propagation of esoteric lore and alchemical methods, especially the Paracelsian school, to many parts of the United States from the mid-twentieth century onward. Like Paracelsus, he was profoundly interested in spagyrics, the laboratory practice of extracting the vital essence of herbs through processes like maceration, circulation, and extraction, to produce synthetic tinctures and elixirs innumerable times more potent than anything the pharmaceutical companies could concoct. His experiential and pragmatic approach to alchemy proved to be an enormous success; neophyte practitioners could acquire a deeper and more tacit understanding of alchemical principles through a gradual and graded immersion in practice as to facilitate a sense of accomplishment and encumber feelings of confusion and being overwhelmed. Between 1960 and 1984, Frater Albertus inaugurated the Paracelsus Research Society in Salt Lake City, Utah, and took hundreds of aspiring alchemists under his wing. Most were members of neo-theosophical movements like the Golden Dawn and the Ancient Mystical Order Rosae Crucis (AMORC), but there were also independent researchers from disciplines as disparately related as parapsychology and chemistry. During the time that the facility was operative, Frater Albertus worked assiduously to educate the public: he initiated and maintained consistent publication of a quarterly journal called *Paralchemy*; he translated many alchemical texts into English from their original German, Spanish, Italian, and French; and he wrote 10 books, with his most renowned being *The Seven Rays of the QBL* (1985) and *The Alchemist's Handbook* (1960).

The mythical aura surrounding Frater Albertus made it very difficult to parse out truth from fiction. Mysterious anecdotes circulated at that time commemorating his success at preparing the oil or essence of lead, copper, and gold. To his devout students, these alchemical triumphs elevated him to the proverbial status of the undisputed adept. He had a way of convincing others of the viability of plant, mineral, and metallic work in practical alchemy. Previously a skeptic, the occultist Israel Regardie (1907–1985) revised his impressions of practical alchemy after visiting Frater Albertus at the Paracelsus Research Society. Whatever he witnessed inside the laboratories there exerted a profound influence on Regardie, enough to galvanize a public retraction of his hitherto myopic impression of alchemy as an exclusive psychospiritual practice in a subsequent edition of his book *The Philosopher's Stone* (1938). Perhaps he was enthralled by the same laboratory operations involving the separation of a dried herb from its vital life force, oil, or essence, which were meticulously described in *The Alchemist's Handbook*. In this concise and eloquently written book, Frater Albertus defines alchemy as the practice of "raising vibrations." This statement is first mentioned in the introduction and then reiterated intermittently throughout the text. Anyone who doesn't know that Frater Albertus and Thomas Lethbridge never met in person would think the two co-created the theory of vibration rates.

In his book, Frater Albertus distinguishes between the Lesser Work, or Lesser Circulation as he calls it, and the Greater Work or Greater Circulation. The first is concerned with the preparation of the plant or vegetable stone, and with the separation of the vital life principle of a herb from its corruptible body; the second alludes to metallic transmutation, a much more coveted and mysterious operation, which necessitates the active involvement of the alchemist himself. "Those who wait for a complete description in similar language, of the Great Arcanum will wait in vain," he warns. "It cannot be given. It is not permissible."[159] According to Albertus, many novice alchemists are easily discouraged from practical and operative work because they perform certain experiments prematurely, and usually without the requisite theoretical knowledge necessary to guarantee success when working with matter pertaining to each of the three kingdoms (i.e., animal, plant, and mineral).

To understand the theoretical premises Frater Albertus was working from, a cursory review of Paracelsian alchemy is necessary here. The esoteric worldview acknowledges the existence of three manifest kingdoms (i.e., plant, animal, and mineral) configured according to three principles affectionately known as the trinity: philosophical sulphur, philosophical mercury, and philosophical salt. Sulphur is negatively charged, mercury is positively charged, and salt, the binding force, is neutral. When alchemists speak of mercury, they are not referring to the crude form on the periodic table of elements but to this life-bestowing power, which animates organic matter. Mercury is also the fifth element, the ether or quintessence of the mystical philosophers and ancient sages. Under the auspices of the esoteric paradigm and its animistic lore, philosophical mercury can be separated from matter using alcohol as a primary saturating agent for the cycle of distillations and the extraction. Frater Albertus claims that philosophical mercury is of a different vibrational rate in each kingdom: lower vibrations in the plant realm, higher vibrations in the animal realm, and the highest vibrations in the mineral realm. In its most refined state, it looks like a yellowish jelloid substance. The exquisite coloration is precipitated by a delicate oil within the mercury. This is philosophical sulphur, a fiery principle which can be isolated from the mercury by subjecting the whole substance to a further cycle of distillation. The separation of mercury and sulphur isn't necessary when using spagyric techniques to synthesize the vegetable stone, but it is mandatory when preparing mineral and metallic tinctures such as oils or sulphurs from the seven planetary metals. Last but not least, the binding force that holds mercury and sulphur together is salt, and can be seen when the dead residue of any herb is reduced to black ash via calcination. Salt contains the defining qualities and is unique to any particular agglomeration of matter—an individual plant, animal, or mineral.

If the claims of Frater Albertus are to be believed, then creating the vegetable stone, or Lesser Circulation, is child's play; all one needs is a preferential herb, a supply of alcohol, a Soxhlet extraction apparatus for the distillation, and a healthy dose of motivation and curiosity. First, the aspirant grinds the herb into a fine powder before placing it into the filter-paper cylinder or thimble of the apparatus. The flask should then be filled with alcohol to about the halfway mark and realigned with the distillation train. The extraction begins once the heat source is ignited. The smoke-like vapors from the alcohol will diffuse through the filter paper cylinder containing the pulverized herb, enter a condenser tube above, and collect there momentarily before running back down into the flask. Subjecting the water-like extract in the flask to about three or four distillations should bring about an observable change; it should lose its transparency and take on a light-yellow coloration. This is the essence of the plant, its philosophical mercury. Changes in the consistency and color are attributable to the presence of delicate yellow oil, its philosophical sulphur. The dead residue of the plant can be separated from the filter-paper thimble, placed in a petri dish, and ignited. This will reduce it to black ash, or philosophical salt.

The aspirant or practitioner is then instructed to scoop up the charred remains of the herb and empty them back into the flask, preferably with the aid of a plastic funnel. According to Frater Albertus, these should be washed over with extract, as much of it as they will soak up. The flask should then be reattached to the Soxhlet apparatus, and the distillation procedure repeated over and over and over again, until there are no further changes to the extract's texture or coloration. At the end, the only remaining thing should be an oily viscid substance that should convert into a runny liquid when the temperature rises and miraculously solidify when it cools back down again. This is the initial manifestation of the herbal elixir, its first state. Frater Albertus asserts that calcination augments its density and renders it more potent; each time this is done, its efficacy doubles. Moreover, the refined extract containing the amalgamation of philosophical mercury and sulphur, as well as the salt which binds them together, can be hermetically sealed in a glass flask and subjected to a low simmering heat to create a plant or vegetable stone, the crown jewel of the Lesser Circulation. The therapeutic potential of the vegetable stone is unprecedented; it can also extract the trinity of any herb or plant through alchemical immersion.

Like a coterie of alchemists before him, Frater Albertus stops well short of revealing the mystery of the Grand Arcanum to his readers. He does, however, kindle within the aspirant the flame of faith by declaring that anyone with the skill, patience and gumption to generate the vegetable stone can surely synthesize the mineral stone. An essential ingredient for the successful completion of the Greater Circulation is a psychospiritual state called readiness—the aspirant must be ready. His assertions are very reminiscent of the Christian ritual of receiving Holy Communion, and all the preparatory inner work, the physical and spiritual cleansing, that must be accomplished before a supplicant can symbolically receive the flesh and blood of Jesus Christ. If there is, indeed, empirical validity to the theory of vibration rates and occult signatures, then the mysterious agent of the Greater Circulation that makes possible metallic transmutation and cannot be named must rest on the shoulders of the individual practitioner, or in their head, rather. The Lesser Circulation can be completed without any active participation on the part of the alchemist, because plant vibratory rates are attenuated in comparison with those of the animal kingdom. The same does not, however, hold true for the Greater Circulation, because the rates of vibration for minerals and metals are much higher than those for animals.

For metallic transmutation to succeed, the aspirant may have to "raise the vibrations" through a premeditated act of creative tension involving the human imagination—in other words, he or she may have to conjure vivid images of transmutation in their mind's eye and keep them alive there during key chemico-operative moments. If human thoughts can be imprinted onto rocks, as Thomas Lethbridge was able to demonstrate with his pendulum, then why can't they also be imprinted onto metals? By the same token, if a pendulum can simulate the rate of a particular substance or object in response to a fleeting thought about it, then who's to say that the thought of gold (which is responsive at the 29-inch rate) or its transmutation can't permanently reconfigure the extract of a metal, especially if the whole enterprise were impelled by focused intention? Mother Nature may also play an integral role in the degree of success; operations conducted during auspicious astrological moments—for instance, during a sun–Mercury conjunction when the base matter in the alembic is mercury, or a sun–Saturn conjunction when the base matter is lead—could somehow force the necessary changes on the atomic level to produce alchemical gold.

Of course, all these flighty speculations could be nothing but the musings of an overactive imagination. But what if?

Endnotes

157   Abraham Eleazar, *The Book of Abraham the Jew (The R.A.M.S. Library of Alchemy) (Volume 29)* (Scotts Valley, CA: Createspace Independent Publishing Platform, 2015).

158 Patrick Harpur (ed.), *Mercurius, Or, the Marriage of Heaven* (Glen Waverley, VIC: Blue Angel Gallery, 2007), p. 451.

159 Frater Albertus, *The Alchemist's Handbook: Manual for Practical Laboratory Alchemy (Revised)* (Maine, USA: Weiser Books, 1987), p. 6.

Chapter 12

Insurrection: The Death of Mechanical Science

Figure 12-1. Mixed medium painting of butterfly-headed goddess and crowned lion with the words *Secret Desire Transformed*. The painting showcases some very common alchemical leitmotifs and symbols associated with transmutation © Elena Ray/ Alamy Stock Photo.

It's only natural for the inquisitive among us to wonder what the current state of affairs is when it comes to relations between alchemy and modern science. Is there any dialogue and rapport between the two, are they sworn nemeses, or are they in the first blushes of a process of reconciliation? We could say they're in the process of working things out. Alchemy, as we know, is an animistic philosophy that acknowledges the mutual interconnectedness and interdependence of organic and inanimate things. Modern science does too, with the difference that it jettisoned the animistic and vitalistic worldview during the seventeenth-century intellectual movement known as the Enlightenment. Ironically, some of the literati who occasioned this were practicing alchemists themselves. Alchemy acknowledges the participatory element between a practitioner and their experiments; the latter are affected by the former's inner mental processes—their intentions and desires, and the emotional valence of their mental state.

Similarly, the orthodox scientific enterprise, or at least some of its disciplines (i.e., theoretical physics), are slowly gravitating away from Kantian-Cartesian mechanical understanding of energy, matter, and human consciousness. In hindsight, they are beginning to see the absurdity of the empirical method with its unrelenting and sanctimonious fixation on extricating the subjective element from research investigations as to discover "objective" nomothetic truths about the cosmos, a cosmos of chiefly unforgiving and rigid determinism. The methodological rigor employed—in other words, the measures taken to prevent confounding variables from contaminating and compromising the experiment's internal validity—is of paramount importance. In evidence-based science, a dearth of methodological rigor or the presence of hitherto unknown confounding variables during the execution phase of an experiment equates to ambiguity regarding the causal relationship under investigation (i.e., in other words, dismal failure) and necessitates immediate replication. The feasibility of this type of questing and the dualistic philosophical position subserving it must in the final analysis be scrutinized, for when we introspect enough, we arrive bloated and bloodied at the following rhetoric: is anything truly objective?

In all guises of scientific research, the data collection and analysis are done by experimenters. Experimenters are human and come replete with their own agendas and expectations. They are driven not by some *a priori* programmed search for an "impersonal truth" but by preconceived emotional judgments frequently indivisible from the self—they come in search of confirmatory evidence for their beliefs. If one looks hard enough at an agglomeration of numbers or data sets, they'll find the patterns they're looking for. Research is, to all intents and purposes, a very personal affair. Moreover, quantum theory has shown that the act of observing a subatomic particle—a concept that does not fit very neatly into the category of "energy" or "matter," I might add—alters its trajectory along the space–time continuum. Loosely labeled "quanta," these pockets of energy do not subscribe to absolute laws per se and prefer marching to the cosmic trumpet of probabilities; apparently, there's a degree of flexibility in the cosmos and all things can exist within that ostensibly paradoxical space. There is a unanimous agreement among quantum physicists that a conscious observer, or participator rather, can affect an experiment and that the result is not predetermined.

Many acknowledged seventeenth-century pioneers of the scientific method went to great pains in coming up with a universal classification system for matter that bifurcated the physical, objective, and measurable, from the mental, subjective, and idiosyncratic. Their prodigious efforts may have been in vain because it's becoming increasingly probable that this division, previously iterated as gospel, is specious and obsolete. An *a fortiori* conclusion is that our perceptual apparatuses are tuned to experience these as distinct entities; however, the two are just disparate energetic densities or wavelengths inextricably bound up with one another. The embodied mind, the microcosm, exists within a complicated set of relations called Nature and can generate unique fields of influence as it cleaves an individual path through the space–time continuum. It is, in turn, influenced by the currents it swims in, the microcosm. The boundaries between the two, microcosm and macrocosm, are permeable and porous. There is an underlying unity, majesty, and coherence to this ineffable Oneness. This is an indelible truth in alchemy, and a rehabilitation venture from many centuries of philosophical scotoma for modern science.

In the wake of the twenty-first century, science attempts to find its bearings on pretty tenuous ground. Our inheritance includes some pretty interesting but spotty ideas about what qualifies as empirically valid and what doesn't. Predicated on the assumption that Nature is internally governed by gravitational, electromagnetic, and strong and weak nuclear forces, which are themselves manifestations of a single force, Occam's razor instructs us to accept as valid comparative theories able to explain existing data sets in simpler and hence more elegant and aesthetically pleasing terms. When conflicted by two competing theories with the same predictive power, always go with the simpler and more parsimonious of the two. This, of course, is an educated guess plucked from the transtheoretical principles pervading science today, but we can never be certain that Nature will subscribe to simplicity just because it's intuitively pleasing and musical to us and extends logically from our operative constructs. The other notable qualifier for scientific merit is Popper's criterion of falsifiability; any hypothesis hoping to be granted airtime in an empirical capacity must frame its predictions in ways that leave them open to unequivocal falsification. This, too, is problematic as it is becoming increasingly clear that phenomena do manifest at subtle nonphysical wavelengths that our sensory organs and perceptual mechanisms are not calibrated to. Their existence is not directly observed nor experienced but deduced through the prudent application of logic. According to Popper's principle, these would be unfalsifiable and unscientific.

Somewhat counterintuitively, this narrower definition of science has also conditioned us to be suspicious and distrustful of our own private thoughts and experience; at our best we're deceptively biased and our capacity to "see" is colored by nonconscious prejudgments, and at our worst we're prone to idiosyncratic perceptual aberrations like hallucinations and delusions, products of defective neural hardwiring or processing, which have no place in scientific progress and discovery. The message communicated is: "You're inconsequential and insignificant in the wider scheme of things; you can't trust your own experience to tell you anything veracious about reality or the truth out there." It can feel like an invalidation of our being. The intransigent commitment to materialism has led us out of a subterranean tunnel and into a Brave New World, where time is an arbitrary epiphenomenon of the Big Bang and matter is the virgin mother and physical cause-and-effect progenitor of human consciousness.

Frankly, a lot of the scientific dogma parroted by experts and exemplary scholars working under tight university budgets is in many ways incoherent and fundamentally untenable. This issue is systemic and deeply ingrained in the developed and capitalist Western world, transcending imposed boundaries on absolute knowledge and consistent across the foundational disciplines of scientific inquiry (i.e., the hard sciences like physics, chemistry, and biology) and the more theoretical and speculative ones (i.e., the soft sciences like psychology, sociology, and anthropology). Let's take a cursory look at some of these. The foundational principles in theoretical physics, like space and time, necessitate a quantum-mechanical description of reality, an essential reconciliation between gravity and quantum mechanics. This conundrum has had theoretical physicists scratching their heads for a long while and then some. There have been no sturdy theoretical bridges built, or even remotely plausible alternatives posed for getting around or over that precipitous impasse.

The biosciences are also fighting demons of their own. To this day, evolutionary biology is unperturbed by its sticky marriage to a multifaceted theory composed of three distinct but interrelated ideas: random mutation, natural selection, and common descent. This, of course, is Darwin's theory of natural selection. There is ample evidence for common descent, but the first two are questionable. The narrative goes something like this: there's a blind, random process operant in Nature able to account for all differences we see between and within species (i.e., why there are differences in color between bottlenose dolphins, and why these exist alongside other creatures like frogs and bats). Random mutations are perpetually cropping up and accumulating in endogenous DNA. Once in a while, a permutation or cumulative permutations may spur changes to structure and body plan that bequeath powerful advantages to one individual of a particular species over others. This could be sharper incisors for an apex predator like a lion to slice up its food, or longer legs for a herbivore of the African savannah like a gazelle to render it nimbler and increase the likelihood of successful evasion from carnivores. Selective fitness augments the likelihood that a creature will survive longer in its niche environment than others of its kind, at least long enough to transmit this valuable mutation onto its progeny. Intergenerational transmission of mutations leads to salient morphological and functional transformations over time, and the rate at which they occur is accelerated under periods of intense environmental stress (i.e., habitat disruption, fragmentation, and loss). Over the span of the earth's 4.5 billion or so-year history, this process has constructed the biochemical mechanisms supporting speciation and biodiversity, everything from the elaborate molecular machinery of cells, to the human genome, to the convoluted, functionally organized, and organizing system of 100 billion neurons in the human brain able to support "consciousness." That's the story the literati pontificate and expect us to swallow whole.

The biochemist Michael Behe gives a very lucid explanation of the egregious limits of natural selection in accounting for some of the wondrous natural phenomena we observe and experience in his groundbreaking book *The Edge of Evolution* (2007). His insights are very refreshing. In a world of disorder, one that moves thermodynamically downward, this thing called a vital life force developed a set of instructions called a genetic code telling a collection of "matter" how to compose and recompose itself within the powerfully disordering tendencies of the inanimate world, and reproduce itself through time in a relatively consistent and unadulterated form. What are the chances that this code, a paragon of coherence and upward ascent to escape erosion, entropy, and decomposition, could have evolved randomly? After an exhaustive, step-by-step, and completely rational micro- and macro-scale investigation, Behe concludes that natural selection via the agency of random mutation is a nuisance tinkerer in stable body plans. It accounts, quite well in fact, for adaptations within niche environments, but the proposed mechanisms cannot account for the creation of the body plans themselves, the origin of species. The accumulation of felicitous mutations, cluster after cluster, needed to produce the coherent features of cells and the vast depth of organic complexity we see on Earth today within a time frame of 4.5 billion years is statistically infeasible unless you're willing to entertain the possibility that they were nonrandom, initiated at propitious moments by an external agency. Behe states that artificial replication of this fine-tuning in Nature—everything from the physical laws and DNA code, to cell types, biological kingdoms, and phyla—would make for an intrepid scientific project. However, the laboratory experiment would require intervention during specific times at the convenience of a creative intelligence, perhaps the mind of an erudite scientist, to "load the dice" and instruct Nature where to go.

Unfortunately, the further we move away from the microscope and direct observation, the murkier things get. The fossil record, scant as it is, has never chalked up anything remotely resembling a transitional form between taxonomic ranks like biological kingdoms and phyla. Nowadays, the consensus among geoscientists and evolutionary biologists is that during the Precambrian period, the earth's first geological eon, a plethora of exotic, soft-bodied multicellular organisms appeared called the Ediacaran fauna. These creatures mysteriously disappeared around 541 million years ago, as if the page containing the instructions to build them had been mercilessly ripped out of the black book of life experiments by a contrite and invisible hand. Immediately following was a paroxysmic eruption of phyla including most animals we recognize today; a frenetic event brimming with novelty and originality called the Cambrian explosion. This is acknowledged as ground zero, the inception of the evolutionary process, which culminated in the anthropic miracle, the *Homo sapiens sapiens*. Creatures appear in the fossil records with fully-formed and sophisticated body plans and no ancestral predecessors to demonstrate an unambiguous line of descent. In subsequent geological eons, the changes occurring within phyla aren't transmutational in nature and conformed strictly to size; animals just got bigger. Iguanas didn't become frogs and crocodiles didn't become hippopotamuses. Increasing complexity over time is a tenuous concept; also, the Cambrian trilobite possessed an extraordinarily complex compound eye with calcite lenses, permitting an acuity of wavelengths and color discrimination within a nearly 360-degree radius of their ecological niche (the ocean) that we could only dream of. Contrary to popular belief, life forms may not have crawled out of the sea and onto the safety of land because things got too noxious and toxic in the aquamarine blue, as Darwin himself believed.

Evidence for Darwinian natural selection is effectively nonexistent in the insect world. During the late Carboniferous and early Permian periods, some 300 million years ago, gargantuan dragonflies with wingspans of up to 28 inches hovered about on Earth like little helicopters. Their life cycle encompassed some very disparate developmental stages: egg, larva, and adult. The carnivorous larva, also known as a nymph, emerged from an egg and spent up to three years underwater, usually at the bottom of a pond, feeding on the larva of mosquitoes or other small organisms, and molting. During its final stage of development, the larva left the aquatic environment; it climbed to the top of a stalk, dried, and then split open at the thorax, permitting a winged "imago" or mature adult to emerge. After the legs hardened, and the wings unfurled and dried out, the dragonfly took to the skies in search of suitable mates, leaving the puffy exoskeleton clinging to the stalk. The metamorphosis from an egg to a sexually mature adult with a set of functional wings is phenomenally phenomenal and nothing short of spectacular. Butterflies and cicadas have very similar developmental stages. The sweeping morphological changes witnessed from one stage of development to another aren't really explicable in Darwinian terms. Larvae confined to a marine environment all their lives might respond to profound environmental stressors (i.e., predation) by developing a form of underwater camouflage—this much is feasible. Conversely, to suggest ancestral larvae would miraculously chalk up something unfathomable and unimaginable to them like flight, and then formulate and execute an action plan that involved steps like leaving their own niche environment, implementing structural innovations to their own bodies, and fine-tuning these ornate innovations to guarantee success in flight does not suspend disbelief.

Having inherited the reductionist and materialist agenda means we have to explain complex biological systems, indeed even the mysteries of our own consciousness (i.e., conscious awareness, intentionality, coherent sense of self) and the opacities of subjective thought, strictly within paradigms like the embodied mind hypothesis. The mind and its illusory sense of self is *embodied* in the sense that it is a direct epiphenomenon of idiosyncratic neurophysiological activation patterns in the brain and ceases to exist when the supporting neural networks perish through irreversible global injury and trauma or natural causes. The mind is an emergent property of the complex activity going on in the human brain, nothing more. The mind = brain equation seems like the obvious deduction for a mechanistic science hoping to explain natural phenomena bottom-up, with corresponding micro- and macro-scale explanations that do not theoretically violate or obviate the established laws. This is all fine and dandy, with one screaming caveat: to imply causality and declare that conscious awareness is "nothing but" a white or pink noise of our cerebral machinery means you also need to give an adequate and plausible account detailing how subjective experience arises from objective events in the brain. You need to explain it.

Referred to as the "hard problem of consciousness" by the philosopher David Chalmers in his book *The Conscious Mind* (1997), the problem has unleashed a Pandora's box for philosophers who try to disentangle conceptual intricacies of what consciousness actually means, and for neuroscientists who have developed a panoply of theoretical and empirical models of specific cerebral mechanisms to explain it. This is no easy feat, and their heterogenous views on the subject have fueled contentious debate and self-righteous polemics in the theoretical neurosciences for decades. How does altering neural activation patterns translate to critical thoughts about the final resting place of Cleopatra VII, or a deceptive machination about how to outmaneuver and outshine worthy competition for a job promotion? How do electrochemical impulses become imagination? There are some ambitious and sensationalist claims made from time to time, but if truth be told, nobody actually knows. Thus far, the hunt for the so-called neural correlates of consciousness (NCCs) using neuroimaging techniques like functional MRI to scour for correlations has come up empty handed. Several brain structures like the mesencephalic reticular formation, the thalamocortical loops, the reticular formation, the intralaminar thalamic nuclei, and the tangential intracortical network of layers I–II have been identified as possible candidates, but how these morphological structures actually "bind" components of mental life together (i.e., intention, awareness, memory, emotion, verbal thinking) to generate an integrated and fluid sense of being is bound to raise many more questions than it can answer.

Our inability to unravel the Gordian knot might have very little to do with our intellectual limitations or imaging equipment and more to do with the kinds of questions we're asking. What we ask is directly and unconsciously informed by our epistemic foundations, our philosophies about the cosmos. Bridging the mental and physical realms, and engaging in painful mental gymnastics to parse out which of the two is fundamental and which is the derivative, is the concern of those with dualist assumptions about the cosmos, a cognitive bias extending all the way back to René Descartes, the father of body-mind dualism. Monism, a position diametrically opposed to dualism, denies any fundamental schism between the elements of mind and matter. A neutral monist like Thomas Nagel, for instance, would conclude there isn't any "hard problem" at all, and rightly or wrongly declare the quest for discovering NCCs to be a futile endeavor. The problem automatically disappears like a desert mirage when we peruse it through a different lens.

Historically, our reasoning is disproportionately skewed toward deductive reasoning. Some of our bigger questions may benefit from a shift of gears into an inductive mode of problem-solving and pattern identification. Nature reveals herself through curious anomalies such as the perceptual excesses, additions to phenomenal experience known as "positive symptoms" by clinicians, induced by diseases of the brain. The author is convinced that some of the greatest insights into the mind–brain dynamic have come from intraoperative clinical observations of patients with intractable epilepsy and tumors. Beginning in 1938 and lasting about 20 years, the brilliant neurosurgeon Wilder Penfield and his associate Herbert Jasper conducted an ambitious surgical procedure on more than 500 patients with temporal lobe epilepsy. It involved the removal of scar tissues that were triggering focal and, in some cases, generalized seizures, with the preferential goal being seizure freedom. The patients weren't under general anesthesia during the procedure, allowing Penfield to attain first-hand experiential reports as he stimulated capacious areas of exposed cortical real estate with an electrode. Having patients give feedback during stimulation allowed him to scrupulously map eloquent cortex [the part of the cortex subserving language] before surgical ablation of the diseased scar tissue. Not only did this minimize damage to collateral healthy tissue and reduce the likelihood of postsurgical complications and cognitive decline (due to unnecessary removal of functional tissue), but it also bequeathed a once-in-a-lifetime opportunity to do something his neurosurgical predecessors hadn't done—that is, map the surface of the human neocortex. This rather invasive technique, called cortical stimulation mapping (CSM), is standard in the contemporary neurosurgical armamentarium for guiding epilepsy and tumor resections. In any case, upon running his electrode over areas of his patients' mesial temporal lobes, they all reported a transient doubling of awareness, with one part of their selves anchored fully to the present and to environmental input from their sensory organs, and the other part immersed in a simulation of veridical reminiscences marching forward at ordinary temporal progression.

In *The Mystery of the Mind* (1975), Penfield relays how, "A young South African patient lying on the operating table exclaimed, when he realized what was happening, that it was astonishing to realize that he was laughing with his cousins on a farm in South Africa, while he was also full conscious of being in the operating room in Montreal."[161] Further, Penfield could prompt an eruption of the exact same reminiscence, over and over, by administering minute voltages to the same location, as if the mesial temporal lobes were an organic VHS tape with fossilized scenes of an individual's life experience. Penfield had stumbled upon dynamite, the physical basis of memory. Under ordinary circumstances, the electrical excitation of neural circuitry necessary for the eruption of a long-term memory replete with olfactory and emotional associations into conscious awareness would be galvanized by intention, by will; Penfield used an electrode in lieu of his patients' intentionality, or when their intentionality was in abeyance. His findings reveal that the predicates for self-as-content, the actual content pouring into the vessel of conscious awareness, are encrypted in neural tissue. But what of self-as-context, conscious awareness itself? Where is that?

Other aberrant perceptual experiences exist that radically violate the said materialistic assumptions, too. Two for which the evidence is robust are out-of-body experiences (OBEs) and autoscopy (AS). The first is a transient phenomenal episode involving disembodiment, the separation of awareness from the physical body itself; the second is characterized by a reduplication of the self or the projection of one's own physical body, a doppelganger, into the space–time continuum. Blanke et al. give the following descriptions: "During an out-of-body experience, the experient sems to be awake and to see his body and the world from a location outside the physical body. A closely related experience is autoscopy, which is characterized by the experience of seeing one's body in extrapersonal space."[161] Repeated stimulation of the superior and middle temporal gyri and the angular gyrus of the nondominant right hemisphere will induce these phenomena.

Let's move on to some experimental research. Owing to the incredible mind-matter experiments of Benjamin Libet, we know that there's salient neural activity in the supplementary motor cortex 350–400 milliseconds (ms), or approximately one third of a second, *before* the intention to move enters conscious awareness. The 150 ms or so separating conscious awareness of the intention to move and the motor act itself is sufficient time for an individual to veto the decision and prevent processes of an unconscious origin from reaching fruition. Since there's no empirical evidence in support of a mandatory role for conscious awareness in the execution of volitional processes or of veto choices being initiated unconsciously, one could interpret the "conscious veto" as an aspect of a higher-order control function in humans not reducible or describable by "objective" physical events. The "conscious veto" may, in fact, be a nonphysical regulator of neuronal activity with top-down or causative control of unconscious brain processes. Together, these clinical and experimental findings undermine the legitimacy of the embodied mind hypothesis and demand philosophical revision.

There's also something else in the cognitive sciences and theoretical neurosciences that doesn't seem to gel very well: computational models for complex biological systems. The late twentieth century ushered in the computational metaphor for the mind–brain dynamic, a milestone in our intellectual history, by drawing a direct comparison with a digital supercomputer. Through the literary device of metaphor, we took our comprehensive knowledge of computers and computational approximations, a human construct and invention, and imposed it onto the most complex piece of organic matter known in an attempt to better understand its internal relations and functions. There was transfer of knowledge from an established vehicle, computer science, to the target, the cognitive sciences. This analogical type of thinking is so deeply embedded in the philosophy of neuroscience that we speak of cerebral relations and functions as if they are actually components of laptop computers: brain modules; encoding, storage, and retrieval of short-term memory; neural networks; coding; processing speed; and representations and maps of objects and faces.

Apt and veracious connections between vehicles and targets lead to enhanced understanding of the new domain, the target, and sometimes quantum leaps in knowledge. Is this the case for the mechanical metaphor of the mind–brain? You could make the metaphor work, but you'd have to ignore much of what makes the brain a functionally organized and reorganizing living system to do so—electrochemical transmission between specialized cells called neurons, bidirectional cross-talk between major body systems like the nervous and endocrine-immune systems, the role of glial cells in the cerebral parenchyma, neurogenesis, neuroplasticity, and literally a horde of other biochemical processes that distinguish the organic from the mechanical. Features with no obvious parallel in information technology have to be explained away somehow, or, in the worst-case scenario, swept under the rug. Damage and disruption to our major organs doesn't always result in deficits or losses. Contingent on their location, structural lesions in the human neocortex may cause hypermnesia (memory enhancement), hypergnosia (exaggerated perception), hypergraphia (excessive writing), euphoria, the doubling of consciousness, disturbances of visual perception like macropsia and micropsia, hallucinatory syndromes, and a myriad of other perceptual excesses. Machines that break down suffer functional losses but never perceptual excesses, or positive symptoms if you prefer the jargon of clinical neurology. The metaphor, while compelling at first glance, falls way short of capturing the quintessence and primary qualities of the mind–brain phenomenon. When subjected to closer scrutiny, the parallel doesn't even appear to be proximal, let alone apt.

I'm sure the ardent technophiles would beg to differ and insist that artificial and synthetic products can be made to mimic the natural—a promethean ambition that extends millennia into the past and was of profound interest to the alchemists of late antiquity. They'll tell you human robots will one day coexist alongside their human architects, equipped with innovative software that allows them to imagine scenarios like you do, feel powerful and overwhelming emotions like you do, and remember an especially traumatic moment in their life like you do. All this will be possible simply by downloading the right software applications into the cluster computers. Unfortunately, or fortunately, a robot can't experience *feeling* or *emotion*, a way of being, in the same way that a human can, disqualifying it from experiential trajectories of development that depend on motivation to gain traction (emotional states fuel sustained action through motivation). Robots don't cycle through stages of development, and they aren't subject to the natural laws in the way that we are—their bodies don't self-organize, reorganize, regenerate, degenerate, and die. In many ways, the computational metaphor has impeded progress in understanding the phenomenology of mind–brain mechanisms.

We're creatures who self-sabotage, apparently. While we're on the subject of obsessive counterfeiting and artificial human life, there's one other proverbial elephant in the room the spotlight has yet to irradiate: the inherent human ambition to usurp the esemplastic powers of the ineffable One and blasphemously manipulate Nature onto flight paths she never intended to pilot through. This is not solely the prerogative of contemporary scientists, for generations of premodern thinkers before them—alchemists, mystical philosophers, and polymaths—got the ball rolling with valid questions about the preparation and grafting of fetal tissue for medical necessity, the prenatal tinkering of neurocognitive and biological traits, and gender selection. The homunculus, a minuscule human grown inside an alembic of a practicing alchemist, was used as a focal springboard from which these other thought-provoking ideas emerged. Pre-Enlightenment, they were nothing but figments of the medieval imagination, but now science has progressed to the point where many of these are not just feasible, they're almost certain. We may, in the not-too-distant future, be selecting physiological characteristics for our progeny like eye color, hair color, and body type, as well as their intellectual level and emotional style (i.e., resilience level, general outlook, social intuition, self-awareness, sensitivity to context, and attention), and whether they'll grow through ectogenesis in an artificial setting somewhere or in a uterine environment. Our technical capacities are becoming increasingly sophisticated: intact DNA within cells grafted from the frozen tissues of dead animals are automatic candidates for cloning using interspecies nuclear transfer, a form of cloning that involves splicing out the DNA to be cloned from the target genome, transplanting it into an enucleated donor cell, and transferring the newly fused product to a host organism. Incorrupt and undegraded DNA salvaged from species recently consigned to the extinct category—for example, the magnificent megafauna of the Pleistocene epoch (c. 2 million to 10,000 years ago)—could also be cloned. Mammoths, elephant birds, and saber-toothed cats, or some genetic imitation of them, could be the superlative attraction at zoos and theme parks at the turn of the twenty-second century.

The only things separating us from the transitional time-traveling reality to a Michael Crichton-like sci-fi novel about necrofauna are the higher valuations and judgments, ethical principles, and ethical standards guiding our choices. Should the boundaries imposed on us by Nature, these judgment-independent conditions, be crossed? If so, under what circumstances are boundary transgressions justifiable and morally defensible, and under what circumstances are they not? Who gets to decide? As a youngster, I was deeply enthralled by *The Mysterious Cities of Gold*, a French-Japanese animated production for children, which first aired in Australia in the early to mid-1980s. The series was a unique synthesis of adventure, sci-fi, mythology, and sixteenth-century history, and appealed to a child's curiosity and sense of wonder about the universe. Late in the narrative, the three child protagonists—Esteban, Zia, and Tao—stumble upon a dwindling population of extraterrestrial, lithe-bodied creatures called Olmecs who have retreated into the subterranean and established their base there. In due course, one learns that their king, the nefarious and wily Master Menator, has vitrified an older, possibly deceased generation of Olmecs and stored them in glass sarcophagi until he can extract living cells from young children and transplant them back into the "sleeping bodies" to rejuvenate them. *The Mysterious*

Cities of Gold may have first aired back in the 1980s, but the sci-fi component eerily foreshadowed discourse in twenty-first-century science and technology around the resurrection of the deceased and possibly even life eternal.

Some might call cryonics the epitome of mortal hubris and conceit; others might call it an absolute zenith of human brilliance, which calls for cautious optimism. It's all a matter of perspective or ethics. Several organizations like the Cryonics Institute in Michigan and the Alcor Life Extension Foundation in Arizona use a preservation technique called vitrification to suspend natural processes of decay in pre-committed individuals who have been legally pronounced dead. These bodies, now in a state of suspended animation, are interred upside down in metal vats of liquid nitrogen, and barring any mishaps or apocalypses, they will remain suspended there until our biotechnologies have developed to the point where revivification is inevitable. That's the plan. The current preservation technique is fairly straightforward. First, representatives from the Cryonics facility inject the "patient" with an anticoagulant like Heparin to keep the blood from clotting. Once the "patient" is back at the storage facility, a team of specialists replace the blood with a cryoprotectant like glycerol, a necessary maneuver that impedes ice crystals from forming inside the body and destroying cell membranes. The institutions involved insist on calling these cryogenically frozen bodies "cryopreserved patients" to reflect the candid belief that death is a temporary and clinically reversible condition; the individual is not "deceased" in the same way that somebody who was cremated or buried would be.

The million-dollar question begging to be answered is how a complex biological system comprising discrete but interconnected systems of specialized cells and organs might respond to being injected with cryoprotectant, desiccated, frozen, and thawed. What happens to human DNA and functional proteins inside cells once they've been inundated with cryoprotectant? Nobody knows, or at least nobody will know until the time comes to thaw out these cryopreserved tissues. The assumptions underlying the entire cryoprotecting process might be flawed and scientifically specious, and if this is so, these patients are woefully condemned to eternal sleep and will never awaken from their century-long or millennia-long slumber. At present, our biotechnologies might not be able to preserve tissues in a form as to render them salvageable for future reanimation. Alternatively, the cryoprotected patient may indeed be a candidate for revival, but only after further enhancements and refinements to the cryoprotecting process have been made that exponentially reduce the amount of stress imposed on the underlying cellular mechanisms. There may be a small window of opportunity for future generations of cryopreserved patients to return to life, but not for the current one. Who knows? It's all speculation for the time being.

The seventeenth-century divorces of chemistry from alchemy, astronomy from astrology, and of atomic-based medicine from the more primordial esoteric systems of magical healing were good in the sense that they allowed our scientific tools of quantitative analysis to develop uncontaminated by the intransigence of religious dogma. An impartial science of confluent determinism, atomism, materialism, and positivism functioned well for a while because many of the faithful proselytes working under its aegis remained loyal to a set of clearly defined spiritual values. This is certainly true of Newton and Boyle, who were both practicing alchemists. However, for generations of scientists who came afterward, the attenuated influence of a spiritual lineage that emphasized the qualitative dimensions of personal responsibility and humility created ideational pockets for personal fantasies of posterity and glory to manifest, perhaps even promethean ambitions to refine our own genetic dowry and become superhuman. The nineteenth-century German philosopher Friedrich Nietzsche (1844–1900) captured the crux of this debased and valueless secularization best with the phrase: "God is dead."[162]

This dearth of personal responsibility, humility, and ethical sensibility is woefully reflected in a third-century Gnostic codex containing a beautiful myth called "On the Origin of the World." In what can only be described as an ingenious reinterpretation of the biblical narrative, the Gnostic myth describes the trials and tribulations of a spiritual aeon named Pistis-Sophia (Faith-Wisdom). She gives birth to a hideous demon named Yaldabaoth, a corrupt and conceited "Son of Chaos" whom the Gnostic sect of Christians equated with the biblical creator Yahweh. Yaldabaoth is the epitome of narcissism; he is also riddled by bizarre delusions of grandeur and cosmic supremacy. Completely unperturbed by his mother's rejection and his steadfast expulsion from the Pleroma, Yaldabaoth proceeds to exercise his own demiurgic powers in the Garden of Eden by projecting himself over the primordial waters and bringing forth several dimensions. Afterward, Pistis-Sophia, intent on shattering his illusions of absolute power, projects herself from the Pleroma to utter a bloodcurdling prophecy: "There is an immortal man of light (Jesus) who has been in existence before you and who will appear among your modelled forms; he will trample you to scorn just as a potter's clay is pounded. And you will descend to your mother, the abyss, along with those that belong to you."[163]

Yaldabaoth's undaunted response to his mother's warning is to procure the assistance of 360 demon minions in molding a clay body in the guise of the luminous spirit of Christ. Yaldabaoth has never actually seen the Christ, so he uses his own vivid imagination in constructing the clay image, hoping the act itself will attract spiritual force from the Pleroma and propitiate the displeasure of the spiritual aeons above. The plot gets thicker still. Pistis-Sophia enters the Garden of Eden as Pistis-Zoe (Faith-Life) and projects an ounce of ethereal light from her mercurial body onto the ground. She then fashions a woman's body and infuses it with a spirit, calling it Eve of Zoe or Eve of Life. Meanwhile, Yaldabaoth and his minions come to realize the futility of their own enterprise and desert their illegitimately created being in Adam, leaving him to the ravages of wind and water; if they can't create humans, they will bide their time corrupting and leading them astray. Eve of Zoe finally stumbles upon Adam's lifeless carcass while meandering around the Garden of Eden. Overwhelmed by a deep sense of grief and pity for her male counterpart, she breathes the divine spark into his mouth with the help of her mother, Pistis-Sophia. "Adam!" she screams. "Become alive! Rise upon the earth!" The divine element moves within Adam like a slithering serpent and imbues him with life. She then leaves a double of her likeness with Adam and infuses herself into the Tree of Knowledge of Good and Evil, the Tree of Gnosis, which stands at the very center of Eden. From here, she can counteract Yaldabaoth's malevolent influence by tempting humans to taste of the savory fruit hanging from the tree's plentiful breaches. Contained within the fruit is the magical seed that dispels ignorance and awakens gnosis, or spiritual knowledge, within the human receptacle.

There are several parallels that might be drawn between components of this myth and orthodox science. The demon Yaldabaoth can be construed as a stand-in for a modern scientific philosopher who is impelled by myopic scientism, a secular religion that has become the same tyrannical oppressor of countercultures and counter-movements it was trying to dismantle in bygone centuries. The paucity of humility and aura of undisputed authority surrounding modern science is reflected in the demands it places on its practitioners for absolute submission to dogmatic assumptions about reality, and in the premature judgment and condescension of research that either doesn't conform to standard quantitative methodologies or dares to examine nonphysical phenomena with candid curiosity and receptivity. The obstinate fixation with Darwinian natural selection and the embodied mind hypothesis, mechanistic theories that cannot accommodate all of the accumulating evidence and in many instances appear to violate rational analysis and logic, has definitely encumbered our progress; a revision, if not a complete overhaul, of our dominant ontological-epistemological paradigms is long overdue. The arrogance and pride of Yaldabaoth is echoed deeply in the modern advances of nanotechnology and cloning, especially where it concerns artificial simulation of human intelligence (artificial intelligence), genetic refinement through eugenics, resurrecting the Pleistocene epoch necrofauna, and the possible reversal of clinical death in cryopreserved individuals seduced by the mirage of a second life or of life everlasting. Are our atheistic scientists the modern Yaldabaoths, reaching sacrilegiously for the stars when our "cognitive closure" forbids direct access to the very mysteries of the cosmos we yearn to understand and emulate?

There's something, a vital life force or essence, that enlivens us but doesn't exhibit any particular feature by which it can be defined. It betrays itself by way of heat and movement, and grants us a coherent sense of self and immutability through time. It transposes electrochemical impulses into imagination, into perception, and into feelings. Consider for a moment Benjamin Libet's conscious nonphysical veto function with no identifiable neural correlates able to inhibit unconscious brain processes from reaching fruition. Or Wilder Penfield's neurosurgical exploration of self-in-context, the unified sense of conscious awareness we possess that is not explicable in terms of neural predicates. Could these phenomena, inexplicable to materialistic science, infer the existence of a discarnate nonphysical entity impinging and cleaving through matter? Could the analogy of electricity coursing through insulated wires or cables be a veracious reflection of the nature of the relationship between this entity and denser forms of matter? Perhaps the wires, or brain, can continue receiving, containing, and expressing electricity or awareness until the former is severed, damaged, annihilated, or simply too weak to encompass it. When this comes to pass, transmission of conscious awareness within the space–time continuum is lost.

In human embryo formation, biologists have observed that the 49-day interval is marked by two fascinating events: the appearance of the pineal gland and differentiation into gender, male or female. Tibetan Buddhists claim that the 49-day interval marks the re-embodiment of a "soul" between lives. The pineal gland, the only unpaired morphological structure in the brain, could serve as a viable entry point; it actually forms in the roof of the fetal mouth out of specialized tissue before migrating to the center of the brain, behind the third ventricle. If this is true, then explicit references in biblical and Gnostic texts to divinities breathing the life principle into a clay body through the nostrils and mouth are apropos, especially if the vital life force enters through an organ that springs forth from the fetal mouth. Here is yet another spanner thrown into the works.

Just like Yaldabaoth who has never seen the luminous spirit of Christ, we too have no direct access to—and hence a very superficial understanding of—this vital life force. Just as Yaldabaoth deserted his illegitimately created being in Adam, we too might awake to the unworkability and futility of our prodigious ambitions one day soon and end up deserting them to the ravages of the natural elements. Even if we do advance and refine our technological potential to the point where many of these anthropocentric experimentations are viable beyond an iota of doubt, will "Pistis-Sophia" permit them to thrive alongside their phenomenally phenomenal prototypes for more than a fleeting moment? The first successful de-extinction candidate was a clone of Celia, the last bucardo to have lived on Earth; it survived for a meager seven minutes before capitulating to a lung defect pervasive in cloned animals. The omniscient author of *The Birth Mark*, Nathaniel Hawthorne, may have said it best with his poignant decree that in truth, Pistis-Sophia "permits us, indeed, to mar, but seldom to mend, and, like a jealous patentee, on no account to make."[164]

Endnotes

160   Wilder Penfield, *The Mystery of the Mind* (Princeton, New Jersey: Princeton University Press, 1975), p. 55.

161   Olaf Blanke, Theodor Landis, Laurent Spinelli, and Margitta Seeck, 'Out-of-body Experience and Autoscopy of Neurological Origin,' *Brain* 127, no. 2 (2004), p. 243.

162   Michael W. McConnell, 'God is Dead and We Have Killed Him: Freedom of Religion in the Post-Modern Age,' *BYu L. Rev* (1993), p. 163.

163   Scott A. Leonard and Michael McClure, *Myth and Knowing: An Introduction to World Mythology* (New York, NY: McGraw-Hill Humanities/Social Sciences/Languages, 2004), p. 171.

164   William R. Newman, *Promethean Ambitions: Alchemy and the Quest to Perfect Nature* (Chicago, IL: University of Chicago Press, 2005), p. 4.

Appendices

Appendix A

The Four Elements

When it comes to the Western esoteric traditions, the four elements are not to be confused with the four corporeal manifestations of the same name. They are merely initial differentiations of the primal virginal substance of all creation, the *prima materia.* All elements exhibit two of four secondary properties: hot, cold, dry, and moist. This theory is a direct import from the Aristotelian nature philosophy, though it most probably took shape under the auspices of the Ionic pre-Socratic philosophers.

Water

The Aristotelian element of water is cold and moist, and its physical manifestation as a composition of two atoms of hydrogen and one of oxygen (H_2O) reflects a quintessential nature—volatility, passivity, amorphousness, colorlessness, and receptivity. Water is characterized by the condition of heaviness, but also of expansion. On a scale that orders the four elements on the basis of their pureness and level of refinement, water would come third, after both fire and air. Unlike fire and air, which tend to rise, water is rather dense and possesses a downward-moving tendency. Nevertheless, it's not as heavy, invariable, and sluggish as the element of earth. In alchemical manuscripts, it is always symbolized by an overturned triangle.

Fire

Fire is the most revered of the four Aristotelian elements. In ancient times, it was justifiably connected to the sun and celebrated as the origin of life and creation. In the temples of many solar deities, fire would burn unremittingly in the innermost sanctuary, or the holy of holies, where it symbolized the undefiled first matter, the Empyrean of God. Heraclitus of Ephesus (535–475 BCE), a contemporary of Anaximenes of Miletus (584–28 BCE), was the first philosopher to identify fire as the most important of the differentiating elements of the original chaos, the *prima materia*, as well as the foremost quality defining it. He posited that fire was the active and only mover behind elemental rotation; that is, the transformation of the four elements into one another—earth into water, water into air, air into fire, and fire into earth again. By this virtue, it made perfect sense that the underlying cause of all phenomena and the natural vicissitudes galvanized by chemical processes including calcination, coagulation, distillation, sublimation, and dissolution could be attributed to the subtle action of fire.

This pre-Socratic notion infiltrated the classical world entirely, for Hellenistic philosophers like Pythagoras, Empedocles, Plato and Aristotle all agreed that the primordial substance, or the receptacle of matter, was probably an intangible fire of sorts. It was theorized to be triune or threefold in nature, possessing a celestial, a subterranean, and a terrestrial correspondent. Fire exhibits the fundamental properties of hot and dry, and its physical manifestation as the oxidization of a particular substance through combustion epitomizes its quintessential nature—boundlessness, inscrutability, and the propensity to purify and generate; the power to rise and illuminate; and inexorable activity and elasticity. In contradistinction to water, which was anthropomorphically imbued with a feminine spirit and connected with the color green, fire was masculine and associated with red. If the elements were ordered according to a continuum for all possible movements, fire would come first. Unlike the other three differentiations of the *prima materia,* which exhibit multiple tendencies, fire remains faithful to just one: the condition of rising. In alchemical treatises, it is always symbolized by a triangle.

Earth

The invention of the four elements of fire, water, earth, and air is more often than not attributed to the speculative thought of Empedocles of Acragas (492–432 BCE). The first person to identify earth as a primary element was the sixth-century thinker Pherecydes of Syros. Both he and Aristotle placed the element at the heart-center of the heavenly rotations, identifying it as the fecund from which the other three—fire, water, and air— miraculously sprung forth. In addition, it was also believed that earth would confer form to all things before they manifested on the physical plane. Aristotle reasoned that the ethereal version of earth must be like its material counterpart, characterized by the conditions of heaviness, solidity, and geometrical, three-dimensional proportions. Hence, it was to be expected that earth-laden principles and substances would be characterized by a gravitational tendency to drop toward the navel of the cosmos. Together with water, earth was considered wholly feminine in nature with a receptive and passive personality. Its two fundamental properties were cold and dry, putting it last on a provisional ladder that orders the four elements according to their finite qualities. Alchemical earth is esoterically and symbolically connected to potentiality, the color white, the concept of generation and life, the cardinal direction of south, and the natural phenomena of heat and electricity. In alchemical theory, earth is equated with the principle of "salt" and symbolized by an overturned triangle bisected by a horizontal line.

Air

For centuries, the ancients believed that water could be transmuted into air through fire. Air is hot and wet, connecting it to both fire and water on the wheel of elemental rotation. Anaximenes of Miletus (mid-sixth-century BCE) was the first pre-Socratic philosopher to attach a special significance to air, identifying it as the base element of which the primary chaos and Empyrean of God was composed. This conviction diffused to the chemico-operative alchemical tradition in late antiquity, and was subsequently immortalized in an eighth-century Arabic text by Jabir ibn Hayyan (*The Emerald Tablet*), which says of the Philosopher's Stone: "The wind carried it in its womb." Air was so important in the esoteric mind that it was even imagined to be the womb that brought forth the elusive and transcendent Stone itself.

Pre-Socratic philosophers, including the likes of Anaximenes of Miletus and Diogenes Apolloniates (c. fifth century BCE), were initially convinced that air, immutable but palpable, was a thread holding the natural world together. Air is an active, masculine element, and its two fundamental properties are hot and moist, or wet. Just like its material counterpart, the element is inextricably associated with volatility, expansion, and becoming, but also with the condition of death and sleep, the cardinal direction of north, the color black, and the quality of falsehood. If the four elements were ordered according to the continuum of all possible movements, air would come second, after fire. Its primary tendency is to rise and extend. In chemico-operative and spiritual-philosophical alchemy, air is symbolized by a triangle bisected by a horizontal line.

The Seven Planets and Metals

The Sun or Gold

According to an old legend, the mysterious author of the *Splendor Solis* didactic treatise, Solomon Trismosin, imparted the secrets of the Philosopher's Stone to Paracelsus of Hohenheim (CE 1493–1541), enabling him to pioneer the field of iatrochemistry. Comprising seven individual tracts that are replete with 20 or so illustrations and accompanied by lengthy quotations, the text informs that "all corporeal things originate in and are maintained and exist of the earth according to time and influence of the stars and planets as Sun, Moon, and the others. These, together with the four qualities of the elements which are without intermission, moving and working therein, thereby creating every growing and procreating thing in its individual form, sex and substance, as first metals originate in the earth of a special and peculiar matter produced by the four properties of the four elements which generate in their mixture the metallic force under the influence of their respective planets."[165]

This is no doubt a condensed summa of the Neo-Platonic cosmos, where Mother Nature is supposed to be a living organism in her own right, and all her creations are not only interdependent and interconnected with one another but also infused with a kind of love or mutual attraction called "sympathy." The *prima materia* is implicitly referenced, from whence the Empyrean of God, the Sphere of the Fixed Stars, the *primum mobile* or rotating heavens, the ether and seven planets, the moon, and the earth itself, composed of the first four differentiated elements—fire, water, air, and earth—all arise. Furthermore, the unique combinations formed by the four Aristotelian elements produce the plant, animal, and mineral kingdoms. While the seven planets are a powerful embodiment of archetypal powers delimited by the Sphere of the Fixed Stars and the Zodiac, the seven metals themselves express unique permutations between the four elements under the auspices of the seven planetary powers. If all that is below is a pale reflection of everything above, as the *Tabula Smaragdina* [Emerald Tablet] would have us believe, then the realms of sky and earth are inextricably linked. Astrology was primarily concerned with the manner in which the heavenly rotations governed the human body and controlled human destiny; alchemy, on the other hand, was deeply concerned with the exploration of metals and elements.

If the Divine Spirit (or pure undefiled consciousness) were personified as a gargantuan ladder stretching from the heavens to the earth, the highest echelon would be hot and dry in nature, masculine in sex, and full of action potential. Alternatively, the lowest echelon would be cold and wet in nature, feminine in sex, and wholly receptive or passive. For the act of becoming or being to register in conscious awareness, there must be a polarization of the Divine Spirit into active and passive poles. There's no valuation of superiority or inferiority placed on any of the archetypes or echelons; they all occupy an undifferentiated space on the continuum with the active and passive forces on opposite sides. The qualities and characteristics of the Divine Spirit are expressed actively through the planetary powers and passively through the earthly metals.

The highest echelon is incarnated light, emanating intellect, and pure essence. Its nature is inflexible, eternal, and immutable. This is why the sun (active manifestation) and the metal gold (passive manifestation) are considered its corporeal counterparts. Both the sun and gold are radiant and magnificent, seemingly indestructible and impregnable, and free of blemishes and tarnish. The qualitative connection between the two remains unacknowledged by orthodox science today. Alchemists believed that everything created under the stars was striving for transmutation or transfiguration into the blessed golden state. According to the abovementioned esoteric correspondences, the sun and gold are physical incarnations of this highest cosmic principle, with the other six generative powers and their constituent planet–metal relationships reflecting substandard echelons of the Divine Spirit. From an esoteric perspective, any echelon other than gold might be described as premature, flawed, or debased.

All symbols for the seven generative powers of the spiritual totem pole are wrought from three rudimentary shapes: the circle, the semicircle, and the cross. The circle, identified by most observers as a symbol of immaculate proportions, is commensurate with the uppermost echelon of the Empyrean of God, pure consciousness itself. It is synonymous with both the sun and gold. The esoteric sun–gold symbol is completed by a single dot midpoint of the circle. In alchemical manuscripts, the sun or gold can also be represented by the figure of a king.

There is archeological evidence to suggest that the metal gold was known from about the fourth millennium BCE onward. In Egypt and Nubia, where gold was "more plentiful than dirt," ancient temple inscriptions have been found detailing the fire-setting and quartz-crushing methods that were used by miners to extract gold from the subterranean. Its therapeutic properties have been known to the human race since time immemorial. Gold gained popularity during the Middle Ages, when the Swiss physician, alchemist, mystic, and philosopher Paracelsus (1493–1541) began administering it to his patients for the alleged purpose of cleansing their circulatory systems of pathogens and impurities. Afterward, the first pharmaceutical institutions of Renaissance Europe created a gold tincture called *Crocus solis* by immersing gold in a solution of nitro-hydrochloric acid. Subsequently, the precipitate was subjected to repeated cycles of distillation with water and mixed with a small amount of potassium as it condensed into a fine powder. Many Renaissance alchemists held the conviction that by preparing gold tinctures or solutions, they were creating the elusive Elixir of Life.

The Moon or Silver

At the opposite end of the wholly active, masculine echelon of the Divine Spirit lies the passive, feminine pole. As we learned in the preceding section, the sun expresses the central qualities of the active, masculine pole; it is a material, superior manifestation of incarnated light, emanating intellect, and pure essence. At the other end, the feminine aesthetic principle exists in a perpetual state of mutability. It is formless yet forming, colorless yet colorful. This principle is a guise of the *prima materia*, the jelloid primordial substance of which the entire cosmos has been hewn. This substance's primary characteristic is to reflect, to imprint, or to be imbued by the natural forms imposed upon it. For that reason, its corporeal counterparts are the moon (active manifestation) and the metal silver (passive manifestation). Both the moon and silver are delicate, malleable, and receptive bodies, passively reflecting and forming gray, black-and-white, or colorless images from external sources of light.

All symbols for the seven generative powers that comprise the wholly Divine Spirit, the multidimensional echelon extending from the Empyrean of God, the highest heaven, all the way down to the crude dimension of earth and dross matter, are fashioned from three rudimentary shapes: the circle, the semicircle, and the cross. The second of these, the semicircle, is identified with the feminine aesthetic principle or pure receptivity itself. It serves as a potent symbol for the physical manifestations that have been linked to the wholly passive, feminine principle, explicitly the lunar satellite and the metal silver. In alchemical manuscripts, the passive lunar–silver principle is sometimes exemplified by the figure of a queen.

As a metal, silver has been mined for domestic use since about the fourth millennium BCE. It appears to have been popular with the cultures of classical Greece and Imperial Rome, who appreciated its inherent properties and versatile applications. Silver was used in the minting of the first coins, and also as an agent for purifying water and preventing contagion. The Arab alchemist Jabir ibn Hayyan revolutionized its usage during the eighth century CE by generating its first metal salt, silver nitrate. Moreover, silver's association with the moon and with the sublunary realm of generation lay at the heart of the earliest homeopathic remedies; if the lunar sphere presided over the healing enterprise, then it was only natural that silver, its earthly counterpart, could be concentrated into a solution and administered to cure ailments of the brain (i.e., epilepsy and vertigo), and to accelerate the remediation of somatic wounds and burns. Working under such premises, many Middle Age and Renaissance alchemists mixed silver nitrate with opium, musk, and camphor in their home laboratories to create a therapeutic tincture known as *pilulae lunaris*, or Pills of the Moon, which they prescribed to patients suffering from the abovementioned ailments.

Venus or Copper

While the two great lights circumnavigating the heavens, the sun and moon, and their associated metals are disparate and at opposite extremes of the Divine Spirit, the other planet–metal pairs, traditionally five in number, are variations of incarnated light (the sun or gold) or reflective potential (the moon or silver). Unlike the solar–gold and lunar–silver pairings, these other formative expressions are restricted in scope and impure by comparison. In the case of the Venusian archetypal force, expressed actively by the planet Venus and passively by the metal copper, the active solar force predominates to such a degree that it overrides all other elemental influences.

According to the fifteenth-century alchemist Basilius Valentinus (Basil Valentine), the Venusian influence is infused by copious amounts of unfixed solar energy, quite like a bromeliad yellowed by overexposure to sunlight. This quality is immortalized in the symbol for the formative force that is fashioned from two other primary shapes: the circle and the cross. The first denotes solar power, and the second denotes the elemental differentiation of the *prima materia* into philosophical fire, water, earth, and air. The arrangement of the circle above the cross indicates that the primary elemental differentiations have not dissolved back into the *prima materia*.

Knowledge of the metal itself goes back to c. 10,000 BCE. Gold and lead, it seems, are the only two metals that were identified and adapted for practical use before copper. Its natural inclination to bind to other metals in the subterranean was not overlooked either. Soon after its discovery, artisans and craftsmen began to alloy it with tin and zinc to produce bronze and brass, respectively. In Egypt, use of copper was quite miscellaneous. It was fashioned into mirrors, statues, vases, pendants, weapons, and other ornaments. The Egyptians also employed it for therapeutic purposes like the purification of water, and the sterilization of wounds and burns. Verdigris, the green oxy-acetate of copper, was used to soothe afflictions of the eyes, and also as a pigment in intricate temple and domestic artwork. In the case of the ancient Greeks, we know that it was used widely for military purposes; Homer reveals in the *Iliad* that Achilles's shield was an amalgamation of silver, gold, copper, and tin. Between the sixth and third centuries BCE, the Romans initiated a trend in which copper was rendered into local currency. Both Julius Caesar and Octavian Augustus had their own coins minted in brass, or an amalgamation of copper, lead, and tin. Under Imperial Rome, the metal was known by the Latin *aes Cyprium*, a term which denotes its autochthonous state as an alloy and its predominance on Cyprus, the Mediterranean isle on which the goddess of love and beauty, Aphrodite, was born.

Mercury or Quicksilver

In contradistinction to the other four planet–metal pairs that symbolize unique ruptures in the *prima materia* or first substance, the volatile and elusive mercurial power is commensurate with the entire process of becoming—in other words, the coming-to-be of form, of self-knowledge, intellect, and incarnated light. Just look at corporeal mercury, a mysterious metal whose nature defies all logic. It is highly volatile, mutable, and protean in character, encompassing the powers of amalgamation, separation, and purification. Baffling to most is how mercury retains its autochthonous state of repose as a liquid without losing density. This is truly a mystery! Together with the element of water, the metal in question can exist in three distinct states: as a liquid at room temperature, as a solid when the temperature drops below 38.8 degrees Celsius, and as a gas when it exceeds 356.73 degrees Celsius. These unique chemical properties—formless but forming, intangible but palpable— inspired alchemists and other esoteric thinkers to perceive it as an androgynous autogenerator of gold and all other metals. They simply remained faithful to the intuit afforded by the laws of analogy; if corporeal mercury could liberate pure gold from its quartz matrix, then shouldn't ethereal mercury be able to extract the vital breath or sulphurous fire of spiritual gold from the amorphous sea of life, also? For many alchemists, this conjecture was an indelible truth. In fact, it was the *primum agens* of their lifelong plight.

Only in the mercurial force do we find the solar and lunar principles along with the four elements reconciled. The esoteric symbol for this quality, comprising geometrical shapes like the circle, the semicircle, and the cross, denotes its inherent nature. The volatile condition of the mercurial spirit is implicit in the arrangement of the parts themselves. The four Aristotelian elements of fire, air, water, and earth are grounded, crystallized into two elemental couplets by the dry, masculine, and seedy solar force fixed directly above it. Mounted atop these, the solar principle symbolizes its potential form in the manner that a eucalyptus seed contains within itself the Platonic Form or Fixed Idea of a grown eucalypt, as well as the dynamic growth process. In mercury, we can see that the circle is capped by a semicircle, meaning that the solar principle or active force is predominated or confined by the lunar principle or passive force. As a whole, the symbol transcribes an unfixed state of being in which all forms of matter that have been, are coming-to-be, or will be in the future coexist as germs in the *prima materia*. Philosophical mercury is in many respects the menstruum or womb bequeathing expression of the universal forces through their planet–plant–metal relationships. The potential for differentiation into solid matter is there, but as the symbol suggests, the inertia of receptivity has not yet been overcome.

Nowhere has the metal enjoyed more popularity than in China, India, and Tibet. In those parts of the world, cinnabar—

the mercurial ore or sulphide—was usually cooked on an iron saucer to unfetter the quicksilver. Iron was used as a medium given that it was the only metal known that resisted dissolution when exposed to metallic mercury. Once reduced to quicksilver, it was used for therapeutic purposes such as accelerating the healing of wounds and prolonging life indefinitely, or so they thought. This rudimentary process for liberating a volatile substance from fixed substances, otherwise known as distillation, was to become standard practice for Alexandrine alchemists, who carried out their chemical operations in laboratory settings centuries afterward. On another note, the ancients were somewhat mistaken in their beliefs; they were convinced that the red sulphide ore of mercury (cinnabar) and the red mercuric oxide (calx), which was obtained by heating it, were one and the same substance. Hence, many alchemists were able to impress their incredulous audiences with a chemical recipe in which the metal's reactions were shown to be reversible; when subjected to a continual cycle of sublimations, the metal passed through manifold transformations before seemingly reverting to its autochthonous, preheated state as cinnabar.

Recipes pertaining to the preparation of quicksilver extend back to at least the second century CE, though it probably wasn't until the Arab conquests of the seventh century CE that a fully-fledged investigation into the properties of the metal were conducted. Under the auspice of a more progressive, intellectual climate, the prominent Arab alchemist Jabir ibn Hayyan (c. CE 721–815) took chemico-operative and practical alchemy to another level. Besides introducing innovations to existing laboratory apparatus, concocting new acids and tinctures, and elaborating upon theoretical premises, Jabir explicitly described the chemical processes through which cinnabar was reduced to red calx and the manner in which mercury perchloride was prepared through sublimation. Moreover, he shifted the focus away from the four Aristotelian elements by introducing the Sulphur-Mercury theory into existing alchemical dogma. In his version of creation, the four ethereal elements of the primordial rupture segregate into two philosophical principles: Mercury and Sulphur. Consequently, polarization of the two principles galvanizes unique configurations between the four elements, which in turn gives rise to all earthly metals under the omnipotent influence of the seven planetary powers. Eight centuries after the life and times of Jabir, the Swiss physician and alchemist Paracelsus of Hohenheim (1493–1541) added a third principle to the Sulphur-Mercury theory: Salt. Paracelsus also discovered a practical application for mercury salts; he administered minute quantities to his patients' wounds and burns to disinfect them and accelerate the healing process.

Mars or Iron

Comprising active planetary and passive metallic energies, the Mars–iron axis stands equidistant from the purely masculine aesthetic power, symbolized by the sun–gold axis, and the purely feminine aesthetic power, symbolized by the moon-silver axis. Quite like the Venus–copper force, Mars–iron is a blunted expression and impure reflection of incarnated light. For the Venusian–copper force, the intangible spirit coagulates the Aristotelian elements under the guardianship of the exalted solar power. The symbol's configuration is an embodiment of the entire process. In the case of Mars–iron, the opposite certainly holds true. The state is characterized by the temporary entombment of spirit in the nascent or inchoate elemental differentiation of the *prima materia* into fire, air, water, and earth. Mars's traditional symbol, the circle surmounted by the cross, expresses this chaotic position. In the alchemical opus, the Mars–iron force is ascribed rulership over *cauda pavonis* or Peacock's Tail, an intermediate stage in the making of the Stone, whereby putrefied matter in the alchemist's alembic generates iridescent blues and greens. Many perceive this stage as a rebirth, reincarnation, reawakening, or reinvigoration of matter.

The metal iron came to prominence during the Iron Age, when it was weaponized for the arrogant exploitation and destruction of Nature. Its properties have been known to humankind since at least the mid-second millennium BCE. This is corroborated by ancient Egyptian bas reliefs portraying the metallurgical procedure of iron smelting, which dates to approximately c. 1500 BCE. In ancient Egypt and the Middle East, iron was regarded with awe and reverence, and held a much more dignified position in metallic hierarchy than gold because the first samples identified were meteoritic or celestial in origin. Indeed, iron was divine in origin—the metal of the gods. An offering of iron was standard etiquette and practice for rulers wishing to quell political unrest and restore peace with their powerful neighbors. The war-loving Hittites, for example, sent Ramses the Great (Ramses II) an iron sword and a lump of meteoritic iron for this exact reason. These profound sentiments extended to classical Hellenistic consciousness, for Homer reveals that the meteoritic iron was a prize awarded to first-place winners of the Olympic Games. During the classical period of Greece proper, the use of iron was extended to medicine. In the *Iliad*, for instance, Homer relates how rust of iron obtained from a spear that injured Telephus was applied to his wound to facilitate the healing process. In another classical myth, the legendary seer and physician Malampus nursed the anemic Iphiclus, the King of Phylacea, back to health by encouraging the daily ingestion of a tincture combining wine with the rust of iron.

There was copious use of the metal during the Middle Ages and early modern period to construct cutting-edge weaponry. Deeply impressed by the qualitative connection between the celestial metal and the astringent, restless nature of blood, sixteenth- and seventeenth-century physicians prepared tinctures of iron as remedial therapies for debilitating physical conditions. Three, in particular, gained widespread exposure: a black oxide known as *Aethiops martial*, a sesquioxide of iron called *Crocus martis*, and an ammoniated chloride named *flores martias*. All three allude to Mars, the Graeco-Roman god of war, and by default the fiery qualities of strength, urgency, and activity.

Jupiter or Tin

The cosmic force expressed actively by the planet Jupiter and passively by the metal tin represents a rupture much closer to the lunar–silver principle than to the solar–gold principle. We know this by looking at where the individual geometric figures on the esoteric symbol stand in relation to one another; the lunar crescent sprouts from the level arm of the cross, meaning that the Jovian–tin force sits between the Saturnine–lead and lunar–silver axes. The Jovian–tin formative power retains the original paradisal state of receptivity and purity. Under the Jovian–tin axis, the soul awakens and incarnates, acquires sentience, and begins to emerge from the chaos and density of dross matter. The upward movement that breaks the spell of inertia, an autochthonous condition of the *prima materia*, is generated by the inspirited powers of the unconscious mind and raises the soul-spirit from the abyssal depths wholly regenerated and transformed. Alchemically speaking, this stage can be equated to the chemical processes of distillation or sublimation, which seek to extract the volatile spirit from its base matter by subjecting the entire body to sweltering temperatures and vaporizing it into a condensate. As a rule of thumb, subjecting the condensate to further cycles of distillation procures a more nuanced level of refinement.

The properties and uses of Jove's metal have been known since about the third millennium BCE. The ancient Persians amalgamated it into their jewelry, while the ancient Egyptians made ample use of its salts as a mordant for dyeing materials. Its chief advocates in the ancient world, the Phoenicians, imported tin from the Near East and Cornwall in South West England; the latter is a place revered and renowned for its tin deposits since the dawn of the Bronze Age. Homer himself, no doubt cognizant of the qualitative connection between the planetary god Jupiter and the metal tin, alludes to it in his epic poem *The Odyssey* when the protagonist, Odysseus, disembarks upon the enchanting shores of Cornwall. Interestingly, the etymology of our contemporary term for the metal can be traced back to the eighth century BCE, a date also agreed upon by the academic consensus to encompass the life and times of this great epic poet.

Living in an area of modern-day Tuscany at this time were the Etruscans, a panentheistic and polytheistic race from either the indigenous Villanova culture or the Near East; they called the Jovian emanation *Tins* and *Tinia*. The linguistic jargon for tin was probably inherited by the Anglo-Saxons after initiating trade and cultivating ties with the aforementioned cultures.

Many centuries afterward, the Romans ascribed to tin the name *plumbum album* [Latin for "white lead"] and proceeded to mastermind an innovation of the highest caliber. The metal was first mined and separated from its ore through searing fires harnessed via metallurgical purification. Following the extraction phase, metallurgists would render the metal into tinfoil and subsequently pass it on to glassmakers whose dexterous hands would work it into the face of mirrors. After the Romans, practical use of the metal gradually dwindled and died out. It wasn't until about the late Middle Ages that tin experienced a resurgence. Of interest to alchemists like Paracelsus and Johannes Agricola, for instance, was the alchemical preparation of the metal's salts; a procedure that involved drenching calcined salts in vinegar and then heating the entire admixture in an athanor (alchemical furnace) to produce salt crystals. Igniting these with charcoal produced the metal oxide. Alchemists of the late Middle Ages and the Renaissance were acquainted with both the stannic chloride or tin tetrachloride, called *sal jovis*, and the metallic binoxide or dioxide, known as *calx jovis* in the vernacular. Their association to the Jovian planet and deity, as well as to the Jovian qualities of expansion, cheerfulness, wisdom, and preservation, is implied by their shared use of the epithet *jovis*. Tin was sometimes sublimated with mercury, sulphur, and sal ammoniac to create a golden crystalline powder called *Aurum musivum* [mosaic gold], which was used for the treatment of sympathetic nervous system disorders like chronic hysteria and muscular convulsions.

At around this time, the metal was also found suitable for amalgamation into pewter, a pliable alloy that could be fashioned into a great many implements including household utensils and ecclesiastical paraphernalia. Like its celestial equivalent, which radiates with a brilliance and magnanimity that seem eternal to our ephemeral eyes, corporeal tin emits light and resists deterioration. Divers who examined eight tons of pewter within a fifteenth-century Portuguese shipwreck off the coast of Namibia claimed that the alloy gleamed dazzlingly, spawning the illusory impression that it had just sunk.

Saturn or Lead

The Saturn–lead axis represents the first rupture of the *prima materia*. This is evident by looking at its esoteric symbol: a cross mounted atop a lunar crescent. The pictogram represents an inchoate differentiation of the Aristotelian elements; they are in a state of passive abasement and have not yet succumbed to the influence of the lunar–silver axis. Moreover, the insurmountable position of the four Aristotelian elements implies that the Saturn–lead formative force stands at the lowest rung of the consciousness ladder. The metal lead (passive manifestation) exhibits the qualities of heaviness, softness, toxicity, and chaos, while the planet Saturn (active manifestation) is the farthest of the seven planets from the center of our solar system, as well as the most "sluggish" in terms of the time taken to complete a revolution around the sun (29.7 Earth years). Saturn and lead both exemplify a quality antagonistic and diametrically opposite of incorruptibility, nobility, eternity, and splendor — qualities embodied by the sun–gold force.

In the alchemical opus, the Saturnine formative force is rendered potent during the lesser circulation or creation of the "white stone" and mediates *necrosis* or *nigredo*, a premature stage in which the base substance in the alchemist's retort or alembic blackens and putrefies. On a psychospiritual level, this state of corruption denotes the inversion and turning inward of the senses. The seventh woodcut emblem from Basil Valentine's *Azoth* series offers an allegorical depiction of this phase as an elderly man in an entombed state of decomposition. Perched atop his hands is a raven, a bird frequently used to symbolize *necrosis* or *nigredo* (a skull or a grave are also used). Two winged entities, the soul and spirit, represent the departure of the vital life force as he expels his last breath.

The metal lead has been known to humankind since at least the seventh millennium BCE. This we know from metal beads unearthed at the Neolithic settlement of Çatalhöyük in modern-day Turkey, which date to c. 6400 BCE. The ancient Egyptians explored the metal's properties and their artificers soon discovered that minium, otherwise known as lead oxide, and litharge, the protoxide, were both suitable for use as pigments. The ancient Egyptians also worked with white lead or lead carbonate; it was extracted by subjecting metal sheets to the evaporating fumes of vinegar. The classical Greeks, who obtained much of their lead from the smelting of silver ores, associated the metal to the Titan Cronus, or Father Time, the youngest of the children born to the dreaded sky god, Uranus, and the earth goddess, Gaea. To this Graeco-Roman god of the harvest we owe the contemporaneous idea of death as a grim reaper who razes lives with his scythe. Use of the metal became widespread during Roman times, when many of the emperors had it worked into pipes, coins, and the system of aqueducts that nourished Rome with water for drinking, bathing, and flushing sewage. Allegedly, the first-century Roman Emperor Titus had some 50,000 or so men delivered to the Iberian lead mines to labor in abject conditions until they dropped dead from exhaustion.

Popularity of the metal doesn't seem to have waned at all. During the Middle Ages, it enjoyed widespread use in the construction of roofs, water tanks, and in the synthesis of pewter. Alchemists and physicians in the seventeenth century were acutely aware of its purpose as a curative agent, too. Many of them prepared a solution of lead acetate and potassium carbonate from which a metallic preparation known as the *Magistery of Saturn* was engendered. This became the basis for an alchemical precipitate called the *Powder of Saturn*, which was supposed to relieve respiratory ailments like asthma and tuberculosis of the lungs. Nowadays, the highly insoluble and stable nature of lead compounds makes it a perfect candidate for the sheathing of electrical wires, acid tanks, and cable hangers, as well as the primary composition for the weights and cable coatings on marine vessels. Psychiatrists working under the biomedical model of mental illness will actively use lithium compounds, known as lithium salts, to stabilize mood disturbances in individuals diagnosed with schizophrenia spectrum, bipolar spectrum, and other cognitive-affective disorders. Despite its acknowledged toxicity, the metal is still used in batteries, glassware, automotive tire balancing, and the coloring of ceramics, as well as for the manufacture of weights used by recreational divers.

Endnotes

165 Salomon Trismosin, *Splendor Solis* (London, UK: Kegan Paul, Trench, Trubner & Co., Ltd., 1981), p. 15.

Appendix C

The Three Alchemical Principles

Sulphur of the Tria Prima

Sulphur first appears as a generative force in an eighth-to-tenth century tractate titled *Liber misericordiae* within the *Corpus Jabirianum*, an alchemical compendium attributed to the Arab polymath Jabir ibn Hayyan, the Pseudo-Geber (c. 721–815). According to Jabir's theory, all cosmic substances are composed of Philosophical Sulphur and Philosophical Mercury (designated Philosophical to distinguish them from the crude elements of the same name) acting on the *prima materia*. Under this idiosyncratic philosophical system, the action of combustible Sulphur (composed of the Aristotelian elements of fire and air, and the secondary qualities of hot and dry) reacted with fusible Mercury (composed of the Aristotelian elements of water and earth, and the qualities of wet and cold) to produce the seven metals under the auspices of the seven planetary powers.

Naturally, Philosophical Sulphur may share qualitative characteristics with the element of the same name on the periodic table, but they are not conceptually commensurate or interchangeable. On the *Tabula Smaragdina* [Emerald Tablet],

Hermes Trismegistus draws attention to 13 precepts that garner an impression of alchemy as the quintessential set of laws and processes that permit creation. From a crude binary perspective, Philosophical Sulphur might be described as a volatile, fiery, and active masculine "spirit" that confers "form" to all created things by binding their vital essence to the corporeal realm. Furthermore, it projects into the sublunary sphere of generation to act upon and facilitate in the transformation of physical matter without being violated by the incumbent process itself. Philosophical Sulphur, according to Jabir, is of an elusive and impalpable nature; it remains concealed when coagulating the "body" of a substance to render it dry and hard, and will only reveal itself during retrograde stages of the alchemical cycle—distillation, putrefaction, or dissolution. Teleologically, Philosophical Sulphur transmutes and becomes pure gold or "spirit" through its interactions with Philosophical Mercury (described in the next section) in quite the same way that a fertilized egg morphs into a human fetus inside the nurturing womb of its mother.

The alchemical symbols act as individual ciphers that map out an entire system of hidden knowledge regarding the processes of creation and can thus impart a wealth of useful information to anyone equipped with a discerning, curious mind and a diligent character. Under Jabir's model, Philosophical Sulphur can act as a stand-in for planetary bodies like the sun, the condition of incarnated light, the state of conscious awareness and metacognition, the ego-self, the diurnal condition, the metal gold, and the splendid mineral diamond. Speaking of the element philosophically, alchemical treatises will warn diligent practitioners to guard against the acidic, corrosive properties of its elementary state. Philosophical Sulphur, they claim, can char, corrupt, destroy, and even invoke the beast within if the aspiring practitioner doesn't arm themselves with the germane prophylactics.

Philosophical Sulphur can also serve as an allegory for the human personality. One's ego-self can be short-sighted, fixated, and concerned only with its own physiological drives, emotional needs, intellectual growth, and personal goals. Left unchecked and unexamined, these can become sabotaging and detrimental, ensuing in behaviors that are both self-destructive and solicit environmental permutations insidious to the collective welfare of the human condition. The way forward is through inner purification, a phenomenon that ironically requires a paradoxical turning outward of our attentional apparatuses—focusing on that which lies beyond personal gain (financial, emotional, or what not) and sacrificing the promise of immediate gratification for longer-term positive outcomes in domains like social security, productivity, and satisfaction. In turning our attention outward, we are orienting ourselves along the yellow brick road leading to self-actualization; firstly, we're inadvertently acknowledging that the cosmos is much grander, awe-inspiring, profound, and mystifying than our own limited and ephemeral ego-selves could ever be, and secondly, we're distancing ourselves from our own intrinsically selfish nature and even sublimating carnal drives associated with them. Humility is weaponized against the inherited shackles of arrogant solipsism.

Matter stays faithful to the same working principles. Contrary to the reductive view of orthodox science, alchemy is heavily anchored in an ancient philosophical humus that assumes all living things are inspirited by a vital principle. The logic behind this conviction isn't hard to fathom; it is, quite candidly, impossible to reduce any living body—mineral, animal, or plant—to its base material without the patent loss of its animating principle. The vital life essence is none other than Philosophical Mercury and Sulphur combined, and can be separated from base matter by subjecting it to ordinary chemical processes like maceration, distillation, and decoction. Originating from the *prima materia*, this dual force is identical for all members of the same kingdom, but proceeds to manifest at a different "vibrational frequency" in each of the mineral, plant, and animal domains. In its unadulterated state, Philosophical Sulphur appears as a delicate oily substance and can be separated from Philosophical Mercury through ordinary distillation. Knowledge of how to alchemically separate these principles from ordinary plant matter also bequeaths competence in the synthesis of homeopathic elixirs with prodigious therapeutic potential. In areas such as China and Tibet, these occult principles are deeply embedded in a body of conventional scientific knowledge that came into existence roughly 2,000 years ago under the aegis of macrobiotics—an Eastern discipline of metaphysical inquiry, which also sought the Elixir of Life.

The esoteric symbol for Sulphur comprises two rudimentary shapes: a cross surmounted by a triangle. The first represents the four cardinal directions and the Aristotelian elements, while the second connotes activity, potentiality, and generation. The triangle is depicted in a superior position in relation to the elements, meaning that the generative force is always acting and fixing the elemental configurations into new forms.

Mercury of the Tria Prima

The idea of organic matter being imbued with a vital essence is a philosophical innovation that probably originated with the Swiss physician, alchemist, and philosopher Theophrastus Bombastus von Hohenheim, or Paracelsus (1493–1541). In his intellectual musings, Paracelsus deduced that the progenitor of the cosmos had resorted to a succession of large-scale distillations of dense matter to produce different hierarchies of being or tiers of consciousness. He assimilated the Jabirian concepts of Sulphur and Mercury into his cosmogony, to which a third was added: Salt. These entities could be found yoked together in the *prima materia* and could be manipulated using chemico-operative methods in a laboratory.

For Paracelsus and his followers, Philosophical Mercury is "spirit," Philosophical Salt is "body," and Philosophical Sulphur is "soul"; the first happens to be positively charged, the second is negatively charged, and the third exhibits a neutral charge and acts as a binding force. Philosophical Mercury or "spirit" is the incorporeal vital essence of an organism that eludes quantitative identification and analysis. Philosophical Salt or "body," on the other hand, binds or fixes the physical form together so that it doesn't disintegrate and reveals itself in the charred ashes once the organism or object is alchemically burned. Finally, Philosophical Sulphur or "soul" is the mediating principle that fuses the disparate "spirit" and "body" together throughout the organism's lifetime and accounts for its physiognomy and growth. Now, it just so happens that while Philosophical Mercury derives from the *prima materia*, it manifests at different vibrational frequencies in each of Nature's three established kingdoms (i.e., plant, animal, mineral). It is lowest in the plant kingdom and highest in the mineral realm. The "rate" for living beings is somewhere between the two just mentioned, a deduction predicated upon the observation that the chronicity of human and animal life is commonly longer than that of plants but paling in comparison with the prodigious durability and longevity we see in rocks, minerals, and crystals. Frater Albertus Spagyricus (1911–1984) transcribes these Paracelsian sentiments verbatim in *The Alchemist's Handbook* and goes on to equate the alchemist's Philosophical Mercury with the notion of *prana* in Vedantic philosophy and the Chinese *Qi*. Philosophical Mercury provides sustenance to the body and can be found in blood and breath. More concentrated amounts abound in semen and vaginal fluid.

Philosophical Mercury is a generative force, sometimes fiery and sometimes watery, responsible for any type of energetic transformation (i.e., physical, psychological, spiritual). It is commensurate with the *prima materia*, the base substance nourishing and transmuting the solar "germ," and it is also the teleological process facilitating the perfection of natural "forms," the *ultima materia*. Both Western and Eastern alchemical treatises sometimes personify Philosophical Mercury as an aerial spirit, cloud, or fumigation. For instance, in the Taoist Chinese text *The Secret of the Golden Flower*, Mercury takes center stage as a hermaphroditic soul with heavenly aspects manifesting as a masculine cloud demon and earthly facets appearing as a feminine white ghost. Its ubiquitous nature evokes images of the primordial chaos, the primeval ocean in most, if not all, creation myths, implying that Philosophical Mercury is the animating spark of organic matter. Ancient concepts like the *anima mundi* or the Platonic World Soul are sometimes equated with Philosophical Mercury. Transposed to the discipline of analytical (Jungian) or archetypal psychology, the demon–ghost pair might be anthropomorphic stand-ins for the *animus* and *anima* within the human psyche.

Carl Jung, who sought to bridge Eastern mysticism with his own analytical psychology through interpretation and commentary of this ancient Taoist text, deduced that spiritual attainment was contingent upon one's acquaintance with the transpersonal realm of archetypes and the introspective conscious withdrawal of psychical projections (i.e., mistaking internal phenomena for external phenomena). This transpersonal realm — described by the Taoist text as the "roots of consciousness and life" and "the blessed country close at hand"[166] — encompasses the true Self, a harmonic state of integration and totality able to reconcile psychological schisms and conflicts, and, more importantly perhaps, render one's life personally meaningful and prosperous. When interpreted accurately, dreams furnish a small window through which this personal transformation can be tracked, as well as offering a symbolic chronicle of the journey from psychological inflexibility and reflexivity to self-actualization. An alchemist might assert that it is the corrosive and disintegrating properties of the "poisonous dragon," Philosophical Mercury, that makes it all possible; there can be no generation and coagulation of a new "form" — in this case, a psychological worldview — if dissolution of the old "form" hasn't occurred first.

Philosophical Mercury is sometimes described by alchemists as "spirit" or "soul." The esoteric symbol is composed of all three rudimentary shapes: the circle, the semicircle, and the cross. In this specific arrangement, the circle fixes the cross of the four Aristotelian elements but is itself dominated by the lunar crescent. This hermaphroditic constitution, unique among the esoteric symbols, describes the inner friction between the fiery masculine and moist feminine generative forces.

Salt of the Tria Prima

Maria the Jewess, a legendary alchemist of late antiquity, reputedly said that "One becomes two, two becomes three, and out of the third comes the one as the fourth."[167] While the Swiss psychiatrist Carl Gustav Jung (1875–1961) referred to this axiom within the context of analytical psychology, esoteric thinkers understand it as the schism generated by the friction between the active, masculine force and the passive, feminine force, to create a third state. This third condition denotes creative unity through synthesis, and also the Adamic state of limitation and confinement. The cross of the elements and the quasi-historical crucifixion of the Christ are figurative representations of this state.

Under alchemical lore, any laws and theorems described are not the sole prerogative or property of one academic discipline but extend to all processes of creation. The Swiss polymath Paracelsus (1493–1541) named the three principles animating all matter Philosophical Sulphur (soul), Philosophical Mercury (spirit), and Philosophical Salt (body). In fact, Paracelsus's compelling oeuvre is yoked together by the conviction that the first exhibited a neutral charge, the second a positive charge, and the third a negative charge: Philosophical Sulphur (soul) is the mediating principle that fuses the disparate "spirit" and "body" together throughout the organism's lifetime and accounts for its physiognomy and growth; Philosophical Mercury (spirit) is the incorporeal vital essence of an organism that eludes quantitative identification and analysis; and, last but not least, Philosophical Salt (body) binds or fixes the physical form together so that it doesn't disintegrate and reveals itself in the charred ashes once the organism or object is alchemically burned.

Frater Albertus's (1911–1984) spagyrical method for the isolation of the vital life force of organic matter (i.e., a plant or herb) is based on the same theoretical premises. In his instructive work *The Alchemist's Handbook*, Frater Albertus reintroduces technical alchemy to a hitherto untutored American audience and makes a startling revelation in the process. The blueprint, signature, life principle, vital force—call it what you will—can in fact be isolated from organic matter using conventional laboratory procedures. According to Frater Albertus, subjecting a fresh or dried herb to the distillatory process generates a twofold division of matter into oil and dead residue. The latter can be charred to black and light gray cinders—this is Philosophical Salt. While the characteristics and vibrations of Philosophical Mercury are uniform across each of the three primary kingdoms (i.e., plant, animal, and mineral), Philosophical Salt differs in that it is idiosyncratic and homogenous for matter belonging to a particular class. This is because Salt carries the individual qualities of the organism or thing, the inner and outer features that give it a unique expression in the cosmos.

Within the repeated conjunctions of Philosophical Sulphur (soul) and Philosophical Mercury (spirit) that enable the alchemical movement from *prima materia* to *ultima materia*, Salt (body) serves as the vessel enabling these powers to infiltrate one another and interact intimately. It is especially characterized by the condition of "fixedness" or *stasis*, meaning it is the part that remains unadulterated and consistent through time. Philosophical Salt permits the human intellect to sense and perceive, to comprehend and to analyze, and to internalize causal and correlational relationships in the natural world. Without it, there would be no way of making sense out of nonsense, or of subjectively experiencing oneself as an integrated whole in the cosmos.

In alchemical esotericism, Philosophical Salt is exemplified by a circle bisected by a horizontal line.

Endnotes

166   Richard Wilhelm, The Secret of the Golden Flower: A Chinese Book of Life (Oxfordshire, UK: Routledge, 2013), p. 95.

167   Mark Haeffner, *The Dictionary of Alchemy: From Maria Prophetissa to Isaac Newton* (London, UK: The Aquarian Press, 1991).

References

Preface

Aristotle, *Meteorologica* (Cambridge, MA: Harvard University Press, 1952).

Richard Wilhelm and Carl Gustav Jung, *The Secret of the Golden Flower; a Chinese Book of Life* (London: UK: Paul Trench Trubner, 1962).

Chapter 1

Lindy Abraham, *A Dictionary of Alchemical Imagery* (Cambridge, UK: Cambridge University Press, 1998).

Aristotle, *Meteorologica*, ed. and trans. by H. D. P. Lee (Cambridge, MA: Harvard University Press, 1952).

Aristotle and C. D. C. Reeve, *Physics* (Indianapolis: Hackett Publishing Company, Inc., 2018).

Emile Brehier, *The History of Philosophy: The Hellenic Age* (Chicago, USA: University of Chicago Press, 1965).

Titus Burckhardt, *Alchemy: Science of the Cosmos, Science of the Soul* (Shaftesbury, UK: Element Books, 1986).

Allison P. Coodert, 'Alchemy IV: 16th–18th Century', in *Dictionary of Gnosis and Western Esotericism*, ed. by Wouter J. Hanegraaff et al., 2 vols (Leiden: Brill, 2005).

Andrea Falcon, 'Aristotle on Causality', in *The Stanford Encyclopedia of Philosophy* (Fall 2011 Edition), ed. by Edward N. Zalta, http://plato.stanford.edu/archives/fall2011/entries/aristotle-causality/.

Charles Mills Gayley, *The Classic Myths in English Literature and Art* (Boston, USA: Adamant Media Corporation, 2005).

Bernard D. Haage, 'Alchemy II: Antiquity-12th Century', in *Dictionary of Gnosis and Western Esotericism*, ed. by Wouter J. Hanegraaff et al., 2 vols (Leiden: Brill, 2005).

Joseph L. Henderson and Dyane N. Sherwood, *Transformation of the Psyche: The Symbolic Alchemy of the Splendor Solis* (East Sussex, UK: Routledge, 2003).

Albert de Jong, 'Zosimus of Panopolis', in *Dictionary of Gnosis and Western Esotericism*, ed. by Wouter J. Hanegraaff et al., 2 vols (Leiden: Brill, 2005).

Noretta Koertge (ed.), *A House Built on Sand: Exposing Postmodernist Myths about Science* (New York City, NY: Oxford University Press, 2000).

Stanton J. Linden, *The Alchemy Reader: From Hermes Trismegistus to Isaac Newton* (Cambridge, UK: Cambridge University Press, 2003).

Michele Mertens (ed.), *Les Alchimistes Grecs: Zosime de Panopolis*, trans. by Michele Mertens (Paris, FR: Les Belles Letres, 1995).

William Royall Newman, *The Summa Perfectionis of Pseudo-Geber: A Critical Edition, Translation, and Study* (Leiden, Netherlands: Brill, 1991).

Lorna Oakes and Lucia Gahlin, *Ancient Egypt* (New York City, NY: Hermes House, 2002).

Michael Rice, *Egypt's Legacy: The Archetypes of Western Civilization 3000–30 BC* (London, UK: Routledge, 1997).

Aldis Uzdavinys (ed.), *The Heart of Plotinus: The Essential Enneads (Perennial Philosophy)* (Bloomington, IN: World Wisdom, 2009).

Chapter 2

Heinrich Cornelius Agrippa, *Three Books of Occult Philosophy* (San Jose, CA: Simon and Schuster, 2021).

Roelof van den Broek, 'Gnosticism I: Gnostic Religion', in *Dictionary of Gnosis and Western Esotericism*, ed. by Wouter J. Hanegraaff et al., 2 vols (Leiden: Brill, 2005).

Roelof van den Broek, 'Hermetic Literature I: Antiquity', in *Dictionary of Gnosis and Western Esotericism*, ed. by Wouter J. Hanegraaff et al., 2 vols (Leiden: Brill, 2005).

Brian P. Copenhaver, *Hermetica: The Greek Corpus Hermeticum and the Latin Asclepius in a new English translation, with notes and introduction* (Cambridge, UK: Cambridge University Press, 1995).

Florian Ebeling, *The Secret History of Hermes Trismegistus: Hermeticism from Ancient to Modern Times,* trans. by David Lorton (London, UK: Cornell University Press, 2007).

Antoine Faivre, 'Ancient and Medieval Sources of Modern Esoteric Movements', in *Modern Esoteric Spirituality*, ed. by Antoine Faivre and Jacob Needleman (Chestnut Ridge, NY: Crossroad Publishing, 1992).

Antoine Faivre, 'Hermetic Literature IV: Renaissance–Present', in *Dictionary of Gnosis and Western Esotericism*, ed. by Wouter J. Hanegraaff et al., 2 vols (Leiden: Brill, 2005).

Bernard D. Haage, 'Alchemy II: Antiquity–12th Century', in *Dictionary of Gnosis and Western Esotericism*, ed. by Wouter J. Hanegraaff et al., 2 vols (Leiden: Brill, 2005).

Stanton J. Linden, *The Alchemy Reader: From Hermes Trismegistus to Isaac Newton* (Cambridge, UK: Cambridge University Press, 2003). William R. Newman and Anthony Grafton (eds.), 'Introduction: The Problematic Status of Astrology and Alchemy in Premodern Europe', in *Secrets of Nature: Astrology and Alchemy in Early Modern Europe* (London, UK: MIT Press, 2006).

Kocku von Stuckrad, *Western Esotericism: A Brief History of Secret Knowledge,* trans. by Nicholas Goodrick-Clarke (London, UK: Equinox Publishing, 2005).

C. J. S. Thompson, *The Lure and Romance of Alchemy* (London, UK: Random House, 1990).

John L. Tomkinson, *Haunted Greece: Nymphs, Vampires and Other Exotica* (Athens, GR: Anagnosis Books, 2004).

Chapter 3

Lindy Abraham, *A Dictionary of Alchemical Imagery* (Cambridge, UK: Cambridge University Press, 1998).

Mary Anne Atwood, *A Suggestive Inquiry into the Hermetic Mystery* (Classic Reprint), (Central, Hong Kong: Forgotten Books, 2012).

Jacob Behmen, *Works of Jacob Behmen: The Teutonic Philosopher V1* (Whitefish, Montana: Kessinger Publishing, 2010).

Jacob Boehme, 'Morgenröte im Aufgang (Aurora)', in *Samtliche Schriften*, vol. 1, ed. by Will-Erich Peukert (Stuttgart, Germany: 1955).

Pierre Deghaye, 'Jacob Boehme and His Followers', in *Modern Esoteric Spirituality*, ed. by Wouter J. Hanegraaff et al., two vols (Leiden: Brill, 2005).

Florian Ebeling, *The Secret History of Hermes Trismegistus: Hermeticism from Ancient to Modern Times*, trans. by David Lorton (London, UK: Cornell University Press, 2007).

Edward Edinger, *Anatomy of the Psyche: Alchemical Symbolism in Psychotherapy* (Chicago, Illinois: Open Court, 1994).

Jon Eklund, 'The Incomplete Chemist: Begin an Essay on the Eighteenth-Century Chemist in his Laboratory, With a Dictionary of Obsolete Chemical Terms of the Period', in *Smithsonian Studies in History and Technology* (Washington DC, USA: Smithsonian Institution Press, 1975).

Antoine Faivre, 'Christian Theosophy', in *Dictionary of Gnosis and Western Esotericism*, ed. by Wouter J. Hanegraaff et al., two vols (Leiden: Brill, 2005).

Nicholas Goodrick-Clarke, *The Western Esoteric Traditions: A Historical Introduction* (New York, NY: Oxford University Press, 2008).

Henry Guerlac, 'John Mayow and the Aerial Nitre', in *Actes du Septieme Congres International d'Histoire des Sciences* (Jerusalem, Israel: 1953).

Wouter Hanegraaff, *New Age Religion and Western Culture: Esotericism in the Mirror of Secular Thought* (Albany, NY: State University of New York Press, 1998).

Harvey J. Irwin and Caroline A. Watt, *An Introduction to Parapsychology* (London, UK: McFarland & Company Inc., 2007).

Ernst Koch, 'Moscowiter in der Oberlausitz und M. Bartolomaus in Gorlitz', in *Neues Lausitzisches Magazin* (Berlin, Germany: 1907).

Lawrence M. Principe and William R. Newman, 'Some Problems with the Historiography of Alchemy', in *Secrets of Nature: Astrology and Alchemy in Early Modern Europe*, ed. by William R. Newman and Anthony Grafton (London, UK: MIT Press, 2006).

G. Starkey, 'The Chymistry of Isaac Newton', *Alchemy Laboratory Notebooks and Correspondence* (2004), http://webapp1. dlib.indiana.edu/newton/reference/glossary.do [Accessed November 23, 2012].

Arthur Versluis, 'William Law', in *Dictionary of Gnosis and Western Esotericism*, ed. by Wouter J. Hanegraaff et al., two vols (Leiden: Brill, 2005).

Andrew Weeks, 'Jacob Boehme', in *Dictionary of Gnosis and Western Esotericism*, ed. by Wouter J. Hanegraaff et al., two vols (Leiden: Brill, 2005).

Alan Williams, 'The Production of Saltpeter in the Middle Ages', in *Ambix* (London, UK: Maney Publishing, 1975).

Chapter 4

Betty Jo Teeter Dobbs, *The Foundations of Newton's Alchemy* (CUP Archive, 1983).

Edward Edinger, *Anatomy of the Psyche: Alchemical Symbolism in Psychotherapy* (Chicago, Illinois: Open Court, 1994).

Henri F. Ellenberger, *The Discovery of the Unconscious: The History and Evolution of Dynamic Psychiatry* (New York, USA: Basic Books, 1970).

Ethan Allen Hitchcock, *Remarks Upon Alchemy and the Alchemists, Indicating a Method of Discovering the True Nature of Hermetic Philosophy; and Showing That the Search after the Philosopher's Stone Had Not for Its Object the Discovery of an Agent for the Transmutation of Metals: Being Also an Attempt to Rescue from Undeserved Opprobrium the Reputation of a Class of Extraordinary Thinkers in Past Ages* (Boston, MA: Crosby, Nichols, and Company, 1857).

Aniela Jaffe, *Jung's Last Years and Other Essays* (New Orleans, LA: Spring Publications, 1984).

Carl Gustav Jung, *Alchemical Studies, Collected Works*, vol. 13 (Princeton: Princeton University Press, 1968).

Carl Gustav Jung, *Mysteries, Dreams, Reflections* (London: Routledge & Kegan Paul, 1963; Fontana, 1977).

Carl Gustav Jung, *Mysterium Coniunctionis, Collected Works*, vol. 14 (Princeton: Princeton University Press, 1968).

Carl Gustav Jung, *Psychology and Alchemy, Collected Works*, vol. 12 (Princeton: Princeton University Press, 1968).

Richard Noll, *The Aryan Christ: The Secret Life of Carl Jung* (New York: Random House, 1997).

Lawrence M. Principe, *The Aspiring Adept: Robert Boyle and His Alchemical Quest* (Princeton, NJ: Princeton University Press, 2018).

Lawrence M. Principe and William R. Newman, 'Some Problems with the Historiography of Alchemy' in *Secrets of Nature: Astrology and Alchemy in Early Modern Europe*, ed. by William R. Newman and Anthony Grafton (London, UK: MIT Press, 2006).

David Sedgewick, *Introduction to Jungian Psychotherapy: The Therapeutic Relationship* (London, UK: Routledge, 2013).

Hereward Tilton, *The Quest for the Phoenix: Spiritual Alchemy and Rosicrucianism in the Work of Count Michael Maier (1569–1622)* (Berlin: de Gruyter, 2003).

Solomon Trismosin, *Splendor Solis: Alchemical Treatises of Solomon Trismosin, Adept and Teacher of Paracelsus... Including 22 Allegorical Pictures... Dated 1582... with Introduction, Elucidation of the Paintings, Aiding the Interpretation of Their Occult Meaning* (London, UK: K. Paul, Trench, Trubner & Company, 1921).

Arthur Edward Waite, *Azoth, or the Star in the East, embracing the first matter of the Magnum Opus, the evolution of the Aphrodite-Urania, the supernatural generation of the son of the sun, and the alchemical transfiguration of humanity* (Whitefish, MT: Kessinger Publishing, 1994).

Richard Wilhelm (trans.), *The Secret of the Golden Flower: A Chinese Book of Life*, with a Foreword by Carl Jung (Orlando, FL: Harcourt Brace & Company, 1961).

Chapter 5

Stanton Marlon, *The Black Sun: The Alchemy and Art of Darkness* (Texas, USA: Texas A&M University Press, 2008).

Salomon Trismosin and Jocelyn Godwin, *Splendor Solis* (Rome, Italy: Edizioni Mediterranee, 2021).

Chapter 6

English Standard Version Bible (2001), Matthew 18:3.

Salomon Trismosin and Jocelyn Godwin, *Splendor Solis* (Rome, Italy: Edizioni Mediterranee, 2021).

Chapter 7

Pamela Rae Health, *Mind-Matter Interaction: A Review of Historical Reports, Theory and Research* (Jefferson, North Carolina: McFarland & Company, 2011).

Meredith K. Ray, *Daughters of Alchemy: Women and Scientific Culture in Early Modern Italy* (Cambridge, MA: Harvard University Press, 2015).

Salomon Trismosin and Jocelyn Godwin, *Splendor Solis* (Rome, Italy: Edizioni Mediterranee, 2021).

Chapter 8

Ikechukwu Obialo Azuonye, 'A Difficult Case: Diagnosis Made by Hallucinatory Voices,' *British Medical Journal*, 315, 1997.

Pamela Rae Health, *Mind-Matter Interaction: A Review of Historical Reports, Theory and Research* (Jefferson, North Carolina: McFarland & Company, 2011).

Albert A. Mason, 'A Case of Congenital Ichthyosiform Erythrodermia of Brocq Treated by Hypnosis,' *British Medical Journal*, 30, 1952.

Arnold Mindell, *Working with the Dreaming Body* (Portland, OR: LaoTsePress, 2002).

Anees A. Sheikh (ed.), *Imagination and Healing* (Oxfordshire, UK: Routledge, 1984).

Salomon Trismosin and Jocelyn Godwin, *Splendor Solis* (Rome, Italy: Edizioni Mediterranee, 2021).

Wilson Van Dusen, *The Natural Depth in Man* (New York, NY: Swedenborg Foundation, 1981).

Chapter 9

Louis Cozolino, *The Neuroscience of Psychotherapy: Healing the Social Brain (Norton Series on Interpersonal Neurobiology)* (New York, NY: WW Norton & Company, 2010).

Richard J. Crisp, *Social Psychology: A Very Short Introduction* (Oxford, UK: Oxford University Press, 2015).

Gerald M. Edelman and Giulio Tononi. *A Universe of Consciousness: How Matter Becomes Imagination* (New York, USA: Basic Books, 2000).

Jonathan Haidt, *The Righteous Mind: Why Good People Are Divided by Politics and Religion* (New York, NY: Pantheon Books, 2012).

Szabolcs Kéri, 'Genes for Psychosis and Creativity: A Promoter Polymorphism of the Neuregulin 1 Gene is Related to Creativity in People with High Intellectual Achievement,' *Psychological Science* 20, no. 9 (2009): 1070–1073.

Stanton Marlon, *The Black Sun: The Alchemy and Art of Darkness* (Texas, USA: Texas A&M University Press, 2008).

Abraham Maslow, *A Theory of Human Motivation* (Reprint of 1943 Edition) (Eastford, CT: Martino Fine Books, 2013).

Lewis Mehl-Madrona, *Healing the Mind Through the Power of Story: The Promise of Narrative Psychiatry* (Rochester, VT: Inner Traditions/Bear & Co, 2010).

Patricia H. Miller, *Theories of Developmental Psychology* (New York, NY: Worth Publishers, 2016).

Robert Plomin, John C. DeFries, Valerie S. Knopik, and Jenae M. Neiderhiser, 'Top 10 Replicated Findings from Behavioral Genetics,' *Perspectives on Psychological Science* 11, no. 1 (2016): 3–23.

Ernest Lawrence Rossi, *The Psychobiology of Mind-Body Healing: New Concept of Therapeutic Hypnosis* (New York, NY: WW Norton & Company, 1993).

Leonard Sax, *Boys Adrift: The Five Factors Driving the Growing Epidemic of Unmotivated Boys and Underachieving Young Men* (New York, NY: Basic Books, 2016).

Daniel J. Siegel, *The Developing Mind: How Relationships and the Brain Interact to Shape Who We Are* (New York, NY: Guilford Press, 2012).

Emanuel Swedenborg, *Arcana Coelestia: The Heavenly Arcana Contained in the Holy Scriptures or Word of the Lord Unfolded Beginning with the Book of Genesis Together with Wonderful Things Seen in the World of Spirits and in the Heaven of Angels.*

Translated from the Latin (Vol. 9) (American Swedenborg Printing and Publishing Society, 1870).

David Tacey, *The Jung Reader* (New York, NY: Routledge, 2012).

Wilson Van Dusen, 'Hallucinations as a World of Spirits,' *Psychedelic Review* 11 (1970): 60–69.

Wilson Van Dusen, *The Natural Depth in Man,* (New York, NY: Swedenborg Foundation, 1981).

Gerald Young, *Development and Causality: Neo-Piagetian Perspectives* (New York, NY: Springer Science & Business Media, 2011).

Chapter 10

Bentley Layton (ed.), *Nag Hammadi Codex II, 2–7, Together with XIII, 2* Brit. Lib. Or. 4926 (1) and P. Oxy. 1, 654, 655: I. Gospel According to Thomas, Gospel According to Philip, Hypostasis of the Archons, Indexes. II. On the Origin of the World, Expository Treatise on the Soul, Book of Thomas the Contender* (Leiden, Netherlands: Brill, 2020).

Chapter 11

Frater Albertus, *The Alchemist's Handbook: Manual for Practical Laboratory Alchemy (Revised)* (Maine, USA: Weiser Books, 1987).

Frater Albertus, *The Seven Rays of the QBL* (York Beach, MA: Samuel Weiser, Inc., 1985).

Abraham Eleazar, *The Book of Abraham the Jew (The R.A.M.S. Library of Alchemy) (Volume 29)* (Scotts Valley, CA: Createspace Independent Publishing Platform, 2015).

Patrick Harpur (ed.), *Mercurius, Or, the Marriage of Heaven* (Glen Waverley, VIC: Blue Angel Gallery, 2007).

Nick Kollerstrom, *The Metal-Planet Relationship: A Study of Celestial Influence* (Eureka, CA: Borderland Sciences Research Foundation, 1993).

Thomas Charles Lethbridge, *Gogmagog: The Buried Gods* (Oxfordshire, UK: Routledge, 1975).

Israel Regardie, *The Philosopher's Stone* (London, UK: Rider & Co, 1938).

Chapter 12

Michael J. Behe, *The Edge of Evolution: The Search for the Limits of Darwinism* (San Jose, CA: Simon and Schuster, 2007).

Olaf Blanke, Theodor Landis, Laurent Spinelli, and Margitta Seeck, 'Out-of-body Experience and Autoscopy of Neurological Origin,' *Brain* 127, no. 2 (2004).

David Chalmers, *The Conscious Mind: In Search of a Fundamental Theory* (Oxford, UK: Oxford Paperbacks, 1997).

Scott A. Leonard and Michael McClure, *Myth and Knowing: An Introduction to World Mythology* (New York, NY: McGraw-Hill Humanities/Social Sciences/Languages, 2004).

Michael W. McConnell, 'God is Dead and We Have Killed Him: Freedom of Religion in the Post-Modern Age,' *BYu L. Rev* (1993).

William R. Newman, *Promethean Ambitions: Alchemy and The Quest to Perfect Nature* (Chicago, IL: University of Chicago Press, 2005).

Wilder Penfield, *The Mystery of the Mind* (Princeton, New Jersey: Princeton University Press, 1975).

Appendices

Frater Albertus, *The Alchemist's Handbook: Manual for Practical Laboratory Alchemy (Revised)* (Maine, USA: Weiser Books, 1987).

Homer and Robert Fitzgerald (trans.), *The Iliad* (New York City, NY: Farar, Straus & Giroux, 2004).

Homer and Robert Fitzgerald (trans.), *The Odyssey* (New York City, NY: Vintage Books, 1990).

Mark Haeffner, *The Dictionary of Alchemy: From Maria Prophetissa to Isaac Newton* (London, UK: The Aquarian Press, 1991).

Hermes Trismegistus and Issac Newton, *The Emerald Tablet of Hermes: The Smaragdine Table, or Tabula Smaragdina* (CreateSpace Independent Publishing Platform, 2017).

Salomon Trismosin, *Splendor Solis* (London, UK: Kegan Paul, Trench, Trubner & Co., Ltd., 1981).

Richard Wilhelm, *The Secret of the Golden Flower: A Chinese Book of Life* (Oxfordshire, UK: Routledge, 2013).

Index

Figures are indicated by *f*, e.g. 326*f*, appendices by A, e.g. A326

MANTRA
BOOKS

EASTERN RELIGION & PHILOSOPHY
We publish books on Eastern religions and philosophies.
Books that aim to inform and explore the various traditions
that began in the East and have migrated West.
If you have enjoyed this book, why not tell other readers by
posting a review on your preferred book site.

Recent bestsellers from MANTRA BOOKS are:

The Way Things Are
A Living Approach to Buddhism
Lama Ole Nydahl
An introduction to the teachings of the Buddha, and how to make use of these teachings in everyday life.
Paperback: 978-1-84694-042-2 ebook: 978-1-78099-845-9

Back to the Truth
5000 Years of Advaita
Dennis Waite
A demystifying guide to Advaita for both those new to, and those familiar with this ancient, non-dualist philosophy from India.
Paperback: 978-1-90504-761-1 ebook: 978-184694-624-0

Shinto: A celebration of Life
Aidan Rankin
Introducing a gentle but powerful spiritual pathway reconnecting humanity with Great Nature and affirming all aspects of life.
Paperback: 978-1-84694-438-3 ebook: 978-1-84694-738-4

In the Light of Meditation
Mike George
A comprehensive introduction to the practice of meditation and the spiritual principles behind it. A 10 lesson meditation programme with CD and internet support.
Paperback: 978-1-90381-661-5

A Path of Joy
Popping into Freedom
Paramananda Ishaya
A simple and joyful path to spiritual enlightenment.
Paperback: 978-1-78279-323-6 ebook: 978-1-78279-322-9

The Less Dust the More Trust
Participating in The Shamatha Project, Meditation and
Science Adeline van Waning, MD PhD
The inside-story of a woman participating in frontline
meditation research, exploring the interfaces of mind-practice,
science and psychology.
Paperback: 978-1-78099-948-7 ebook: 978-1-78279-657-2

I Know How To Live, I Know How To Die
The Teachings of Dadi Janki: A warm, radical, and life-
affirming view of who we are, where we come from,
and what time is calling us to do
Neville Hodgkinson
Life and death are explored in the context of frontier science
and deep soul awareness.
Paperback: 978-1-78535-013-9 ebook: 978-1-78535-014-6

Living Jainism
An Ethical Science
Aidan Rankin, Kanti V. Mardia
A radical new perspective on science rooted in intuitive
awareness and deductive reasoning.
Paperback: 978-1-78099-912-8 ebook: 978-1-78099-911-1

Ordinary Women, Extraordinary Wisdom
The Feminine Face of Awakening
Rita Marie Robinson
A collection of intimate conversations with female spiritual
teachers who live like ordinary women, but are engaged
with their true natures.
Paperback: 978-1-84694-068-2 ebook: 978-1-78099-908-1

The Way of Nothing
Nothing in the Way
Paramananda Ishaya
A fresh and light-hearted exploration of the
amazing reality of nothingness.
Paperback: 978-1-78279-307-6 ebook: 978-1-78099-840-4

Readers of ebooks can buy or view any of these bestsellers by
clicking on the live link in the title. Most titles are published
in paperback and as an ebook. Paperbacks are available in
traditional bookshops. Both print and ebook formats are
available online.

Find more titles and sign up to our readers' newsletter at
www.collectiveinkbooks.com/mind-body-spirit. Follow
us on Facebook at facebook.com/OBooks and
Twitter at twitter.com/obooks